Quran and Reform

THEION

Studien zur Religionskultur/Studies in Religious Culture

Herausgegeben von/edited by
Wilhelm-Ludwig Federlin, Edmund Weber und/and Vladislav Serikov
Johann Wolfgang Goethe-Universität Frankfurt am Main

Band XXXI

Zur Qualitätssicherung und Peer Review der vorliegenden Publikation

Die Qualität der in dieser Reihe erscheinenden Arbeiten wird vor der Publikation durch einen Herausgeber der Reihe geprüft.

Notes on the quality assurance and peer review of this publication

Prior to publication, the quality of the work published in this series is reviewed by one of the editors of the series.

Katharina Völker

Quran and Reform

Rahman, Arkoun, Abu Zayd

Bibliographic Information published by the Deutsche Nationalbibliothek
The Deutsche Nationalbibliothek lists this publication in the Deutsche
Nationalbibliografie; detailed bibliographic data is available in the internet at
http://dnb.d-nb.de.

Library of Congress Cataloging-in-Publication Data
Names: Völker, Katharina, author.
Title: Quran and reform : Rahman, Arkoun, Abu Zayd / Katharina Völker.
Description: Frankfurt am Main : Peter Lang, 2017. | Series: Theion ; 31 |
Includes bibliographical references.
Identifiers: LCCN 2016050419 | ISBN 9783631675311
Subjects: LCSH: Quran–Criticism, interpretation, etc.–History–20th century. |
Islamic modernism. | Rahman, Fazlur, 1919-1988. | Arkoun, Mohammed. | Abu
Zayd, Nasr Hamid.
Classification: LCC BP130.45 .V65 2017 | DDC 297.1/2260904–dc23
LC record available at https://lccn.loc.gov/2016050419

ISSN 0943-9587
ISBN 978-3-631-67531-1 (Print)
E-ISBN 978-3-653-06937-2 (E-PDF)
E-ISBN 978-3-631-71212-2 (EPUB)
E-ISBN 978-3-631-71213-9 (MOBI)
DOI 10.3726/ b10650

To my three warriors

Abstract

This thesis engages with three Modern Muslims accounts of the nature of the Quran and its interpretation as basis for reform schemes. I investigate how the three Muslim intellectuals Fazlur Rahman (d. 1988), Muhammad Arkoun (d. 2010), and Nasr Hamid Abu Zayd (d. 2010) view the revelation process and the role of Muhammad in it. This leads to a better understanding of how the three thinkers wish to interpret the Quran. Furthermore, I look into their ideas for reform on the levels of individual consciousness, society and scholarship and relate these ideas to their understanding of the Quran and its exegesis.

All three thinkers acknowledge the centrality of the Quran to Islamic faith and culture. In their unique ways Rahman, Arkoun and Abu Zayd call for an intense engagement with the Quran, which they feel is often overshadowed by reliance on traditional interpretation, various instrumentalisations of the Quran for the sake of ideological endeavours, and dependency on secondary Islamic sources. This study reveals that, despite their critique, these portrayed reform thinkers are nonetheless reliant on tradition (*turāth*), religious discourse, and secondary Islamic literature such as *hadith*, *sunna* and *sīra*.

Analysing the three scholars' interpretation methods displays innovations but also reveals some shortcomings. However, the main finding of this thesis is that all three intellectuals propose ways of understanding Islam as being highly significant to a contemporary world. Rahman and Abu Zayd propose the possibility of living a Muslim life today while successfully encountering challenges of modernity. Arkoun's ideas are more concretely directed at a reform of thinking in Muslim and non-Muslim circles, and predominantly in the academy.

This thesis argues that the overall scholarly dynamic of the three academics is based on a philosophical attitude, which exposes itself as a humanistic project. All three accounts of Islam stress the importance of ethical norms. Those shall serve as foundation for the reconciliation of cultures that often seem fatally opposed. As bridge-builders and border-crossers between so called Western and Islamic thought Rahman, Arkoun and Abu Zayd contribute to the spirit of solidarity amongst civilisations.

Preface

Transliteration

Arabic terms are transliterated according to the system established in the *International Journal of Middle East Studies (IJMES)*. In English frequently used words such as Islam, Muslim, Quran, *hadith*, and *sunna* lack diacritical marks. These exceptions are found in the *IJMES* Word List (Except Chart). Transliterations, especially those with diacritics are italicised. Transliteration in quotations remains unchanged and might follow different rules. An apostrophe is used for the letter *hamzah*. An inverted superscript comma is used for the *'ayn*, except where it appears spelled as ᶜ*ayn* in quotations or titles.

Translation

Translations from German into English are my own, if not otherwise indicated.

Quran citations are extracted from the approximate meaning of the Quran in English by Arberry (*The Koran Interpreted: A Translation*). Citations of the Quran are in the form 'chapter (sura): verse'. Quran citations within citations remain unchanged.

Further Spellings

Out of respect for the religious beliefs of the three thinkers discussed in this thesis words like Prophet, God, and the Divine are spelled with capital letters.

Abbreviation of key works

EI[(2)]:   Encyclopaedia of Islam (2nd edition)
EQ: Encyclopaedia of the Quran

Acknowledgments

I am obliged to express my gratitude to Nasr Hamid Abu Zayd and Muhammad Arkoun who warmly welcomed me in their homes, spending their valuable time communicating their philosophies. I am grateful to have had the opportunity to meet with them in 2009, before both died a year later. I feel deep sorrow for their loss and wish their inspirational work will come into fruition within the hearts of their students all over the world.

Bärbel Beinhauer-Köhler and Hans Daiber are given thanks for having brought me onto the track of studying Islamic intellectualism.

For taking on the supervision of this project I want to thank Gregory Dawes. His insights shed light on the sometimes gloomy path of doctorate research. Moreover, he gave me the opportunity to experience amazing New Zealand.

For the sponsoring of study, travel, conference attendances and publishing I am indebted to the University of Otago, New Zealand Education, the New Zealand Federation for Graduate Women, and the People of New Zealand.

Importantly, without the support of my beloved father as well as my patient husband, this publication would not have been possible. I thank my entire family for being there and dedicate this work to my sons Orion Morfeus, Jason Herbert and Aeneas Athanasios.

This book is based on original research undertaken for the doctorate degree at the Department of Theology and Religion, University of Otago (2012).

Contents

Chapter I – Introduction

1. A Common Theme: Rethinking Islam through Rereading the Quran

The three Muslim intellectuals discussed in this book dedicated their work and life to change in contemporary Islam. This change Fazlur Rahman, Muhammad Arkoun and Nasr Hamid Abu Zayd hoped to achieve through a rereading of the Quran. A re-reading constitutes a rethinking of the role of the Quran in Muslim thought and society. This discourse generally goes hand in hand with re-considering the role of religion in the contemporary world. In the course of rereading, the three thinkers reassess their own tradition and at the same time open their horizons for inspiration from outside their belief. Numerous commonalities emerge between the three accounts of Islamic thinking, as they share the longing for progressive developments in theology, politics, society, and scholarship. In addition they rest many of their hopes on their understanding of the Quran and the proposed exegesis. A common theme through out the writings of these scholars is the centrality of the Quran and its reception history within Islamic culture and thought.

Different terminology is used to describe the group of Muslim intellectuals to which Rahman, Arkoun and Abu Zayd belong. Categorising these scholars may not be helpful, as a detailed analysis of their thinking reveals an abundance of perspectives and influences. However for the sake of communicating their ideas, a labelling might be appropriate to a certain degree. Many descriptive terms are used to describe them: progressive, modern, reformed, protestant, rational, and enlightened. Even more specific terms can be found. Rahman is called *neo-conservative* or *neo-traditionalist*; Abu Zayd is referred to as *neo-Mu'tazilite* and Arkoun is labelled *deconstructivist*, *structuralist* or *postmodern*. Still, all these labels must be viewed critically. Plus, it is yet unclear whether these thinkers perceive themselves as a group, or whether they happen to be individuals who express similar ideas. It appears it is more the concern of outward observers to categorise these thinkers for the sake of discussing contemporary Islam. Even though I consider myself an observer – and I make use of certain general labels when conversing about this stream of Islamic thought – it is not the task of this thesis to determine decisive classifications. Nonetheless, when referring to secondary literature on the works of the three thinkers, one might need to come to terms with the applied labels. However, the analysis attempted in this work might provide insights that could promote more detailed classifications that do justice to the complexity of their thought.[1] And in practice, I do not avoid using descriptions such as 'progressive' or 'liberal' as long as I feel they are mainly adequate.

Many ideas expressed by Muslim intellectuals, such as the three under scrutiny, sound liberating and innovative to Western audiences. Hence, this line of thought gained considerable attention in recent years within scholarship of religion and also the public media. For several reasons, the attention given within Western discourse

---

1   For a recent attempt of classifying trends in Islam and clarifying terminology see the article *Contemporary Trends in Islam: A Preliminary Attempt at a Classification* by the Islam scholar Abdullah Saeed.

is not unjustified. The most prevalent reason is the well-meant advocacy of Western observers in pointing out similarities between this kind of 'Islamic' thinking and the mentalities of liberty and democracy which are broadly perceived as important dimensions of Western societies. In this regard the reason for the presence of 'progressive' Muslims in the media is a good-willed attempt to bring the two sides, the 'Western' and the 'Islamic,' closer together. These efforts are aimed at presenting Islamic views as welcomed alternatives to the, however often grossly distorted,picture of Islam in tabloids. Hence, interest in these alternative voices are unfortunately often triggered by crises and events that let Muslim culture appear questionable to Westerners.

By and large I am inclined to oppose generalized images of Islam that promote distorted perceptions non-Muslims develop of Muslims, and their diverse beliefs and cultures. Hence I like to point out the multiplicity of religious thought within Islam, not only to highlight more liberal Muslim voices that formulate alternatives towards fundamental or extremist Muslim stances, but also to highlight the depth and vast facets of Muslim thought in general. What we can say at first glance, is that Rahman, Arkoun and Abu Zayd appear to be progressive, future and development orientated.[2]

The scholarly and public interest in these new voices is comprehensible when one looks at the titles published by modern Muslim writers in Western languages (here English examples): *Towards a humanistic hermeneutics* (Abu Zayd, 2006), *Reformation of Islamic Thought* (Abu Zayd, 2006) *Islam and Modernity* (Rahman, 1982), *Rethinking Islam* (Arkoun, 1994), *Islam: To Reform or Subvert* (Arkoun, 2007), *Quran and Liberation* (Esack, 1997), *Islam and the Secular Mind* (Akhtar, 2008), *Radical Reform: Islamic Ethics and Liberation* (Ramadan, 2009), *Islam, Secularism, and Liberal Democracy* (Hashemi, 2009). These titles include various buzzwords such as humanism, reformation, modernity, liberation, secularism, democracy, which instantly remind a Western audience of intellectual developments that are primarily dedicated to Western societies. Moreover, these words are often regarded as sole fruits of Western intellectual endeavours. Such new connotations of Islam bring the reader of these titles at odds with already established images of Islam. Western Orientalist images of Islam are often as incompatible with those values that are now also being called for by Muslims.

Critical investigation of modern Muslim writings by Western intellectuals can lead to very distinct conclusions. One example is the extensive investigation into Tariq Ramadan's work by the French author and journalist Caroline Fourest in her book *Brother Tariq: The Doublespeak of Tariq Ramadan* (2008). She concludes that the media should be more critical of Ramadan. According to Fourest, Ramadan portrays two different accounts of Islam and a Muslim life in contemporary times. What he says while addressing a Western audience might be very different from what he expresses in front of Muslim listeners. She accuses Ramadan of being two- faced, which renders him untrustworthy. In contrast, studies of other Muslim thinkers such as Ursula Günther's investigation of Arkoun's work conclude that the positive impact of the author's

---

2   I am content in using the term 'progressive' as an explanatory adjective, because common among the thinkers is the general idea of the enhancement of human conditions. At this point, I will not differentiate between those who are progressive (according to certain criteria) and those who merely think of themselves as being progressive. But it might be worth pointing out that there exists a difference and that a researcher needs to be aware of it in the course of enquiry.

work might be and should be felt in the future, because of its valuable impulses and prospects for both, the Muslim and non-Muslim audience.

So far we have identified two reasons for interest in contemporary Muslim intellectuals. The first reason is that contemporary Muslim intellectuals offer accounts of Islam as alternatives to extremist and exclusivist interpretations. The second reason is that their work can be interpreted as an attempt to reconcile Islamic values with values that are regarded as precious in the Western world. Of course these two reasons are interconnected on different levels. I also want to point out a third motivation for engaging with this kind of thought from a non-Muslim perspective. What makes some of these Muslim thinkers interesting for a Western audience is that they make use of, or show parallels to critical research, argumentation, and methods which are widely applied in Western academia. They are not shy of directing analytical investigation to their religious and cultural heritage. In doing so, they are perceived by Western scholars, theologians and the media as role models of a future-oriented, well-informed Muslim scholarship. Commentators on their work express the hope that such Muslim thought could lead Islam into a reformation.[3] Linked to this development are prospects of establishing peaceful intercultural and interreligious encounters that further constructive coexistence. Non-Muslim supporters, promoters or mere sympathetic commentators of this kind of Muslim thought are often Christian theologians, who critically engage with Muslim thought and are looking for parallels to their own religion's history, values and beliefs. Time and time again they carry anticipations for an irenic co-operation with such representatives of the Muslim faith in Western spheres. Especially in Western countries with large Muslim minorities these inter-faith attempts are crucial. Examples of such Christian theologians who support and promote the liberal attempts of modern Muslims and speak in favour or at least refer to them as positive models are the Catholic scholars Joachim Valentin, Christian Troll, Felix Körner and Gregory Baum.[4]

The three incentives for Western scholars to engage with contemporary Muslim thought seem to be valid motivations. In addition, I will attempt to explore the three accounts of Islam by Rahman, Arkoun and Abu Zayd with regard to the 'centrality of the Quran.' The notion of the centrality of the Quran lies at the heart of what I consider an authentic (or genuine) account of Islam. In the formulation of such an account one needs to think about the nature of the Quran, how it ought to be dealt with and how it informs Islamic thought and life. The Quran is the founding stone of Islamic religion, namely, it embodies the experience of revelation. Hence, any explanation of Islam needs to attempt to understand the Quran, its revelation and interpretation.

Rahman, Arkoun and Abu Zayd each formulate the centrality of the Quran in similar ways. In addition they develop concrete wishes for social reforms that are intended

---

3   Here one needs to recognize that many 'Western' perceptions of Islam, also of Islam's moderate voices, are often Euro-centric in perspective. Often commentators fail to engage with the very own terms of these Muslim accounts.

4   Cf. Troll, *Plurality of Religion – Plurality in Religion*. Troll refers to Abu Zayd and Arkoun as carrier of hope for a scientific and contemporary hermeneutic of the Quran. See also Troll's interview: "Es fehlt eine zeitgemäße Hermeneutik des Korans." Valentin mentions Abu Zayd and Arkoun as representatives of a new understanding of the Quran and possible bridge-builders between Western and Islamic theological thought. Cf. Valentin, *Is There Rationality in Islam? Theological Backgrounds of the Current Conflicts*, 75–89.

to affect how Muslims express and live their religious beliefs. The main challenge is to show how they desire to achieve these concrete reforms and a changed perception of Islam through a re-reading of the Quran. It might be anticipated that a rethinking of the Quran's nature has already led to new ways of envisaging Islam.

Examples of new views of Islam can be found in Felix Körner's presentation of core texts of the Ankara school in his book *Alter Text – neuer Kontext* (Old Text – New Context), 2006. It features the rereading of the Quran and the rethinking Islam as practised by Turkish scholars who hope for a general renewal of Muslim thinking, not just a change of conditions to suit demands of modernities. Ömer Özsoy, one representative of the Ankara School, expresses his hopes for a re-thinking of the Quranic nature in order to gain back its relevance for Muslim life today. To view the Quran as a *non-hyper-historical* (*übergeschichtlichen*) text would enable Muslims to find adequate answers to the challenges of modernity.[5] Another member of the Ankara School, Mehmet Paçaci, discusses the 'historicity' of the Quran,[6] and expresses the expectation for the establishment of a new culture by today's Muslims.[7] He also rethinks the character of the Quran as a revelation, not only a fixed text, and wants to avoid 'going back to the Quran in the course of a quasi-Protestant textualism.'[8] These two examples, by Özsoy and Paçaci illustrate how a contemporary rethinking and re-reading of the Quran takes place in connection with reforming Islam and Muslim culture.

Rahman, Arkoun and Abu Zayd pose similar ideas They recognize the centrality of the Quran, and develop methods of interpretation that will lead to what they regard as an account of Islam more suitable for contemporary life. They consider not only the nature of the Quran but also the process of revelation, the role of Muhammad, the need for historical awareness, and for social reform. The fact that the three thinkers engage intensely with theological themes proves that their accounts differ from merely political, philosophical or sociological schemes.[9] They are genuinely Islamic, since the common denominator in their overall thinking is the centrality of the Quran. Of course upon closer examination *Islamic* is not synonymous with *Quranic*. However, it may be that there exists a connection between Quranic interpretation and society throughout Islamic history. Since the three thinkers suppose such link and hope that a shift within Islamic world views could affect society positively, this research will follow the assumption Expecting a link between the treatment and understanding of the Quran and cultural expressions of Islam, Rahman, Arkoun und Abu Zayd also address the role of religion in contemporary society inclusive of the challenges a religious life might face. For this reason it is helpful to call to mind some of these challenges.

---

5 Cf. Özsoy, "Erneuerungsprobleme zeitgenössischer Muslime und der Koran," and "Rede, nicht Text." Ömer Özsoy is currently professor of Islam at the J.W. Goethe University in Frankfurt.

6 For a discussion of Paçaci's problematic use and translation of the term 'historicity' and its different meanings and connotations see Körner, *Alter Text – neuer Kontext*, 75–6.

7 Paçaci, "Der Koran und ich – wie geschichtlich sind wir?" 33.

8 "Rückgriff auf den Koran als quasi-protestantischen Textualismus." (Körner, *Alter Text – neuer Kontext*, 74.)

9 In this course Arkoun seems to pose somewhat of a special case, because although he dedicates most of his work to questions of Islam, he does not unlike Rahman and Abu Zayd, openly admit endorsing a religious world view. I will mention this problematic later in the main analysis.

2. Challenges to Religious Thought

Religions are challenged by ever changing circumstances in politics, society, and economy. If religion wants to avoid becoming obsolete for society it has to react to changes in a way that it successfully preserves its relevance. Euro-centrically said, the adaption of religion to contemporary challenges is often regarded as an outcome of modernity and associated changes including: enlightenment, progress, and social improvement. Certain factors of the adaption of religion pose special challenges, such as privatization and individualization (Kaufmann, 1989),[10] submission under value-universality (Nielsen-Sikora, 2005),[11] relativization (Callaway, 2007),[12] inner reformation and with it globalization of human rights (Lund, 2006),[13] secularization (Willems, 2002),[14] loss of welfare function via substitution through social states, and pluralisation. In the context of the 'World Values Research' Müller (2009) reflects on some of these effects on religious traditions:

> The pluralisation of 'life worlds' leads to differing religious worldviews, which make the persistence of one single legitimizing religious worldview impossible to maintain, the "plausibility structure" of religion becomes severely undermined (cf. Berger & Luckmann 1966). A relativization of religious beliefs and decrease of societal importance of religion takes place. With religion's separation of other parts of the society and the increased demand for scientific and technical knowledge, it becomes increasingly difficult to socialize younger cohorts into traditional belief systems. Yet with the loss of its former all embracing functions for society, religion is forced to retreat from the public into the private sphere, losing its influence and significance for other parts of the society. On an individual level, decreasing individual religious beliefs and a disengagement from religious rites follow.[15]

Challenges for religion based on secularization and modernization theories predict some kind of vanishing of religion. This process of evaporation entails first a disappearing from the public sphere and secondly the loss of significance, also for private individuals. On the other hand, Casanova has shown that the differentiation between religion and public sphere alone might under various criteria continue to privatise religion but does not necessarily do so. He mentions several criteria that can lead to the privatization of religion and concludes that religion on the basis of civil society can still be active in the public sphere and even foster the de-differentiation between religion and public. With this Casanova seems to attribute religions quite a subversive power and hence the

---

10 Thomas Luckmann worked out the process of privatization of religion in modern society. cf. *Das Problem der Religion in der modernen Gesellschaft*, (Freiburg 1963). English version: *The Invisible Religion. The Problem of Religion in Modern Society* (London/New York 1967). Cf. Franz Xaver Kaufmann, *Religion und Modernität*, 72.

11 Nielsen-Sikora speaks of the 'universal term' of political culture in his article "'Verfassungspatriotismus' in der Europäischen Union?", 184–5.

12 For the relativity of values cf. Callaway, *The Rhetoric of Asian Values*, 112–21.

13 Michael Lund speaks about the globalization of human rights after 1500 (reformation), in his article "Human Rights," 39–63.

14 See also Willems' study about the debate of values with regard to secularism in: *Religion als Privatsache?* Here is also discussed the ambivalence between the theoretical separation of state and church, e.g. in the USA, and the subversive demand for more influence of religion in governing society. 88–112.

15 Müller, "Religiosity and Attitudes towards the Involvement of Religious Leaders in Politics," 3.

potential to significantly shape society despite a differentiation between religion and public sphere.[16] On the other hand Halman and Pettersson (2004) find in their study on European values no "widespread preference for religion to be a potent actor in the political and public realm."[17] These examples show that discussions on the future role of religion in private and public spheres are likely to raise questions about future challenges to religious thought. What is more, religions as part of specific cultures and mentalities have been touched by encounters with other cultures and beliefs. What might be special in the present is the extent to which people are connected by new media and hence have much more and easier access to foreign news and beliefs around the world. In addition, the different ways of living become competitive in the constant strive for economic strength. There seems to be a mutual relation between religions, politics and societies. When one thinks of the role of religion – whether its role seems crucial or peripheral, – religious beliefs seem to either influence, or be influenced by world dynamics. As such they are part of something bigger then themselves.

Rahman, Arkoun and Abu Zayd reflect on the role of religion and try to discover which contribution a rethought Islam could make to the dynamics of a changing world. In this they also reflect critically on the different answers already given by Muslims to challenges of modernity.

3. Specific Challenges to Islamic Thought

Because the research in this work is about Muslims' answers to challenges for religions, it might be worth considering those challenges that seem to be specifically faced by Muslim cultures. Most obvious are the existential plights which stem from the underdevelopment of majority Muslim countries.[18] Statistics show that the overlap of Muslim majority and underdeveloped countries is significantly higher than such of historically and dominantly Christian countries.[19] Much research has tried to find reasons for the phenomenon of this underdevelopment. One line of research suggests that the strong links between religiosity and political leadership might be a factor that hinders development. Tim Müller finds that amongst the Muslim public the acceptance of the idea that religious spokespeople influence politics is high. The Arab world shares

---

16 Halman refers to Casanova, *Public Religions in the Modern World*, 1994, (*European Values at the Turn of the Millenium*, 319).

17 Data for this study was collected 1999/2000 (Halman & Pettersson, *European Values at the Turn of the Millenium*, 16+336).

18 Works mentioning underdevelopment are: Kuran, *Islam and Mammon*; Amirpur, *Der Islam am Wendepunkt*; von Kügelgen, *Averroes und die Arabische Moderne*; Norris/Inglehart, *Sacred and Secular*; Müller, "Religiosity and Attitudes towards the Involvement of Religious Leaders in Politics;" Global Gender Gap Report; United Nations Human Development Report (UN-HDR)/ United Nations Arab Development Report (UN-ADR); Rahman, Arkoun and Abu Zayd but also Abd al-Jabri, Fatimah Mernissi, Amina Wadud, and Leila Ahmad often speak of the crisis or morass of the Muslim world. In their critiques they use various terminologies which are intriguing to discern. Numerous sociological researches suggest that this difference between the West and Muslim countries comes down to deviations in economic development. The role of an explicit Islamic mentality as cause of underdevelopment is strongly debated.

19 In this thesis 'development' is understood to consist of complex factors and criteria as put forward by the UN Human Development Report.

this overlap of high acceptance of 'religious influence' and lowest development in the world only with Sub-Saharan countries.[20] This result hints at a possible link between the acceptance of religious leadership within politics and underdevelopment. Here secularization theorists hit upon a verification of their view that a differentiation of religion and state fosters development. Others, such as sociologists of religion like Ulrich Oevermann (2006) find that a sociological reading of the Quran reveals an Islam-inherent impediment to development. He claims that this limitation goes back to the lack of the rationalization dynamic.[21] One conclusion of this sociological reading is that Islam bears an inherent impossibility of a differentiation of state and religion. If this were true also here the development of democracy-awareness (*Demokratiebe-wusstsein*) seems prevented.[22] Oevermann asserts that in his sociological ('objective') hermeneutics he scrutinizes the literal readings of the Quran, as put forward by what one could call 'more fundamentalist' streams of Islamic thought. According to this logic, I speculate that a 'more humanist' reading such as proposed by Rahman, Arkoun and Abu Zayd might exempt Islam from these consequences.

Such sociological theories and Müller's study are echoed in Riaz Hassan's research *Faithlines* (2002), which shows how the majority of Muslims interviewed in his study stated that an Islamic society would "have to be based on the Quran and Sharia."[23] Still, other studies display different results. Political scientist Inglehart finds that public support of democracy in Islamic countries is as strongly developed as for example, in the USA. Intriguingly, the widest gap between Western and Islamic civilizations is found in different moral and sexual values.[24] This finding suggests that it is not the

---

20 Müller, "Religiosity and Attitudes towards the Involvement of Religious Leaders in Politics": "Since 2002, the United Nations has three times commissioned the so-called Arab Human Development Report. There, Arab scientists explore the factors that contribute to the 'halt of the Islamic world', which they certainly do not deny. They come to the conclusion that in the Arab world substantial deficits in the areas of freedom, rights for women and education prevail. In all these areas, only sub-Saharan Africa has worse figures than the Arab world. In Egypt, the illiteracy rate of men is 40 percent, of women around 60 percent. Only two of one thousand Arabs have internet access. Could not these numbers be much more responsible for the "halt of the Islamic world," than the written, in the Quran preserved word of God? One might reply that all these deficits are basically based on the Quran: for it cements bondage and oppression of women and prevents development. But if all this would actually be derived from the wording of the Quran, then how has this society, which relies on the Quran as a constituent element, brought forward a high culture? This sounds not entirely logical."

21 In contrast, Oevermann claims that this dynamic is fostered by Biblical narratives, particularly those of the story of the fall.

22 Oevermann and also the sociologist Johannes Twardella (2006) claim further Islam-inherent blockades of modernisation, one of them being the dependence of Muslim populaces on clerics in matters of knowledge. I believe this dependence must be contrasted with the reliance of gaining knowledge through non-religious education.

23 "93 Prozent aller von ihm befragten Indonesier, Pakistanis und Ägypter erklärten, dass eine islamische Gesellschaft auf dem Koran und der Scharia fußen müsse (F 124)." (Amirpur/Amman *Islam am Wendepunkt*, 19.)

24 Norris/Inglehart (2004), in *Sacred and Secular* discuss the value of 'democracy.' The sociologist of religion Inglehart conducts quantitative data collection through projects such as the World Values Survey. Studies of 1995–2001 say that faith in democracy can be found on the middle level with USA and Islamic countries. The biggest gap between

lack of supporting democratic systems that divides Islam and the non-Islamic West, but maybe differences in ethics. A discussion based on these indications might reveal further challenges to Muslim countries if a plausible connection between moral values and religious belief could be shown.

History of Islamic cultures shows another detail. It is the enormous time hiatus between the end of the high time – or Golden Age – of the Islamic empires up to approximately the 12th century and the beginning of confrontation with Western civilization. There are different theories about when and why the decline of the Islamic era took place. Some even doubt that a decline took place or negotiate the extent of the decline. The fact that in at present the Muslim world is far from a golden age and consists of mostly underdeveloped countries is, I believe, evidence enough for a decline of some sort. This observation leads to various interpretations of reasons for the stagnation within Islamic cultures also from within the Muslim realm. For example, contemporary scholarship of Islam in Ankara, the aforementioned *Ankara School*, laments "the burden of Western imperialism, which paralysed the development of Islam since hundreds of years."[25] One characteristic of Islamic revival movements for example – and I would exempt the Ankara School from this class – is the linking of the effects of imperialism to a weak Muslim culture. Some representatives of this group find imperialism to be the cause for the current underdevelopment. Hence liberation from imperialism and its effects is required. Others say the weak Islamic profile of Muslim cultures allowed imperialism to succeed in the first place. They then conclude that the solution must be the re-formulation of a strong Islamic agenda for Muslim culture. Others see in the confrontation with the colonial powers that pressed into the Near- and Middle East an excessive demand on Islamic cultures through material and ideological development of the West. This excessive postulation probably fostered a purposive-rational reason (*Zweckrationalität*).[26] *Zweckrationalität* functions selectively and is applicable in current situations that need current solutions. It does not attempt to be a holistic account of rationality that spans to humanities or mental endeavours. However, we must see that the challenges address not only economy but also thought. This close link can be found in the history of economic growth in the Western hemisphere. Within Muslim countries the exposure to new economic systems and technologies led to different attitudes within the populace and political leaders. Some welcomed the implementation of technology but rejected the economic system for religious reasons. Some strengthened their identity as *Muslim* or *Arab* through rediscovering and intensifying faith. At the same time, the technological achievements of the West were welcomed with the argument that they rooted in the sciences that Islam developed in its golden age and then transferred to the West.[27] Others point out the sudden confrontation of Islamic culture with Western colonial powers. The effect of surprise they claim was harder for Muslim societies to process because most of them lacked the gradual development from medieval ages via renaissance towards enlightenment into present times. At least

---

beliefs in democratic values could be found between Eastern Orthodox countries and Western countries, not between Islamic and Western countries. Although Norris and Inglehart admit that the biggest gap between West and Islamic countries can be seen with regard to sexual conduct.

25 Körner, *Alter Text – neuer Kontext*, 243.

26 Hendrich, *Islam und Aufklärung*, 8.

27 Cf. Hendrich, *Islam und Aufklärung*, 246.

24

it is suggested that this development did not take place to a degree comparable to that in the West.[28] Within this line of criticism, the Egyptian professor of philosophy Murad Wahba claims that "the lack of renaissance and enlightenment in the Muslim world almost equates the lack of Averroism in this part of the world."[29] Wahba alludes to the anticipation that the marginalization of certain streams of thought was carried out by the dominant Islamic zeitgeist roughly since the 12th century. Now, Wahba refers to the Islamic philosophical-rational thought which in the form of Averroism essentially contributed to Europe's intellectual development. This shows, according to Wahba, how such trends within Islamic thought need to find fertile soil – as it did find in the West – to carry fruits. Wahba says:

> Averroisimus als ein philosophischer Trend hat eine wirksame Rolle bei der Heraus-bildung des europäischen philosophischen Bewusstseins gespielt, während es sich im Übergang vom Mittelalter über die Renaissance zur Aufklärung befand. D.h. die islamische Zivilisation – in Gestalt des Averroismus – hat zur Entwicklung der menschlichen Zivilisation im Westen beigetragen, während Averroes von der islamischen Kultur vollkommen abgelehnt wurde.[30]

Could therefore the marginalization of rational thinking, and with it, the lack of comparable development towards renaissance and enlightenment be a cause of the current underdevelopment?[31] Often strong links between religious leadership and state affairs are blamed for this. These links might have been encouraged by idea of a necessary inner unity of religion and state. Geert Hendrich (2004) claims that the idea of such unity was traditionally a theological one and only introduced by politics from the 11th century on.[32] Ammann (2006), who also acknowledges the underdevelopment writes

---

28 Valentin, "Rationalität im Islam?" 76.
29 von Kügelgen cites the Egyptian philosophy professor Murad Wahba (1979), *The Paradox of Averroes*, 260. (von Kügelgen, *Averroes*, 1)
30 Ibid: "Averroism, as a philosophical trend, has played an effective role in the formation of the European philosophical consciousness, while it was in the transition from the Middle Ages, through Renaissance to the Enlightenment. This means, the Islamic civilization – in the form of Averroism – has contributed to the development of human civilization in the West, while Averroes was completely rejected by the Islamic culture."
31 Valentin, "Rationalität im Islam?" 75. Joachim Valentin warns to not uncritically praise Western enlightenment and he tries to indicate the need of accepting Islamic mental history as also part of Western history. He suggests to say at least partially "good-bye to the irreligious conception of rationality in French Enlightenment." Valentin also mentions Abu Zayd in his assertion that 'enlightenment' "is generally understood first as paraphrase of a European phenomenon which obviously has no direct counterpart in Islam" (Valentin, ibid, 88+76).
    Another possible cause is mentioned by the Muslim scholar Abed al-Jabri. He mentions in his critique of Arabic reason the inner struggle for power of contesting Muslim leaders and Islamic groups which led to the downfall of the early Arabic high culture [Hochkultur] (cf. Al-Jabri, *Kritik der Arabischen Vernunft. Naqd al-ʿaql al-ʿarabi*). This line of argument holds the deconstructive politics responsible for the demise and not primarily aberrations within philosophical theological thinking. (This is not to say that Jabri does not bring forward also a critique of the decline of philosophical thinking in Islam.)
32 Hendrich, *Islam und Aufklärung*, 48.

about the supposed connections between Islam and its alleged inability to develop. He doubts that the reasons can be found in the sacral nature of the Quran:[33]

> Seit dem Jahre 2002 haben die Vereinten Nationen dreimal den so genannten Arab Human Development Report in Auftrag gegeben. Arabische Wissenschaftler untersuchen darin, welche Faktoren zum 'Stillstand der islamischen Welt', den sie durchaus nicht leugnen, beitragen. Sie kommen zu dem Schluss, dass in der arabischen Welt erhebliche Defizite in den Bereichen Freiheit, Rechte für Frauen und Bildung herrschen. In all diesen Bereichen wird die arabische Welt nur noch von Schwarzafrika unterboten. In Ägypten liegt die Analphabetenquote bei Männern um 40 Prozent, bei Frauen um 60 Prozent (...).
> Könnten diese Zahlen nicht weit mehr für den „Stillstand der islamischen Welt" verantwortlich sein als das geschriebene, im Koran festgehaltene Wort Gottes? Entgegnen könnte man, dass all diese Defizite im Grunde auf den Koran zurückgehen: weil er Unfreiheit zementiert und Frauenunterdrückung und Entwicklung verhindert. Aber würde sich all dies tatsächlich eins zu eins aus dem Wortlaut des Koran ableiten lassen, wie hat dann diese Gesellschaft, die sich auf den Koran als konstituierendes Element beruft, eine Hochkultur hervorbringen können? Ganz logisch klingt das nicht.[34]

In my view Ammann rightly points out that the Quran and its content are often blamed too quickly for the crisis of the Muslim world. It is the understanding of the people that the written word lies at the bottom of creating values, life-styles and decision-making. So we can assume that, yes the Quran potentially delivers certain mental material to Muslim cultures; but on the other hand it is still the people who decide

---

33 "Immer wieder wird der Islam als demokratieresistent beschrieben. Die meisten, die so argumentieren, suchen die Gründe für diese angebliche Resistenz im Sakralen, also in dem Text, der diese Religion stiftete, dem Koran. Doch verschließt die Fixierung auf den Koran nicht den Blick für die eigentlichen Hintergründe und Ursachen des 'Stillstands der islamischen Welt', der zu Recht konstatiert wird?" (Ammann in the introduction to Amirpur/Ammann, *Islam am Wendepunkt*, 16–7.)

34 Amman in the introduction to Amirpur/Ammann, *Islam am Wendepunkt*, 16–7: "Since 2002, the United Nations has ordered the so-called Arab Human Development Report three times. Arab scientists are investigating the factors contributing to the 'halt the Islamic world', whose existence they do not deny. They come to the conclusion that in the Arab world exist significant deficits in areas of freedom, rights for women and education. In all these matters the Arab world is only underscored by Sub-Saharan Africa. In Egypt, the illiteracy rate of men lies at 40 percent, of women at 60 percent (...). Could it not be these figures that are responsible for the "standstill of the Islamic world," rather than the written word of God, captured in the Quran? Could the reply be that all these deficits go basically back to the Quran: because it cements bondage and the oppression of women and suppresses development. But could all this actually be derived from the wording of the Quran one by one, then how could this society that relies on the Quran as a constituent element, have produced a high culture? This does not sound quite logically."
I believe it also needs to be investigated to which degree Islamic societies were actually conducted through ideologies that were inspired by a particular Quranic interpretation. To discover the most influential ideas during the time of the high culture of Islam, might mean to find potential inspiration for today's encountering of reality.

which readings of the Quran they prefer. In any case it is not clear to which degree the Quran is the source for the expressions of life and thought in the Islamic realm.

Another idea comes to mind when reading Ammann's citation. If his critique was to be expanded and one concluded that it is not the Quran but that there are other causes (Ammann points as example to the high illiteracy rate), then the idea of a re-reading of the Quran as a possible solution out of the crisis also needs to be rethought. We will see in how far Rahman, Arkoun and Abu Zayd find solutions in a re-reading of the Quran, or a reconsidering of its role, a rethinking of the role of religion in general and which other factors for the underdevelopment they identify.

Also Nader Hashemi (2009) tackles the task of Islam's development towards liberal conduct of society put forward the idea that "liberal democracy requires a form of secularism to sustain itself, yet simultaneously the main political, cultural, and intellectual resources at the disposal of Muslim democrats today are theological."[35] Hence the author pleads for developing a genuinely Islamic theory of liberal democratization via reformation of religious thought, on which I believe interpretation of the scriptures lies at heart.[36] He also states the importance, not only for Muslims but for all, of engaging with the challenges to Islamic thought and the offered solutions:

> The topic of religion and democracy, after September 11, is now one of the most important and pressing questions of our age. This is especially true in light of the general absence of democracy and respect for human rights throughout most of the Muslim world. The destabilizing effects that emanate from the Middle East now affect us all.

Hashemi argues

> that there is an inherent link between the reformation of religious thought and political development. [...] This relationship between religion and liberal democracy is especially important in societies where religion is a key marker of identity and where religious values shape the political culture. Recognizing this point can help democratic theorists untangle the complicated relationship between religion, secularism, and democracy in the Muslim world today.[37]

As part of democratization within Islamic cultures Katajun Amirpur (2006) stresses the point of an open discussion culture (*offene Diskussionskultur*): "Who wants an open reform debate, should exclude no one."[38] With this she signifies the mechanisms within Islamic societies such as Egypt and Iran, which often exclude reformist thinkers and

---

35 Hashemi, *Islam, Secularism, and Liberal Democracy*, 1.
36 Hashemi, *Islam, Secularism, and Liberal Democracy*, 22. He attributes great importance to Muslim intellectuals in fighting for a liberal democratization: "Personalities such as Shireen Ebadi, Yusuf Saanei, Mohsen Kadivar, and Abdolkarim Soroush remind us of the critical role played by what we might call "religious intellectuals" in promoting political development in conservative religious political environments. By situating their moral arguments with one foot in tradition and the other in modernity, they act as a critical bridge in the transition from authoritarianism to liberal democracy. This is particularly true when it comes to introducing new philosophical and theological innovations in societies with nonexistent or weak liberal-democratic traditions." (101)
37 Hashemi, *Islam, Secularism, and Liberal Democracy*, 21–2.
38 Amirpur/Ammann, *Der Islam am Wendepunkt*: "Wer eine wirkliche offene Reformdebatte wünscht, sollte niemanden ausschließen" (11).

their arguments from crucial public debates. This current marginalisation could hinder intellectual development and reduce offers of solutions for developing Islamic cultures.[39]

As we see, possible reasons for the contemporary state of Islamic cultures seem to be manifold and cannot be reduced to one single component. For us it is interesting to see which connection Rahman, Arkoun and Abu Zayd anticipate and tackle with their specific views on the Quran and the proposed hopes for reform. Obviously, in the course of recent history (18/19th -21st century) numerous answers were given by Muslims to offer solutions to these challenges. Among the various streams of thought many demanded first of all a new reading of the Quran. And these streams are of interest to us. Within them the stipulated degree of forming society by a certain Quranic interpretation varies and also does the quality of argumentation. In contrast to those approaches, where the agenda is set first and only secondly is looked for support in the Quran, in this study such genuine Islamic schemes of thought are of interest that demonstrate a more systematic approach to the Quran.

4. Research Question

This research critically investigates the thinking of Rahman, Arkoun and Abu Zayd, in order to find an approach towards evaluating the socio-intellectual potentials of contemporary Muslim thought.

Rahman, Arkoun and Zayd plead for mental individualization various freedoms, such as of choice of religion, opinion, teaching, research, and suffrage. Especially Rahman and Zayd, have experienced oppression of freedom in one or more of these realms thus it is possible that some of their scholarly foci result from their biographies. All three thinkers are specifically interested in the social manifestations of a rethinking of Islam and the Quran. Neither of them always deliver an analysis of the probable connection between specific Islamic thought and the current situation in Islamic countries. At the same time they often mention such connections and hence aim at offering alternative views, on which they rest hope for a development towards enlightenment, reformation and democracy.[40] From our initial considerations of the challenges for Islamic thought and the propositions by contemporary Muslim thinkers for reform, numerous questions could be addressed at the thinking of Rahman, Arkoun and Zayd: Do Rahman, Arkoun and Zayd aim at an Islamic enlightenment, reformation, renaissance, modernity? If they use such terms of describing a kind of transformation, how do they define them? Are they considering the changes and dynamics within other cultures that effected religious thinking and living? Do they draw parallels to other religions which went through similar processes? If they call for similar changes in Islamic religious societies, do they consider the consequences for religion, for example do they address the possible surmounting of religion or withdrawal into the private realm?

For our investigation, the centrality of the Quran plays a crucial role. So if the three thinkers refer to values or so-called achievements of modernity such as secularity,

---

39 Cf. Wielandt, "Wurzeln der Schwierigkeit innerislamischen Gesprächs." Wielandt writes about the marginalization mechanisms that also led to Abu Zayd's expulsion. Cf. Thielmann, *Nasr Hamid Abu Zaid und die wiedererfundene hisba*, 126–7.
40 Owing to the complexity of these terms it must be one of the objectives of this thesis to observe how Rahman, Arkoun and Abu Zayd utilize them.

democracy and freedom do they anticipate that those can be also derived from the Quran? Or do they at least observe that the Quran does not entail material that could hinder the achievement of these values? How much importance do they attribute to the Quran in finding answers for contemporary Muslims in current affairs? In view of these questions and with regard to the assumption that inner consistency is a criterion for credibility of any thinking, I have decided on the following leading question: How does each thinker understand the Quran and can this understanding lend support to their reform ideas?

This question entails the sub-questions: how do Rahman, Arkoun and Zayd understand the nature of the Quran? This comes down to their understanding of the revelation process and the role of Muhammad as Prophet. How then does their comprehension of the Quran's nature influence their interpretation methods? Which core ideas of their reform hopes can be supported by their Quran exegesis?

5. Choice of Thinkers

I choose to examine the thinking of three Muslim intellectuals who seem to have numerous motivations in common. Fazlur Rahman, Muhammad Arkoun and Nasr Hamid Abu Zayd offer perspectives on Islam and the Quran that are alternatives to revivalist and fundamentalist accounts. In addition all three thinkers are regarded as belonging to a rational stream of Islamic. Nevertheless, they tend to assign great importance to religion as a social factor. They link their hope for social change to the demand for a reconsideration of the Quran's nature and its interpretation. Their sources of inspirations can be found in the Islamic and non-Islamic heritage of philosophy, history, sociology and literary studies. References to diverse sources of knowledge suggest that they practice a inclusive scholarship that considers not only intellectual accounts from within Islam. Rahman has a background in traditional Islamic studies and is committed to rethinking Islamic law and philosophy. Arkoun mostly works within the realm of history and sociology of religion and has particularly interest in anthropological approaches. Then, as a literary scholar, Abu Zayd examines the effects of language and applies literary theories to the study of the Quran. The borders between the different disciplines are ultimately intertwined and all three thinkers seem to appreciate the fruitfulness of inter-disciplinary approaches. Rahman, Arkoun and Abu Zayd show – even though to varying degrees – that scientific thinking should not be restricted by cultural and religious boundaries.

Further commonalities are found in their research interests. They tackle the relationship between religion and scientific knowledge, the role and tasks of religion today, the significance of an Islamic *weltanschauung* in a global context, the relationship between state and religion, Quran reception throughout Muslim history and the treatment of Islam and the Quran by Western scholarship.

Furthermore the three thinkers share some biographical experiences. They received scholarly training in their Muslim home countries but also at Western universities. It is here in the Western academy where they taught for longer periods. Rahman joined the North American University of Chicago in the 1960s whereas Arkoun spent most of his teaching career in the West (mostly at Paris' Sorbonne). Abu Zayd taught in Japan and Europe. All three thinkers are in many ways border-crossers.

A further commonality, between Rahman and Abu Zayd in particular, is that their published work caused Muslims and non-Muslims all over the world to either oppose or support their thought. They initiated a notable public and scholarly debate within theological and scientific circles in the West and in Islamic countries. In addition, their publications caused harsh reactions within Islamic legal and governmental levels. Abu Zayd's publications, as witnessed at the book fair in Cairo 2005, where still banned by the government. This shows how significant his work seems to the leading Egyptian intelligentsia, which has strong links to state politics. Maybe it was the coincidence of time and place of their publications, making their cases relevant for a wider even world-wide discussion. The Islamic studies scholars Rotraud Wielandt and Jörn Thielmann have shown that the cases of Rahman and Abu Zayd are good (but sad) examples for the cooperation between religious authorities and state. Also Bassam Tibi (1998) with reference to the Abu Zayd case concludes that there has been an "institutional intrusion of the state by fundamentalists."[41] In this way both thinkers can be regarded asgalvanisers of grievances in parts of the Islamic world. Unfortunately, both have also in common that they lacked support from their own states (Pakistan and Egypt), which rather listened to the accusations of religious leaders than to Rahman's and Abu Zayd's propositions for an improvement of social state of affairs. Often, these states and their men want to secure what they construct as a unity of the people, while simultaneously striving to gain and secure power and high positions. It seems not paramount to improve the social conditions of their people. As Abu Zayd says, his case of persecution was only a symptom of an afflicted Muslim society that is afraid of re-thinking and re-formulating faith, and disinterested in reforming society. Similarly, Rahman was abandoned by his former supporter, the president of Pakistan Ayyub Khan, when religious authorities raised their voices against Rahman's stances on Islam. Although Arkoun was not exposed to the same threats that Rahman and Abu Zayd had to face, Bassam Tibi points out that also he put himself at risk of being threatened by fundamentalists. Simply the titles of his publications, such as *Rethinking Islam*, could have been reason enough for attracting opponents.[42]

Because Rahman, Arkoun and Abu Zayd were partially trained in Western universities, their style of writing and argumentation is likely to be understood by Western readers. All their major works appeared in Western languages (as well as those of majority Muslim countries) and they are widely referred to in Western scholarship on Islam. This is because all three thinkers are proclaimed Muslims with a genuine and primary interest in developing and critiquing Islamic thinking. Rahman and Abu Zayd proclaim their Muslimhood explicitly, whereas Arkoun tries to keep it out of his writings, to the extent that one cannot judge his affiliation. However I anticipate that he considered himself a Muslim. Also the fact that he contributed his scholarly life to the study of Islam and the Quran points to his dedication and appreciation of Muslim culture and religion.

Another parallel, next to the ones mentioned above, is that Rahman and Abu Zayd were both so called *Carriers of the Quran* at young age, which means they memorized the entire Quran by heart.[43]

---

41 Tibi, *The Challenge of Fundamentalism*, xxvif. Tibi cites Abu Zayd in an interview where he speaks about the subversive danger of fundamentalist ideology which infiltrates state and schools.
42 Tibi, *The challenge of Fundamentalism*, 156.
43 Abu Zayd memorized the Quran at 8 and Rahman at 10 years of age.

I also find worth mentioning that Rahman, Arkoun and Abu Zayd originate in majority Muslim countries but come from different cultural and linguistic backgrounds. The mother tongue of the Pakistani Rahman is Urdu, while Arkoun from the Kabylie spoke Berber and Abu Zayd was the only native Arabic speaker amongst the three. With this diversity, they represent a complex Muslim community, of which only the minority have Arabic as their first language.

Common amongst them is that their first major scholarly studies were explorations of medieval Muslim scholars. Rahman gained his doctorate with a work on the psychology of the Persian Aristotelian philosopher and ethicist Ibn Sina (980–1037, Latin: Avicenna). Arkoun worked on the Persian neo-Platonic philosopher and ethicist Ibn Miskawayh (932–1030) and Abu Zayd on the Andalusian philosopher and mystic Ibn Arabi (1165–1240). These three luminaries of Muslim erudition belonged to what some scholars call the *Golden Age* of Islam,[44] in which numerous disciplines in human and natural sciences developed rapidly through the minds of Muslim scholars.

Neither Rahman, nor Arkoun or Abu Zayd are interested in delivering a complete interpretation of the Quran (*tafsīr*). Their major interest is to initiate a shift in perceiving and treating the Quran and redefining the possibility of living as a Muslim in a contemporary, also sometimes non-Muslim, environment. Although they do not produce an entire exegesis of the Quran, they provide guidelines for Quranic interpretation (and to various degrees practice exegesis). Those guidelines they hope will lead to the above mentioned change of approaching the Quran, so that it can today still inform Muslim life. Hildebrandt (2007) however points out that a reassessing of daily life matters would "not require a systematic new definition of the revelation concept and with it the corresponding method of exegesis."[45] In spite of this statement I see how the three thinkers establish exactly this link between a new perspective on revelation and interpretation methods and the reflection on life-concerning issues. This is not to say they proclaim that the Quran provides answers for all questions. But they see that, given the importance of Islam and with it the magnitude of the Quran in Muslim cultures, a rethinking of Quran, revelation and exegesis indeed must impact Muslim cultures. It is exactly this link which I attempt to examine. The study will look at the relationship between their reform hopes and their arguments, which seek support in their proposed Quran treatment. In this study we have to be reminded that Rahman, Arkoun and Abu Zayd do not rest all hopes on a re-reading of the Quran. Still much of what they hope for arises from their views on what the Quran, and therefore Islam has to offer to a contemporary world.

---

44 Cf. Ahmad Y. Hassan, Bernard Lewis, Seyyed Hossein Nasr.

45 Hildebrandt writes: „So macht Jansen drei Perspektiven der modernen muslimischen Koranbetrachtung aus: die Beschäftigung mit Alltagsfragen diesseitiger Art, mit naturwissenschaftlichen Fragen und mit Philologie. Was die erste Perspektive betrifft so kommt sie ohne systematische Neudefinition des Offenbarungskonzepts und der damit korrespondierenden Exegesemethoden aus." Jansen finds three perspectives within modern Muslim Quranic interpretation, namely "the engagement with questions of every day life of temporal kind, with questions of natural sciences and philology." (*Neo-Muʿtazilismus?* 361)

Chapter II – Quran

The concepts of the Quran's nature shall guide my enquiry through the complexity of the philosophies of Rahman, Arkoun, and Abu Zayd. Their thinking addresses multiple social spheres and their accounts are not always easily linked to their specific understanding of the Quran. Since I anticipate that all three thinkers put forward (each in his unique way) the thesis 'rethinking Islam requires rethinking the Quran', it seems paramount to investigate their accounts of the Quran. The subsequent query into their interpretation methods (chapter V) will depend on our findings in this chapter. Both, investigations made here and in chapter V, will reveal whether they tackle this thesis in the same way.

In this chapter I present their accounts of the Quran according to 6 foci, namely the Quran's *'corruption', function, complexity, orality* and *writtenness, universality,* and *accessibility* via *intelligibility/rationality*. These foci are all more or less specifically addressed by the three intellectuals and seem to contribute to their methods of interpretation. At the end of each section dedicated to the three thinkers, I reflect on the most significant findings and questions that surface from the investigation. Finally, a comparison of the three Quran accounts will be given.

Rahman

Rahman believes that any development within Muslim societies must occur through taking a fresh look on the Quran. He asks: "What kind of man does the Koran aim at producing? If this question can be successfully answered by Muslims, all questions can be answered."[46] The centrality of the Quran to Rahman's thought is unquestionable. He demands constant reflection over current social conditions and in response to them he hopes to formulate adequate religious requirements for running an Islamic society. In that course the re-reading of the Quran and re-application of its interpretations renders an endless process.

1. The Uncorrupted Quranic Essence

Despite Rahman's focus on the Quran, he does not reject the reference to secondary Islamic literature.[47] The Quran is also for Rahman in need of further explanatory literature, if only to a certain degree and purpose (cf. chapter V. Rahman). But at the same time Rahman grants the Quran highest authority within the religious corpus. This becomes lucid in Rahman's statement: "except the Qur'ān, all else is liable to the corrupting hand of history."[48]

What does he mean by that? According to my reading of Rahman, the moral laws entailed in the Quran are part of the divine sphere, 'as concrete as God,'[49] hence (theoretically) not exposed to corruption. Since Rahman's methodology ultimately

---

46 Rahman, "Roots of Islamic Neo-Fundamentalism," 35.
47 Saeed, "Fazlur Rahman," 55.
48 Rahman, *Islam and Modernity*, 147.
49 See my reading of Rahman, *Major Themes*, 15–6 in chapter II Rahman 2.

aims at revealing these divine laws it seems he regards the Quran generally as uncorrupted. His silence on the controversial history of the Quranic text might support the conclusion that he either was not highly critical with the Quran's historiography, or that he refers to the yet unwritten and orally known Quranic revelations. On the other hand he was by no means uncritical with Quranic interpretations produced throughout Islamic history. In his eyes interpretations are man-made, open to corruption and always dubious, while the Quran, remains coherent and uncorrupted. This understanding again points to the dichotomy of the Quran in its unspoiled and un-written state, and the written text, that is surface for multiple human and fallible renderings.

2. Guide towards Moral Perfection

The function of the Quran is to mediate divine guidance to humankind. Man is is hence encouraged to fulfil God's will, in the present and hereafter. The Quran also brings correction, which seeks to abolish errors of peoples which had been given scriptures in the past and which had corrupted them through misinterpretation. Following the divine and 'most comprehensive guidance for man' (*hudā li'l-nās*) in the present leads ideally to the perfection of humankind,[50] and in the hereafter to eternal life in paradise. In all efforts to engage with the Quran, the reader should approach the text in the knowledge that the Quran seeks to be a guide (and not a dictator).

Rahman writes: "The Qur'ān, as the Word of God is as concrete as the Command or the Law of God–indeed, as God Himself–and represents the depth and breadth of life itself; it will refuse to be straight–jacketed [sic] by intellectual and cultural bias."[51] I understand this to mean that the moral law is divine, since it is itself a part of God,[52] and hence in the end cannot be corrupted in any way. The main function of the Quran is guiding humankind towards moral perfection. That God's guidance ideally leads to the "moral improvement of man,"[53] means that both soteriological explanations and practical instructions for social conduct conjoin.

How does the Quran gain its purpose as guidance? Rahman endorses the traditional Islamic view that the Quran was revealed to Muhammad as reaction to numerous real situations (social, political, military etc.) over a certain period of time. Put differently, the condescension of the divine speech is a response to historical circumstances. It attempted to guide a certain people at a time of definite circumstances, which evolved chronologically.[54] Still, for Rahman the Quran's content – the

---

50 Rahman, *Islam and Modernity*, 155.
51 Rahman, *Major Themes*, 15–6.
52 Rahman, *Islam*, 32–3.
53 Rahman, *Islam and Modernity*, 2.
54 A similar thought was expressed by the Protestant Christian theologian Semler who holds that first of all the exegete today needs to be aware of the time gap between the emergence of the text and its exegesis at any given time afterwards. Secondly, the interpreter knows that Jesus and the authors of the New Testament had (in order to transmit a message) to use language and expressions, which were known to the audience. The Muslim scholar of the Ankara School Mehmet Paçaci explains Semler's account of the accommodation theory in his essay *"Der Koran und ich – wie geschichtlich sind wir?"* (cf. Körner, *Alter Text-neuer Kontext*, 36; Paçaci refers to Werner G. Jeanrond, *Theological Hermeneutics*, London, 1991.)

divine law – transcends the passing time. We will later see in the discussion about Rahman's exegesis how he tries to reconcile these two notions: the condescension of God's words, and its universal character. For now we keep in mind that Rahman advocates for their compatibility.

Another function of the Quran is the enabling of humankind to fulfil the purpose of God's creation.[55] By following the Quran's guidance and serving God (*ʿibāda*) humankind brings the potential creation into actuality.[56] The task of serving God, Rahman asserts, must be taken on by humans via free submission to God's guidance. Humankind is free in its decision to accept or refute God's invitation to the right path.[57] Importantly it seems that 'coming to the right path' requires not only free will but also to rationally think and decide. Rahman accordingly emphasises the didactic role of the Quran as *hudā li-l-nās* towards the *good* and *just*.

Rahman expresses the function of the Quran also in different terms: The Quran is the incorporation of the concept of God, "the ultimate source of creative energy that can be appropriated by individuals and societies in certain ways."[58] Within Rahman's understanding, one concept of God is to lead humans to justice and this concept of justice is embodied in the Quran. Rahman seems to suggest that not God himself but God's concept of justice incorporated in the Quran. Rahman would most certainly not want to breach the doctrine of *tawhīd*, the oneness of God, which in Rahman's view is "imperative."[59] In that regard Rahman follows a doctrinal understanding of *tawhīd* and subsequently of God's justice, as stressed by the Muʿtazila, a rational school of Islamic thought which was briefly mentioned in chapter I. The concept of *tawhīd* would be (at least in the view of the Muʿtazila) violated if one considered an essence of God to be manifested in the book Quran. Rahman must not have had it in mind to attribute justice to God's nature as another divine entity. However, he asserts that the concept of justice, since it is as eternal as God, gives the Quran a certain totality (or in Rahman's words: total 'coherence'). Also here Rahman adheres to the stance of the Muʿtazila that justice is, after oneness (*tawhīd*), the second chief principle of God's nature. It is this nature of the Quran as God's words, essentially entailing divine justice, which prevents the Quran from corruption. The Quranic and divine principle of justice has invigorating effects, since it initiates creativity amongst humankind. The creative energy is potentially entailed in the Quran and must be appropriated by humankind in order to develop God's creation further towards the ideal of a just society: "The goal of man is to study the universe, the laws of his own inner psychic constitution and the process of history and then to press this knowledge in the service of the good and that this purposeful activity – the *ʿibāda* or "service to God"– is the purpose of his creation and, indeed, the purpose of all creation."[60]

---

55 Rahman, *Major Themes*, 8.

56 Rahman, *Major Themes*, 8–9.

57 Rahman, *Major Themes*, 20. see also Rahman, *Islam and Modernity*, 2+155.

58 Rahman, *Islam and Modernity*, 154.

59 Rahman, *Major Themes*,[2] xv.

60 Rahman, *The Qurʾānic Concept of God, the Universe and Man*, in Islamic Studies (March, 1967) 10, cited in Berry, *Islam and Modernity*, 113.

3. As complex as Life

The Quran is essentially linked to the complexity of life: "[...] a book like the Qur'ān, which gradually appeared over almost twenty–three years, is highly complicated–as complicated as life itself."[61] The Quran incorporates dynamics of change that occurred in the period of its emergence. It is an established notion in Islamic theology to recognize the links between the divine message and human affairs. The acceptance of the idea of context-related revelations allowed to draw distinctions between verses revealed before and after the exodus (*hijra*), into Meccan and Medinan verses. In addition, many volumes of Islamic secondary writings claim to deliver material on the historical and social occasions of revelations. We will see that Rahman understands the connectivity between Prophet, people and the divine messages as that of an emanation,[62] which means in the context of the Quranic revelations the 'gradual coming down from God'. He refers to social circumstances of the pre-revelation time (*jāhiliyya*) and the changes the Quranic message brought about. Hence Rahman argues for the "interconnection" of the Quran with human conditions.[63] However – and this is an important aspect of Rahman's account – the Quran's complexity does not prevent the text from entailing universal messages.[64]

One question, whose answer could help to shed more light on Rahman's understanding of the nature of the Quran, is whether or in how far he ascribes eternity, degrees and forms of universality and divinity to the text. Of course these questions are ultimately linked to Rahman's views on the human aspects of the Quran. Farid Esack (1997) sees Rahman assigning an ontological otherness to the Qur'ān, believing "that the Qur'ān really originated outside this world."[65] But Rahman deems that this otherness of the Qur'ān should be linked "to the work and religious personality of the Prophet,"[66] and concludes that it becomes thus relative to human conditions. According to Abdullah Saeed (2004), Rahman's attention to the connectivity of the Quran to human affairs seems a way of avoiding excessive focus on the otherness of the Qur'ān.[67] Both Saeed and Esack refer in this context to the most controversial passage in Rahman's book *Islam* on page 31:

---

61 "In a sense, of course, the Qur'ān is simple and uncomplicated, as is all genuine religion-in contradistinction to theology-but in another and more meaningful sense a book like the Qur'ān, which gradually appeared over almost twenty-three years, is highly complicated-as complicated as life itself." (Rahman, *Islam and Modernity*, 137.)

62 Cf. chapter III on Rahman.

63 Rahman, *Islam and Modernity*, 5.

64 In the scope of Rahman's thinking the idea of interconnection might even go further, namely develop into that of an interaction. For example, as we explore in chapter III, he claims that the Quran was closely interlinked with Muhammad's psyche. He alludes to an Islamic belief (without actively endorsing it) that the entire Quran came down to the heart of the Prophet, who released it piecemeal in the appropriate situation.

65 Esack, *Qur'an, Liberation and Pluralism*, 64. Esack refers to Rahman's *Islam* (1966, 30–1).

66 Rahman, *Islam*, 31.

67 Saeed, "Fazlur Rahman," 47. As remark, the temporal rejection of externality of the Quran is also one characteristic of the Christian idea of condescension as mentioned above.

The Qur'an itself certainly maintained the 'otherness,' the 'objectivity' and the verbal character of the Revelation, but had equally certainly rejected its externality vis–à–vis the Prophet … But orthodoxy (indeed, all medieval thought) lacked the necessary intellectual tools to combine in its formulation of the dogma the otherness and verbal character of the Revelation on the one hand, and its intimate connection with the work and religious personality of the Prophet on the other, i.e. it lacked the intellectual capacity to say both that the Qur'an is entirely the Word of God and, in an ordinary sense, also entirely the word of Muhammad.[68]

This passage is controversial for a number of reasons. The most obvious reason is that Rahman's idea of a participation of the Prophet in the revelation process violates certain established understandings of the Quran's total divinity and otherness in contrast to everything human. This is because although tradition recognizes that revelations were brought contextually, it does not embrace the notion of any participation or contribution of Muhammad to the Quran and its wording. Rahman was aware of the tensions arising from considering 'intimate connections' between Muhammad and the Quran. But he did not cease to support this notion, even while facing death threats.

Since the notion of the *total otherness* of the Quran is widespread within Islam, and because also Muhammad Arkoun and Abu Zayd will address it, I mention here a few doctrines related to it. One is the doctrine of the uncreatedness of the Quran, which was developed after Muhammad's death and is often argued for with reference to the Quranic term *al-lawḥ al-maḥfūẓ*. This term, translated as *the preserved tablet*, only appears once in the Quran,[69] but nevertheless received considerable attention in various streams of Islamic thought. Kenneth Cragg (1964) describes the doctrine built upon this term:

The Revelation, here in its initiation and throughout, is understood as the coming down of a pre–existent Book, a transaction that extended over some twenty–three years during which the contents of the original Book ('The Mother of the Book') preserved in Heaven with God were uttered, recorded, and then perpetually recited in devotion, on earth.[70]

Rahman holds that this understanding of the Quran's origin rejects the idea of God's reaction to earthly circumstances, denies any situational interaction between the Divine and humankind and portrays Muhammad, the seal of all Prophets, as an empty vessel lacking autonomous will. It also supports the notion of determinism which, as Rahman finds, finds no support in the Quranic message. In other words, a literal understanding of *tablet* supports the doctrine of the uncreatedness of the Quran. It suggests that the Quranic written text, as circulating today, is God's word: entirely, holistic, exhaustive, because all that it entails was already written on the tablet, which is with God – uncreated and divine. The idea of the tablet was steadily manifested in later traditions, a process accompanied by the establishment of a fixed text of the Quran (*muṣḥaf*) which then became the source and authority for various competing

---

68 This passage is also cited in Saeed, *The Qur'an*, 31, and Esack, *Qur'an, Liberation and Pluralism*, 65.
69 Q. 85:22.
70 Cragg, *The Call of the Minaret*, 78.

theologies and political agendas.[71] In contrast, Rahman rejects a literal understanding and offers following account: What is revealed equals God's command (*amr*). Such Rahman renders to be the *tablet* or *mother of books*, the source from which all revealed books stem from.[72]

In summary, Rahman's ideas on the Quran's complexity point to the interconnected character of the Quran. Ideally the content of the Quran needs to be expressed in an intelligible fashion. Hence it finds its way through a human Prophet and descended to humankind in response to concrete historical circumstances. Throughout, Rahman grants the Quran divine origin and therefore its ontological otherness, but at the same time points to its relevance, accessibility and applicability in the earthly realm. Only there it can motivate humankind to develop towards moral perfection and fulfil the purpose of creation. Rahman's understanding of the *tablet* as command (*amr*), renders the idea that the Quran needs to be interconnected with the human souls in order to ignite creative energy and action towards goodness. Through '*ibāda* (the service to God) the goodness of God (the divine justice as incorporated in the Quran) can evolve into the goodness amongst humankind.

4. *Ratio Legis* and *taqwā*

We have already discovered that in Rahman's view the main function of the Quran is its incorporation and communication of the divine concept of justice. Justice as the main principle of the Quran guarantees the Quran's overall coherence and prevents its corruption. In addition, the Quran captures universal ethical instructions in concrete patterns which originally referred to actual situations. The Quran is dedicated to lead humankind towards the formulation of "universal ethical values" which constitute the basis for society.[73] For Rahman the Quran is always explicit or at least delivers 'semi-explicit' (implicit[74]) *ratio legis* about the actual purpose of each moral law. In what we will see are the verses of contingent character, the Quran "simply gives an answer to a question or a problem, but usually these answers are stated in terms of an explicit or semiexplicit *ratio legis*." In addition "there are also certain general laws enunciated from time to time."[75] The aim of the Quran – here

---

71 Today, a number of Western scholars have the impression that the dominant Muslim view on the Quran renders it uncreated. With this perspective certain difficulties arise. Beatrice Schuchardt in her book *Auf der Grenze: postkoloniale Geschichtsbilder bei Assia Djebar* mentions the idea of the Quran as eternal script and supposes that inherent to the Quran would be a "Logozentrismus, demzufolge die Welt als ein Buch und Gott selbst als ein Text zu verstehen ist. Aus diesem Logozentrismus leitet sich wiederum der Ewigkeitsanspruch dieses Buches als Ort der Verkündung einer unveränderlichen göttlichen Wahrheit ab." Schuchardt, *Auf der Grenze: postkoloniale Geschichtsbilder bei Assia Djebar*, 113. Schuchardt also refers to Malise Ruthven (*A very short Introduction to Islam*, 2000:46) who believes that the emphasis of the *preserved tablet* and the subsequent notion of the unaltered word of God being preserved in the written text was an attempt to achieve a united Arab identity.
72 Rahman, *Major Themes*, 98. Rahman speaks about the tablet in the context of exploring notions of prophecy and revelation (Cf. Chapter III, 1).
73 Rahman, *Islam and Modernity*, 160.
74 Rahman, *Islam and Modernity*, 20.
75 Rahman, *Islam and Modernity*, 5–6.

with regard to its *rationes legis* – is to awaken *taqwā*,[76] the awareness of observance of the universal laws, and of the external judgement that will await each person with reference to the degree of such observance.[77] This means that the Quran hopes that its instructions will help human individuals to develop *taqwā* which ought to go hand in hand with the discernment of the *rationes legis*. We will see in chapter V that it must be the goal of the exegete to extract the generality of each moral law while being in this "mental state of responsibility" which appears to be what the 'Quran attempts to induce in man.'[78] Frederick Matheson Denny in his article on Rahman in 1989 points out: "*taqwā*, the 'reverential fear' that Rahman wrote much on, is itself a kind of knowledge that is much more than the basic fear of the supernatural that comes at the threshold of religious experience."[79] In Rahman's opinion *taqwā* requires a constant reflection on one's beliefs and knowledge. Rahman asserts: "One cannot take God for granted, since no individual or community in the world can at any time appropriate Truth; in fact, the very claim, whether made by an individual or a community for itself or by a community on behalf of its real or putative founder, amounts to a confession of lack of *taqwā*."[80] Hence, certainty is not a product or aim of *taqwā*, but rather this constant re-consideration of what God might expect from each individual.

Arkoun

Arkoun's perspectives on the Quran are of suggestive character and not expressed in the affirmative manner of the devotee. Therefore it is difficult if not even impossible to deduce any conclusions about his religiosity. Some researchers have tried to do so,[81] but I find it rather difficult. This is because his writings on Islam and the Quran are formulated in explicitly scientifically and distanced. Rahman and Abu Zayd much more obviously state their own beliefs, even within their scholarly works. Therefore, while investigating Arkoun's thought, it seems important to distinguish between his scientific statements and what may be his own beliefs. This means that if his private views remain in the dark, his academic work should not be mistaken for his own views. Nonetheless, it is possible to extract enough material from Arkoun's writings for well-informed conjectures about his own accounts concerning particular topics. Although of course Arkoun's scientific engagement is our main interest, I generally think it is important to be aware of the possible influence of personal beliefs. In short,

---

76 Rahman, *Islam and Modernity*, 155.
77 Cragg reflects on Rahman's concept of *taqwā* which is the "moral responsibility 'squarely anchored within the...limits of God' [...]. Linked with the Day of Judgement, so vital in the Qur'ān, *taqwā* can mean, as Fazlur Rahman explains it, a sort of personal 'X–raying of one's mind', anticipating the 'hereafter', the essence of which, he averts, 'consists in "the ends of life"[*Al–Akhirah*].'" Cragg, *The Pen and the Faith*, 102. He refers to Rahman, *Major Themes*, 29, 108+120. Also Ibn Taymiyya believed that *taqwā* is the most important inner constitution according to which humans are judged before God.
78 Rahman, *Islam and Modernity*, 155.
79 Denny, "Fazlur Rahman," 1.
80 Rahman, *Major Themes*, 12; cf. ibid, 31.
81 E.g. Ursula Günther.

Arkoun's distance from affirmative expressions of what he holds true about matters of belief poses a specific challenge.

Arkoun's scientific engagement with Islam reveals his main interest: the analysis of Quranic interpretations and their socio-political applications throughout Islamic history.[82] Arkoun expresses preferences for and rejections of particular treatments of the Quran. Highlighting these preferences could show what Arkoun holds expressible about the Quran and which research and interpretation methods he finds suitable. In order to extract his preferences I need to find out how Arkoun understands the nature of the Quran. More specifically, I am interested in how Arkoun might want the Quran to be understood and treated today.

1. A Product of Selection and Distortion

From an explicitly claimed anthropological viewpoint,[83] Arkoun is particularly critical of three ideas of Islamic accounts of the Quran: the belief in the Quranic text as being God's words per se (*ipsissima verba*); secondly the idea of this word's preservation on a *heavenly tablet*;[84] thirdly, the exceptionality of the memories of the followers (*ṣaḥāba*) of Muhammad which preserved the verses as uttered by Muhammad.[85] Arkoun admits that the Quran was (possibly) partially written down during the lifetime of the Prophet and until the compilation process under 'Uthman began, various partial compilations circulated.[86] He might be alluding to an idea derived from hadith material stating that one of Muhammad's companions, Zayd b. Thabit,[87] "used to write down the revelations for the Prophet."[88] Then the written accounts of the Quran underwent a complex genesis of omittance, selection and marginalization of other different compilations also known as codices. What is known as the Quran today was at the time of agreeing on a final version, the *muṣḥaf*. The *muṣḥaf* is part of the corpus of religious literature which was from a certain time on consolidated and considered as a final collection of literature that was meant to be the source for all future religious formulations of faith. This process of closing the collection and formulation of secondary literature such as *hadith* and *sunna* results for Arkoun in an authoritative codex, namely the Official Closed Corpus (OCC). With regard to the *muṣḥaf* we can assume Arkoun refers here to the 'Uthmanic text, a consonantal script (*scriptio defectiva*) lacking punctuations.[89] Important for us is that Arkoun recognizes the Quranic text as a product of distortion, omission and selection. It seems imperative for Arkoun to mention that other extant versions next to the OCC were destroyed, "in order to avoid feeding dissent about the authenticity of

---

82 For a discussion about Arkoun's Quran-understanding compare with Völker, Katharina (2014), "Mohammad Arkoun: The Quran Rethought – Genesis, Significance, and the Study of the Quran." *Journal of Religious Culture*, no. 189.

83 Arkoun, *Rethinking Islam*, 35.

84 *al-lawḥ al-maḥfūẓ/* cf. II 1.3. (Rahman)

85 What I call *exceptionality* Arkoun terms *infallibility* and *superhuman*.

86 Arkoun, *The notion of Revelation*, 65–66/ Arkoun, *Rethinking Islam*, 35.

87 Böwering, *Recent Research on the Construction of the the Qur'ān*, 82.

88 Welch, Paret, Pearson. "al-Kur'ān," EI; Krawulsky in *Eine Einführung in die Koranwissenschaften* mentions also the role of Zayd b. Thabit. She refers to Ahmad Hanbal's *Musnad*, 127.

89 But also of this kind, different versions of the proclaimed officially closed *muṣḥaf* existed.

40

the revelations selected."[90] Indeed, Islamic tradition has not only one but different accounts of the Quran's compilation process. One common version is described by Welch, Paret and Pearson:

> 'Uthmān obtained the "sheets" from Ḥafṣa[91] and appointed a commission consisting of Zayd b. Thābit and three prominent Meccans, and instructed them to copy the sheets into several volumes following the dialect of Ḳuraysh, the main tribe of Mecca. When the task was finished 'Uthmān kept one copy in Medina and sent others to Kūfa, Baṣra, Damascus, and, according to some accounts, Mecca (*Gesch. des Qor.*, ii, 112 f.), with an order that all other copies of the Ḳur'ān were to be destroyed.[92]

Even though this account is one of the more traditional ones, neither Western scholarship nor Islamic theologians agree on only one possible version.[93] Whichever compilation story Arkoun has in mind, it could be any account that allows for a selection or modification process. Arkoun seems to be aiming at evoking awareness among contemporary readers and students of the Quran, that there existed marginalised versions and the reason for excluding them from the canon might have had other reasons than divine intentions: practical, political, social purposes. Arkoun contends that the *muṣḥaf* was over time perceived as entailing God's word per se, which emanated right from the *mother of the book*:

> Politically, in the absence of democratic mechanisms, the Qur'an plays an indispensable role in the process of legitimation in the new states. Psychologically, ever since the failure of the Muᶜtazili school to impose its view of the Qur'an (mushaf) as created by God in time, Muslim consciousness has incorporated the belief that all the pages bound together as mushaf contain the very Word of God. The written Qur'an thus has become identified with the Qur'anic discourse or the Qur'an as it was recited, which is itself the direct emanation of the Archetype of the Book.[94]

His emphasis of the history of the Quran as that of human manipulations allows doubt about how much revelation, or original divine word, the Quranic text really contains. Arkoun seems to exclude any participation of the Divine in these manipulations, as it is sometimes put forward by Islamic teachings. Mythological elements like the idea of Jibreel and Muhammad editing the text conjointly, or that God gave Muhammad's followers superhuman memories, is excluded in Arkoun's account. As an example of this belief in the latter notion I cite contemporary *hadith*-scholar Fazlur Rahman Azmi who in his essay *Shabe Bara'at* counts these 'exemplary' memories amongst the criteria for *hadith*-authenticity. He writes that "Allah Ta'ala endowed certain chosen servants with exemplary memories; Enabling them to memorise thousands of narrations with their chain of narrators; [...]."[95] While Azmi writes here in the context of the nature of *hadith* transmission, it does seem representative of the view against which Arkoun is reacting with regard to

---

90 Arkoun, *Rethinking Islam*, 35.

91 Ḥafṣa was the daughter of 'Umar, the second so-called righteous caliph in Sunni Islam. She has also been one of Muhammad's wives.

92 Welch, Paret, Pearson, "al- Kur'ān," EI.

93 Welch, Paret, Pearson, "al- Kur'ān," EI.

94 Arkoun, *Rethinking Islam*, 36.

95 Azmi, *Shabe Bara'at – The Fifteenth of Sha'bān in the light of Qur'ān & Hadeeth*, 3.

the transmission of Quranic wording. I presume that those contemporaries who transmitted Quranic verses also partially transmitted sayings of the Prophet. The belief in the infallible memories of Muhammad's followers Arkoun regards as part of the mythological consciousness. His emphasized scientific perspective does not want to ignore the mythological but – in the course of a "welcoming sort of rationality"[96] – wants to recognize these fabled aspects of the Islamic depictions as psychological components of the *imaginary* of human thinking.[97] Also in need of socio-psychological analysis are certain religious notions that seem to have primarily social functions. For example he makes clear that the establishment of the first so called authoritative compilation (*muṣḥaf*) aimed pre-eminently at uniting and consolidating the Muslim community. This is why in the process of text compilation social and psychological factors play a role. Theological constructions for justifying these concepts such as the *muṣḥaf* and the infallibility of the chain of transmission must be read with one eye on social and political aims. I conclude that even though Arkoun rejects the idea of the infallibility of the *saḥāba*'s memory, his perspective on the Quran regarding different reports of alteration, compilation and editing of the Quranic texts finds support in the Sunni tradition. Surely this view of the history of the Quranic text seems to take on critical features which greatly exceed what the tradition would assert.

2. Deliverer of *ḥaqq* and Being-in-the-World

Arkoun believed that the way Muslims shape their lives, is partially influenced by standards and world views which are derived from Quranic interpretations. In this way Arkoun affirms the centrality of the Quran for faith and existence in the Muslim world. The idea of the Quran as underlying current for numerous social phenomena is reminiscent to Arkoun's idea of religion as a force which penetrates societies. Quranic interpretation is linked to the hegemonic reason, which is the dominant thinking at a certain time and place in a society. The hegemonic reason puts forward standards of life, which instruct social conduct and decision making. These standards embody what is held to be true about the world, God and his laws. Even though Arkoun grants the Quran and hence religion importance, and makes them a central theme in his analysis, he is still critical of a reductionist view that says the Quran and its readings are responsible for all occurrences in the Islamic world. In Arkoun's view, this wrongly reduces the complexity of human thinking to a minimalistic world view, which is of no help to the current affairs of our all *being-in-the-world*. He consciously employs the expression *being-in-the-world* to express the existential importance of social systems such as religions.[98] It is this context of

---

96   Arkoun, *Rethinking Islam*, 37.

97   In other words, such mythological notions must be analysed via the application of the anthropological category *imaginaire*.

98   The concept of *being–in–the–world* occurs in Okakura Kakuzo's *The Book of Tea* in which he discusses the Chinese perception of Taoism as the "art of being in the world." It also expresses an idea formulated by Heidegger in his *philosophy of being* (Seinsphilosophie). Heidegger used the expression *Das–in–der–Welt–Sein*, which means literally *that–in–the–world–being*. Arkoun occasionally refers to Heidegger's metaphysics but does not say whether he derived this term from Heidegger. Arkoun

explaining the Quran's ability to give meaning to our *being-in-the-world* in which the engagement with the text (its reception and exegeses history) should take place. In other words, what Muslims believed to be true and worth basing their decisions on should be subject to investigation. In that one also discovers the development and changes of mentalities throughout history. Hence Arkoun hopes for a sketching of the history of mentalities.[99] This latter idea entails also the study of values and their generation throughout human history. Obviously the study of mentalities and values goes beyond the study of Islamic culture, which only serves as a starting point for Arkoun's overall research proposals. Thoroughly scrutinizing the evolution of values will lead to a broader comprehension of claims to truth and faith. Now, in the context of Quranic studies which interests us here, he points out the role of the Arabic term for truth, *al-ḥaqq* and its reference to the book Quran itself, the Quranic message, Islam and God.[100] Arkoun reckons that the function of the Quran to shape humankind's *being-in-the-world* necessitates that the Quran delivers truth (*truth-right/ḥaqq*). Faith emerges then in the course of people's appropriation of what they hold to be true according to the Quran (or other religious scriptures). Along the line of *ḥaqq* one can study the history of values and mentalities, as mentioned before. In all this, the role of the Quran is that of a deliverer of truth concepts, therefore of faith and subsequently of social standards. But why does Arkoun think the Quran has the power to deliver all this? This is for one reason because of the Quran's self-proclamations as God's message of the ultimate monotheistic religion and as the final truth. Arkoun then writes on *ḥaqq* from a more theological perspective: "[...] the term *ḥaqq*, a concept expressed in the Qur'an [and notably enriched by the great mystics of the classical period.] The term 'truth' (*ḥaqq*) refers at the same time to truth, justice, what is right, the actually real."[101] It constitutes a new set of values, or from the devotee's view: it restores the original values that make the covenant (*mīthāq*) between Allah and God's people. From this finalizing perspective the Quran calls for an Islam which equals truth as such and is hence superior to other religions, which, if they contain truth at all, entail a distortion of truth. Islam hence is also referred to as *dīn al-ḥaqq*, the true religion/belief. When studying Islam and

---

might have derived it from his readings of Dilthey or Foucault who utilize Heidegger's philosophy. It is also a concept similar to the 'Life-World' as employed within Husserl's phenomenology, that influenced Hasan Hanafi's philosophy (Hanafi was a teacher of Abu Zayd amongst others). In all its variations, also related to Gadamer's 'melting of horizons', the *being-in-the-World* always relates to 'experience', that can never be absolutely objectified. Also for Abu Zayd it is part of the ongoing creation, set free through the 'interaction' between humans and God's signs.

99   The German word equivalent to the 'history of mentalities' is *Mentalitätsgeschichte*.

100   The term *al-ḥaqq* appears numerously in the Quran with different connotations and in different contexts. The *Corpus Quran Project* detects 191 occurrences of *al-ḥaqq* (and in its derivations; cf. http://corpus.quran.com/search.jsp?q=truth&s=1&page=1).

101   Arkoun, "The Reflexive History of Thought Seen as a Problematisation of Truth," 14. On page 1 of this (to my knowledge) unpublished essay, Arkoun cites the following as an introduction: "« *However, the number one obstacle to the search for light is quite probably the* will to power, *the desire to show off one's virtuoso abilities or to provide a shelter against too evident objections.* Truth *is a limit, a standard which is higher than individuals, most of whom harbour a secret animosity against its power»* André Lalande, *Vocabulaire technique et critique de la philosophie"* Préface, PUF 1926."

43

the Quran the concept of *truth-right* must be recognized as a fundamental theological idea with consequential social effects. Although Arkoun claims that the Quran entails the mechanisms for having impact on people and societies, he does not yet explain how exactly these mechanisms operate.

3. Multi-Level-Transition

Arkoun believes in a *multi-level involvement* of the Quran with human affairs. Although his account reminds us of Rahman's idea of the interconnectivity of the Quran, Arkoun approaches it from a different perspective. If one considers, as Arkoun does, not only the written text – which is complex literature by itself – but also its emergence and reception by human thought, it can be seen that human rational engagement with the Quran is actually shaping human thought and society. Arkoun's conception of the relationship between Quran and person avoids – in contrast to Rahman's – any admitting of revelation having been an actual event. Arkoun's research draws the human understanding of 'what is perceived as revelation' into the foreground.

Arkoun notices – as does Islamic tradition – the difference between the time of revelation and the following periods. We know that the classical categorization of verses with regard to the geographic whereabouts of the Prophet in either Mecca or Medina is programmatic for the acceptance of the idea of condescension.[102] In comparison, Rahman in a way weakens the significance of the difference between both periods in order to support the idea of the Quran entailing the universal principal of justice which gives coherence to the entire message. In contrast to Rahman, Arkoun accentuates such historical developments of the text. For instance he distinguishes between Quranic reality/QR (*fait quranique*) and Islamic reality/IR (*fait islamique*). In addition it is important for him to distinguish the oral from the written Quran. Introducing the concept of QR makes explicit the chronological gap between the instance of revelation and the following period IR. QR refers to what was manifested in the course of history of what Muslims generally believe to have been revelation, sent by Allah to Muhammad ibn Abdullah to restore monotheism.[103]

---

102   The Arabic word for 'to descend' is *nazala* and its derivation *tanzīl* (which means 'something sent down') are used to term the process of message transmission between God and the angel Gabriel. (cf. Abu Zayd's chart of revelation in chapter III, Abu Zayd 2)

103   Arkoun prefers to refer to the Islamic Prophet Muhammad with his worldly name in order to avoid his research to be linked to a specific theological a priori. With this, Arkoun wants to underline the character of his work as socio-historical research. Günther describes him: "Er begreift sich als Historiker bzw. historien penseur der islamischen Geistes- und Ideengeschichte, der eine Perspektive der philosophischen Vernunft einnimmt." Günther, *Mohammad Arkoun*, 218). Arkoun writes: "By the Qur'anic fact I mean the historical manifestation, at a time and in a precise socio-cultural milieu, on an oral discourse which accompanied, for a period of 20 years, the concrete historical action of a social actor called Muhammad ibn Abdullah." (Arkoun, "Present-Day Islam," 58.)/ Günther writes that the 'fait coranique' is "God's appeal to human conscience, which took place in a language and in the context of particular economic, social, ethical and political experiences in the Arabic peninsula of the 7th century, in order to make alert the existential

In the QR takes place the act of revelation (chapter III) and the discourse between text, Muhammad, and the first follower generation. Arkoun does not yet speak of 'text' regarding the initial situation between Muhammad and the Divine. He prefers the term 'discourse.' The Quran understood as initial discourse also includes the first meaning production by the people (*al-nās* or the final addressee). This first meaning production is partially reflected in the Quran's reaction to certain responses by the first audience towards Muhammad's utterances. Since Arkoun denies the possibility of researching the communication between the divine sphere and Muhammad, explaining the term revelation will have to entail a discussion about the discourse on the horizontal level (Prophet-Text-People) which takes place in the physical realm. One characteristic of QR – if one assumed a divine agent as communication source – is immediacy on the vertical level. On the other hand QR is shaped by communication of three parties: the speaker (God/ Jibreel), the first (Muhammad) and the final addressee (the people: *al-nās*). The term Quran refers within QR to an oral transmission of messages among those parties. More precisely it means a transmission of messages, uttered by Muhammad and presented as God's words, to *al-nās*. The investigation of the actual encounter between the divine sphere and Muhammad is out of the scope of Arkoun's research.

Hence the transmission between God and the final addressee will in the following be referred to as the transmission between Muhammad and the people, thus referring to the realm that is a possible research object according to Arkoun. He describes the QR: "For a period of at least twenty years there occurred an explosion of values, a kind of continuous creativity in which symbolic language constantly elevated and opened social and political behavior to the realm of transhistoric [sic!] meanings. This was the role of Qur'anic discourse, which is always to be distinguished from the hadith, [...]."[104] When Arkoun uses the term 'text' in discussions about this initial situation, it means the divinely initiated oral utterances of Muhammad. I read from Arkoun's reflections, that he renders it possible that some of the utterances were already put into writing within QR. Still the significance of the writing is minor since memorization and orality were – in contrast to writing – the common tools of transmitting information within that given cultural realm.[105] It seems Arkoun's scholarly perspective avoids a detailed discussion about *tanzīl* or *waḥy*, since he is more interested in the meaning of revelation for society.[106]

---

conditions of a belief in the one God." (Günther, *Mohammad Arkoun*, 269)/ "The concept of the One God comes to be reworked, not for the sake of its own content, but in order to repudiate, right from the start, the manner in which it is asserted by other 'Peoples of the Book'. [...] The Jews and Christians are called upon to correct their errors (in other words, to do *tawba*) in the same vein as the idolaters or polytheists are required to do." Arkoun refers here explicitly to sura 9. (Arkoun, "Revelation Revisited," 31.)

104   Arkoun, *Rethinking Islam*, 44.

105   Hawting, "Pre-Islamic Arabia and the Qur'ān," EQ; Kermani points out that the oral character of the Quran is relived in the recitation of the Quran. While the performance of recitation the listener absorbs the Quran not via reading scripture but by listening to it. Therefore the Quran has also today high significance in its orality. Kermani, *Gott ist schön*, 208–9.

106   Despite his distanced approach to the phenomenon 'revelation' Arkoun does not consider using a different expression (although he sometimes speaks of 'notion of

Onto QR followed Islamic Reality (IR), which began after revelation and was marked by the compilation of a variety of written texts that meant to resemble the oral discourse or (in theological terms) God's words. Those compilations became a new authoritative reference point in the course of establishing the upcoming religion. In a second stage IR is marked by the gradual replacement of the oral discourse with theological interpretations of written texts. As we will find these developments within the formative period of Islamic religion raise certain questions which lead beyond the mere problem of authority. We will not engage in Arkoun's project of deconstructing Islamic thought, but at this point we need to become aware that the two concepts QR and IR and their distinction are the backbone of Arkoun's critical investigation into Islamic thought. This is because the distinction between QR and IR admits three crucial transitions in the history of the Quran: oral text evolution within a multiple-parties discourse, transition of authority from orality to writing, and transition from authority of text to authority of interpretation.

According to Arkoun these transitions have to be explored by applying adequate sorts of disciplines (e.g. history, anthropology, philology, linguistics, discourse analysis, psychology, sociology). Those can and sometimes must be intertwined, resulting in pluralistic, broad approaches to the Quran, Islamic thinking and cultures. It seems with the demand of multiple approaches Arkoun wants to do justice to the complexity of the research objects (see chapter IV Arkoun 2). The first transition (the evolution of an oral text within a multiple-parties discourse) marks the actual emergence of what will later be believed to have flowed into the written accounts. The concept of this transition recognizes the Quran's emergence in connection to the linguistic system of seventh-century Arabia, its penetration by symbolic language, in the socio-political conditions of Oriental cultures, in a realm of world perception infiltrated by myths and expressed by rites and certain practices characteristic of religions in oral societies.

4. From Orality to Written Authority

The second transition (from orality to writing) raises the question of the authority of the written in contrast to the oral Quran, or vice versa. The religious environment of QR was mostly functioning on the basis of oral transmission of general as well as metaphysical knowledge. Of course also the art of Arab poetry was mainly presented in an oral event. So the concept of oral transmission of knowledge was known to the first audience. This does not mean however, as Arkoun points out, that the new religious message's legitimation was not subject to substantial challenges and critique by the first hearers. The mere fact of its oral nature might not have been a sufficient

---

revelation'). In the analysis of Arkoun's thought I suggest to refer to the Muhammad's first proclamations (which were presented as revelations from God) as *'initiated oral utterances.'* This expression leaves open the source for the initiation and hence does justice to Arkoun's stance. As we have seen also he leaves out the discussion about whether and how Muhammad was inspired but at the same time considers a psychological examination of the experience of revelation. The expression *initiated oral utterances* avoids the inclusion of a specific divine agent, as portrayed in this specific religious tradition.

tool of persuasion, but at least it established a common ground of communication and understanding.

With the approval of a written Quranic text and the marginalization of other written versions, and especially in the course of struggling to proclaim one final ultimate text, the fact that the Quran was originally an oral communication act gradually receded into the background. The Quran primarily known as the oral discourse transformed into the *muṣḥaf,* which is "in the current linguistic sense of that term" what is referred to as the Quran.[107] The third transition (from authority of text to authority of interpretation) was fuelled by the concept of a *muṣḥaf* which generated a tendency to claim that since there is one Quran it has only one meaning. This claim will lead to what Arkoun targets as 'instrumentalization of the Quran'. Still, until now Arkoun has not given convincing reasons for believing that the awareness of the original orality of the Quran could avoid such instrumentalization. But it is understandable that the OCC came to represent unity, freedom from doubt, and totality and underwent a process of sacralisation.[108] The sanctified status of the Quran made it the central textual source (in contrast to other, what I call 'secondary sources' like *hadith* and *sīra*) for the formulation of Islamic faith. The artificial construct of an OCC supported the promotion of the Quran as the true, final and only scripture. In consequence it "became an object of infinite interpretation aimed at all believers [...]."[109]

> The Qur'ān as an object of research is a collection of initially oral utterances put into writing in historical conditions not yet elucidated. These utterances were then elevated, by the industry of generations of historical figures, to the status of a sacred book which preserves the transcendant [sic] word of God and serves as ultimate and inevitable point of reference for every act, every form of behavior and every thought of the faithful, who themselves are to be considered as communally interpreting this heritage.[110]

This shift, from addressing a limited circle of people at a certain time to addressing all humans at all times is of utmost significance.[111] It becomes clear that this transition from orality to writing is related to our above exploration into Arkoun's stances on the corruption of the Quranic text. Arkoun's concept of the compilation allows for possible meaning alteration, due to different consonant spellings in different versions of the *muṣḥaf.* Although Arkoun refers to only one final compiled *muṣḥaf* the anticipated

---

107   Arkoun, *Rethinking Islam,* 41.

108   Arkoun. "Revelation Revisited," 2; Tilman Nagel mentions the sacralization process within Islamic tradition from the 11th century on. Cf. Nagel, *Allahs Liebling,* 115.

109   Arkoun, *Rethinking Islam,* 37–8.

110   Arkoun, "Contemporary Critical Practices and the Qur'an."

111   Hawting discusses the crucial changes the Quran must have brought about after its emergence in Arabia. He points out the tension (which is also a question of debate within Rahman's Quran understanding) namely how specific messages can entail universal meanings: "There is a certain tension between the idea that the Qur'ān is a revelation relevant for and applicable to all peoples and all times, and the view that at least some of it was revealed with reference to a specific society and time and to particular incidents in which the Prophet was involved." Hawting, *Pre-Islamic Arabia and the Qur'an.*

practice of omission and selection makes it likely that the text was altered.[112] It appears on a closer look that Arkoun may refer to the *idea* of a *muṣḥaf* rather than the actuality of one. Here I must stress that the OCC includes of course also other literature, secondary to the Quran, but which is also believed to be finally closed by the various orthodoxies. But the *muṣḥaf* is, of course, part of this OCC. Arkoun seems to say that most Muslims are kept in ignorance of the textual variations of the *muṣḥaf* of which Muslim scholars are aware. However, Arkoun himself is still oversimplifying the tradition.[113] He does not elaborate on the history and variants of the Quranic texts. Before the background of these different accounts of the history of the Quranic text, Arkoun's term 'OCC' seems for his purposes a practical reduction of what has probably been a complex phenomenon.

Abu Zayd

Similar to Rahman, Zayd endured rejections of his approach to the Quran. His scientific treatment of the Quran and the emphasis on its human nature were interpreted as blasphemy.[114] Abu Zayd held that in order to communicate with humankind, God had to allow for communication in human language. In other words, the Divine 'came down to the human level.' Similarly, Abu Zayd promoted the study of the Quran within human sciences like linguistics, history, semiology etc. But in Egypt the time was not ripe for such an approach to the Quran. Attacks were mounted against Abu Zayd's person, family and academic achievement. A report by one of his accusers alleged that Abu Zayd had denied the Quran's divine source.[115] This report, its media reception as well as the influence of critics on the sermon preaching in mosques stirred a hostile atmosphere, eventually leading to Abu Zayd's escape from Egypt. The core of the critique rests on the alleged compromising of the Quran's divinity. However, as well as Rahman, Abu Zayd emphasised the human nature of the Quran but at the same time granted the Quran its divine origin. It will be interesting to see how his views possibly try to reconcile the two aspects of the Quran, namely its divine origin and human nature. Let us take a look at Abu Zayd's statement about the twofold character of the Quran, which remind strongly of Rahman's own view. Abu Zayd says:

---

112 Zwettler, *The Oral Tradition of Classical Arabic Poetry*, 122–4.

113 This understanding of Arkoun's notion of the *muṣḥaf* as part of the OCC would also represent a more adequate stance with regard to the factual existence of Quran text variations today. For example, even after the possible compilation-ruling of 'Uthman, there existed various *qirā'āt* (readings/citation methods), which differ in *ḥarakāt* (diacritic vowel pointing system) but not necessarily in the *i'jām* (consonant pointing). The record of variants of reading the Quran shows that even those were not merely different in *ḥarakāt* but there appear occasionally variants in the *rasm*, the base structure of consonants. Cf. Donner in his article "The Quran in Recent Scholarship" shows that also some variants of *qirā'āt* have different *rasm* (42). As an example he refers to: "Paret, citing A. Fischer, in *EI2*, 'Kirā'a.' A salient example is found in the text of Q. 3:19, where for the phrase "inna l-dīn 'inda llāhi l-islām" we find in Ibn Mas'ūd's reading "inna l'dīn 'inda llāhi l-ḥanīfiyya" (Jeffrey, *Materials*, 32)." (footnote 61 on page 50)

114 Cf. Thielmann, *Nasr Hamid Abu Zaid und die wiedererfundene hisba*, 205.

115 Ibid, 136.

When it comes to questions like: What is the Quran? I'm ready to say, the Quran is the word of God, absolutely divine. And the Quran is the word of man, absolutely human. The question will always be: How do we understand the Quran? Only looking into the divine aspect, we are in trouble. Looking only to the human aspect, we are in trouble; we have to find a way to see this dialectical relationship as it is expressed in the Quran and that would give us more power to understand the Quran without feeling that we are deviating from divinity.[116]

With this citation we are reminded of Rahman's idea that Muhammad actively took part in imagining the Quranic content and that therefore the Quran would be divine and to a certain extent human at the same time (cf. chapter III Rahman, 2). Despite the similarities between Zayd's and Rahman's philosophy, there are differences in conceptualizing the revelation process.

1. A Human and Literary Text

Abu Zayd believed that the Quran was in some sense originally God's words.[117] This notion makes Abu Zayd's enquiry into the literary qualities of the text even more noteworthy. Because, for a believer to regard the revealed scripture of their own religious tradition as a subject to scientific scrutiny, is challenging.

Abu Zayd seems to acknowledge traditional Islamic accounts of the history of the Quranic text. He holds that the Quran "was recorded in writing early on."[118] However, he also demanded the publishing of all scientific data arising from studying the earliest Quranic writings, in order to shed light on its history. Furthermore, he criticized that these oldest versions of Quranic writing remain in the custody of few experts. This insistence points towards Abu Zayd's awareness of the importance of these early scriptures, which entail numerous textual deviations, also compared with today's available Quran versions.[119] For Abu Zayd, when approaching the Quran as a literary text, all possible human contributions need to be considered while studying the text. All the same, Abu Zayd is, like Rahman and Arkoun, more concerned with the treatment of the Quran and the meaning production and implementations of its interpretations in Muslim lives and does not spend too much effort in discussing the authenticity of the widely available Quranic written accounts and their histories. He leaves these studies to others, while pointing out the importance of this research.

---

116 Abu Zayd, "Im holländischen Exil."

117 Abu Zayd revealed to me that it is easier for him to engage with the Quran as a literary text in a scholarly manner while studying (for example) an English translation. His lifelong dedication to the study of the Quran and Islam, and his affirmed emotional ties to the Arabic Quran suggest that Abu Zayd believed in a divine origin of the Quran. Although he was accused of apostasy he asserted throughout his career that he was a wholehearted Muslim. Cf. Thielmann, *Nasr Hamid Abu Zaid und die wiedererfundene hisba*, 206.

118 Abu Zayd states: "Unlike the Quran, which was recorded in writing early on, the Sunna was transmitted orally before the compilation of the collections of tradition by the end of the 2nd/8th century." (*Reformation of Islamic Thought*, 27; section 3.5 on Rethinking *sunna, hadith* criticism: the Emergence of a New Exegesis of the Quran). He does not though discuss this suggestion of an early recording of the Quran, nor does he refer to the sources he has in mind.

119 Such text derivations were found by the *Berlin Corpus Coranicum Project*.

2. Creative Communication

The Quran is essentially communicative and Abu Zayd refers to it not only as text but also as a discourse.[120] Even when God speaks in first person (often expressed as royal 'We'[121]) the speech is at all times addressed to someone and never presents a monologue.[122] Hence, it aspires to teach, inform and "initiate a specific action" from the addressees.[123] Another function of the Quran is to be a reminder (*dhikr*) of the covenant (*mīthāq*) between the Divine and humankind. In addition, the Quran describes itself as guideline towards the establishment of justice and the gaining of salvation.[124]

Abu Zayd considers the Quran as a tool for God's ongoing creation, by inspiring man to beliefs, deeds, and the transformation of reality. On a larger scale the Quran influences the mentalities of entire societies and hence becomes a 'producer of cultures'. However, it is important to recognize that Abu Zayd refuses the suggestion that the Quran serves as sole source for cultural formation, nor for answering all current social questions.[125] To stress this point he often refers to the first followers of Muhammad, who were distinguishing between rulings based on prophecy and such based on the Prophet's private consideration.[126] If they were not sure about the nature (divine or personal) of particular rulings, they would have asked the Prophet for clarification. In this line of argument belongs also Abu Zayd's refusal of the idea that the Quran delivers answers to all aspects of life and religious belief.[127] For him the Quran is first of all a spiritual and inspirational text, not a recipe book for all challenges.

The Quran is a human text (*naṣ insānī*) in two ways: the meanings derived from it are human interpretations and the primary function of the Quran is to address humans. In addition, the Quran is not only *muntaj thaqāfī* (product of culture) but also *muntijan li-l-thaqāfa* (producer of culture).[128] It is a product of culture in the sense that it is conditioned by the cultural life of the Hijaz, its pre-Islamic language, semiotic understandings and functions. The Quran created a 'new' culture distinct from but influenced by the pre-Islamic Hijazi culture. To demonstrate the distinction Islamic tradition uses the term *jāhiliyya* to indicate time and life without Islam. Abu

---

120   Over time Abu Zayd developed his approach to the Quran from regarding it as a literary text, towards looking at it as a product of discourses taking place amongst the parties of the Divine, Muhammad and the people.

121   Abu Zayd, *Rethinking the Qur'an*, 19.

122   Abu Zayd, *Mohammed und die Zeichen Gottes*, 58–60.

123   Abu Zayd, *Mohammed und die Zeichen Gottes*, 59.

124   We will find out later that justice seems also for Abu Zayd (as for Rahman) to be the essence of the Quran's message. (cf. chapter IV, e.g. re gender equality. See also Abu Zayd, "The Qur'anic Concept of Justice.").

125   Twardella, *Religiös-philosophische Profile*, 50.

126   Abu Zayd, *Politik und Islam*, 40.

127   In that regard Abu Zayd differs much from revival movements wanting to revive the 'original' state of affairs.

128   Abu Zayd, *Gottes Menschenwort*, 88. See for Arabic terms Hildebrandt, *Neo-Muʿtazilismus?* 373+411, and Sukidi, "Naṣr Ḥāmid Abū Zayd," 184: "a 'product of culture' (muntaj thaqāfī), a 'producer of culture' (muntijan li al-thaqāfa)." Sukidi refers to Abu Zayd, *mafhūm al-naṣṣ*, 24.

Zayd discusses the difficulty of the term *jāhiliyya* and the different contemporary understandings (religious and political) of it in his *Islam und Politik* (*naqd al-khitāb al-dīnī*).refer to MA Abu Zayd maintains that the then new emerging Muslim culture was informed by this *jāhiliyya* culture even though the Islamic culture was to become a culture in its own right, now modelled by its understanding of the new message. Still, it derived modes of expression from the culture it emerged from. Abu Zayd states: "The fact that the Quran text was understood and one took it to heart had an irrevocable impact on the surrounding culture."[129] In order to take on this task of cultural and mental transformation the Quran, its language, the narratives and the figures depicted in them had to reflect cultural notions that the audience could relate to. In other words the Quranic revelation recycled linguistic material which was already available and mirrored some key cultural elements which were familiar to the audience. After connecting to the addressees and gaining their attention, the Quran could begin the transformation of thinking, knowledge and perception.

In the process of motivating individuals and social groups, the function of the Quran as a literary and partially poetic text comes into play. This is because one way of gaining immediate connection was the use of poetic language, with which the Hijazi people were familiar. Like Arkoun, Abu Zayd keeps in mind that the Quran was initially transmitted orally and perceived only by hearing. Abu Zayd also emphasizes the oral use of the Quran in Muslim's daily lives and speaks of the almost magical effect of the Quranic recitation on the people. Such effect should not be underestimated or even ignored in Quranic and Islamic studies, which often concentrate on the writings and their interpretations. Hence, Abu Zayd, like Arkoun, keeps in mind the manifold nature of meaning production and prefers to speak of plural Muslim cultures. The Quran-aided production of cultures is an ongoing process, resuming as long as world views are to a certain degree informed by the various understandings of the Quranic message.

Regarding the Quran as a contributor to culture production, also means to define the Arabic-Islamic culture as a culture of the text. Abu Zayd give the example of the development of vital disciplines within the humanities and social sciences along the line of rational engagement with the Quran.

> Zum Beispiel führte die Lehre von der Vokalisation des koranischen Textes zur Entstehung der Wissenschaft der Grammatik (*nahw*). Und die Erläuterungen des Korans führte zur Scholastik (ᶜ*ilm al–kalam*). Die Diskussion über das Thema des *idschaz* (Unnachahmlichkeit, Wundercharakter des Korans) führte zur Entstehung der Rhetorik (*balagha*). Die Untersuchung der koranischen Geschichten führte zur Entstehung der Geschichtswissenschaft. Die Untersuchung der im Koran erwähnten Orte führte zur Geographiewissenschaft. Also gingen vom Koran als Zentrum und in seinem Dienst eine Gruppe von Wissenschaften aus, die die Essenz der arabisch–islamischen Kulturwissenschaften darstellen.[130]

---

129   „Die Tatsache, dass der Korantext verstanden wurde und man sich ihn zu Herzen nahm, hatte unwiderrufliche Auswirkungen auf die ihn umgebende Kultur." (Abu Zayd, *Gottes Menschenwort*, 88)

130   Abu Zayd, *Politik und Islam*, 194–5: "For example, the teaching about the vocalization of the Quranic text led to the emergence of the science of grammar (*nahw*). And explanations of the Quran led to scholasticism (ᶜ*ilm al–kalam*). The discussion on the topic of *idschaz* (inimitability, miraculous character of the Quran) led to the emergence of

If these advancements go back to the engagement with the Quran, they prove the Quran as a prevailing contributor to the evolution of Islamic sciences and culture of knowledge (*Wissenskultur*).

3. Humanity and Historicity

The 'human nature' of the Quran is derived off two central aspects: the dialectical character (or dialectic relationship) of the Quran and historicity (*tārīkhiya*). The dialectical character of the Quran is based on thinking the Quran as *discourse,* an oral long-term interaction between the Divine, Muhammad's utterances and the first audience. To understand the Quran as a human text comes essentially down to its initial oral character as discourse. Another expression Abu Zayd uses is 'humanity of the text.' Both terms, the 'human text' and the 'humanity of the text,' emphasize amongst other aspects the human capability of understanding, on which God's revelation relies to be appropriated. It also means that the text exists *for* humanity. It serves humans throughout history and hence functions within the historical sphere of humanity. While making these points, Abu Zayd in no case denies the divine origin of the Quran: „Ich habe bereits klargestellt, dass mit der Historizität des Koran als ein Text nicht gemeint ist, dass es sich bei ihm um einen menschlichen Text handelt.“[131] This citation reflects Abu Zayd's constant awareness that the origin of the Quran is found in the divine sphere and not in the human sphere. To resolve the conflicting tension between the divine origin and the Quran's existence in the human sphere Abu Zayd shifts attention to the transmission process between these two spheres. Referring to Abu Zayd's *naqd al-khitāb al-dīnī,* we read that the "text changes its character from the first moment of its sending – which means since the Prophet cited it in the moment of revelation. It transformed from a divine text, became a concept and hence a human text."[132]

Linguistically, the Quran's dialectical character is expressed by four elements: the presentation of various dialogues in the Quran, the Quran's address of different listeners, the relation between message-sending and historical circumstances, and the use of language current in the addressed culture.[133] The dialectical relationship (*'alāqa jadaliyya*) between the divine message (*risāla*) and the human understanding of it is expressed by various dialogues in the Quran. Here different groups of Muhammad's first audience, believers, non-believers, and peoples of the book are given voices in multi-dialogues among each other, with Muhammad or with the Divine itself. Hence Abu Zayd describes the Quran as a polyphonic text:[134] "In it we again find the voice of the early Muslim community, when they retrieved from Mohammed information

---

rhetoric (*balagha*). The investigation into the Quranic narratives led to the emergence of the discipline of history. The investigation of the places mentioned in the Quran led to the science of geography. So, from the Quran, as center and in its service, emerged a group of sciences, which are the essence of Arab-Islamic cultural sciences."

131   Abu Zayd, *Gottes Menschenwort,* 86.

132   Abu Zayd, *Politik und Islam,* 87. Sukidi, "Naṣr Ḥāmid Abū Zayd," 184 refers to Abū Zayd, *Naqd al-khiṭāb al-dīnī,* (original Arabic version of *Politik und Islam*), 126. (human text, Arabic: *naṣ insānī*)

133   Sukidi, "Naṣr Ḥāmid Abū Zayd," 187. Sukidi refers to Abū Zayd, *Naqd al-khiṭāb al-dīnī,* 203.

134   Abu Zayd, *Rethinking the Quran,* 18–21. Abu Zayd, *Mohammed und die Zeichen Gottes,* 69. (See also chapter V, Abu Zayd, 4)

on certain matters, but also the voices of those who mocked or attacked Mohammed – whether they were Meccans, Medinans or Jews. All of these talks and discussions can be found in the Quran."[135] The Quranic voice in addition also addresses explicitly chosen listeners,[136] or as Yusuf Rahman (2001, a student of Abu Zayd's hermeneutics) states a "variety of addressees."[137]

On a different level the dialectical relationship is expressed in each human attempt, from the beginning of the revelations until today, to engage with the Quran. Engagement here means on one hand the act of intellectual interpretation and on the other hand the act of recitation, which, in Abu Zayd's view, always carries individual interpretation.[138] Either way the believer thinks to be in communication with the divine intention, as s/he expects such to be embodied in the Quran. The Quran consciously works within this realm of linking its message to the horizon of the reader. Clearly the intention of the text is to initiate a communication between the reader and the Divine. In this perspective, Abu Zayd conceptualizes the Quran as discourse – he mainly refers to its communicative function as *risāla* (message) and *waḥy* (revelation),[139] – in order not to perceive the Quran as mere text, which can be a projection surface for various ideologies. The "re–invoking" of the Quran's "living status" becomes superior to the plain emphasis of the fact of historicity in all engagements with the text.[140] To unveil the living status of the text, Abu Zayd detects within the Quran a unique way of coding the divine message in human language. The Quran's "dynamics of coding," which include poetic language, were of course recognized by the Arabs. These dynamics Abu Zayd understands to be those 'specifics from which emerged the idea of the absolute 'inimitability' (*iʻjāz*) of the Quran.'[141]

The second aspect of the Quran's human character is its aforementioned historicity (*tārīkhiya*), which refers to all processes that effected the formation of the Quran. These include revelation, the processing of the message via the person Muhammad (inspiration/*waḥy*), the communication between Muhammad and the first audience (Prophetic speech) and finally the collection and editing process of the Quranic text. Abu Zayd believes that the original communication between Muhammad and the Divine took place in a certain time and space, namely in history. Furthermore, the Prophetic words are conditioned by the language, metaphors and other modes of expression used in Muhammad's linguistic community. As a fallible human Muhammad

---

135 Abu Zayd, *Mohammed und die Zeichen Gottes*, 65: „In ihm finden wir die Stimme der frühen muslimischen Gemeinschaft wieder, wenn sie sich bei Mohammed in bestimmten Angelegenheiten Auskunft holte, aber auch die Stimmen derer, die Mohammed verspotteten oder angriffen – ob Mekkaner, Medinenser oder Juden. All diese Gespräche und Diskussionen finden sich im Koran wieder."

136 Abu Zayd, *Mohammed und die Zeichen Gottes*, 58.

137 Rahman, Y. *The Hermeneutical Theory of Naṣr Ḥāmid Abu Zayd*, 133.

138 Abu Zayd, *Rethinking the Quran*, 13.

139 Rahman, Y. *The Hermeneutical Theory of Naṣr Ḥāmid Abu Zayd*, 122.

140 Abu Zayd writes: "It is also not enough to invoke modern hermeneutics in order to justify the historicity and, therefore, the relativity of every mode of understanding claiming in the meantime that out modern interpretation is the more appropriate and the more valid. These insufficient approaches produce either polemic or apologetic hermeneutics." (Abu Zayd, *Rethinking the Qur'an*, 11)

141 "Aus diesen Besonderheiten [...] entstand die Idee der absoluten "Unnachahmbarkeit" (*iʻjaz*) des Koran." (Abu Zayd, *Gottes Menschenwort*, 89)

received messages in specific circumstances that provoked revelations.[142] Revelation therefore has a historical dimension and this comes down to the fact that "where there is no addressee there cannot be a message." From this perspective it makes sense that Abu Zayd explicitly refutes the literal understanding and embraces a metaphorical interpretation of the preserved tablet (*al-lawḥ al-maḥfūẓ*).[143]

> Die Idee der Zeitlosigkeit des Koran ist also kein Teil des Dogmas, und die Aussagen des Heiligen Koran über die 'wohlverwahrte Tafel' (*al-lauh al-mahfuz*, 85:22) müssen, ebenso wie die Aussagen über Gottes „Stuhl" (2:255), seinen „Thron" (7:54, 9:129, 10:3 u.a.) und ähnliche Dinge, allegorisch und nicht wörtlich verstanden werden. Das „Bewahren" (*hifz*) des Koran durch Gott meint nicht ein Bewahrtsein im Himmel, ein Aufgeschriebensein auf der wohlverwahrten Tafel, sondern ein Bewahrtsein im diesseitgen Leben und in den Herzen derjenigen, die an ihn glauben. Gottes Wort „Wir haben die Mahnung hinabgesandt, und wir bewahren sie (*wa-inna lahu la-hafizun*)" (15:9) meint daher keinen direkten göttlichen Eingriff in den Prozess des Bewahrens und Niederschreibens des Koran durch den Menschen, sondern es ist ein Eingriff in den Menschen, der an diese frohe Botschaft glaubt, sowie eine Motivation und ein Antrieb für ihn, die Bedeutung dieses Bewahrens zu erkennen.[144]

The Quran is preserved in the hearts of the believers, and hence is part of present reality, not of the metaphysical realm. In this sense must also be read 15:9, which then does not mean 'God preserves the written Quran' but the 'original Quran in the heart of the people.' Abu Zayd also reads the term *umm al-kitāb* in verses 43:2+3 metaphorically. He understands it as "divine knowledge" in contrast to a literal meaning of "mother of the book."[145] As I have mentioned before in the analysis of Rahman's views on the Quran, the literal reading of 'the tablet' supports the idea of the uncreatedness of the

---

142 The practice of studying the occasions of revelation and the distinctions made between Meccan and Medinan verses demonstrates that Islamic tradition recognizes this link between the message and history. See also for Abu Zayd's emphasis of Muhammad's humanhood, *Gottes Menschenwort*, 87.

143 Hildebrandt (*Neo-Muʿtazilismus?* 407) refers to Abu Zayd's *mafhūm an-nās*/ Wild (*Die andere Seite des Textes*, 258) refers to Abu Zayd, *mafhūm an-nās*, 48–50. Cf. Kermani, *Das Konzept* wahy, 61./ Sukidi, "Naṣr Ḥāmid Abū Zayd," 185./Rahman, Y. *The Hermeneutical Theory of Naṣr Ḥāmid Abū Zayd*, 129.

144 Abu Zayd, *Gottes Menschenwort*, 94–5 (the chapter "Historizität. Der missverstandene Begriff" is a translation of Abu Zayd's article *mafhum al-tarikhiya al muftara alaih.*): "The idea of the timelessness of the Quran is not part of the dogma, and the testimony of the Holy Quran about the 'well-preserved tablet' (*al-lauh al-mahfuz*, 85:22), as well as the statements about God's "chair" (2:255), his "throne" (7:54, 9:129, 10:3, etc.) and similar things, must be understood allegorically, not literally. The "Preservation" (*hifz*) of the Quran through God does not mean preservation in heaven, to be written on the well-preserved tablet, but preservation in the life here and in the hearts of those who believe in it. God's word, "We have sent down the reminder, and we preserve it (*wa-inna lahu la-hafizun*)" (15:9) means therefore no direct divine intervention in the process of preserving and writing down of the Quran by the people, but it is an intervention into human affairs, for those who believe in the good news, as well as a motivation and an incentive to recognize the importance of preservation."

145 Abu Zayd, *Mohammed und die Zeichen Gottes*, 71.

Quran, which also Abu Zayd rejects.[146] Abu Zayd employs the Mu'tazila argument against reading the tablet as uncreated: „[D]enn sonst kommt man dazu, eine Vielzahl ewiger Wesenheiten anzunehmen [...]. Wenn die 'wohlverwahrte Tafel' aber nun erschaffen in der Zeit hervorgebracht ist, wie kann er auf ihr geschriebene Koran dann ewig und zeitlos sein?“[147] One consequence of understanding the Quran as created and of rejecting a literal reading of the terms 'mother of the book' and the 'preserved tablet' Abu Zayd dismisses the notion of determinism.

4. Original Speech and *mushaf*

The original Quran understood either as original divine saying or as actual recitation by Muhammad cannot be subject to scientific inquiry. However, one can speculate about the perception of the first audience. Such can be potentially reconstructed to the extent our knowledge about the original culture, time and language of seventh century Arabia allows it. Also susceptible to scientific "inquiry are all written Quranic texts and interpretations.[148]

Abu Zayd distinguishes between the moment of revelation, its first recitation by Muhammad and today's text material. He admits the existence of different Quran versions.[149] With that admittance and in absence of assertion that the text compilation into the final *mushaf* was somehow divinely guided, Abu Zayd's account allows for the possibility that those texts deviate from the original citation by Muhammad.

---

146   Abu Zayd, "Historizität. Der missverstandene Begriff" (*mafhum al-tarikhiya al muftara alaih*), in: Abu Zayd, *Gottes Menschenwort*, 95.

147   Abu Zayd, "Historizität. Der missverstandene Begriff" (*mafhum al-tarikhiya al muftara alaih*), in: Abu Zayd, *Gottes Menschenwort*, 98; Y. Rahman writes "Concerning the Preserved Tablet [...], which is believed to contain the Qur'an before it was sent down, is also considered by Abū Zayd as created. If it is eternal, how could be there many eternal beings besides God? Abū Zayd asks hypothetically." (Rahman, Y. *The Hermeneutical Theory of Naṣr Ḥāmid Abū Zayd*, 156. He refers to Abu Zayd, *al-Nass, al-Sulta, al-Haqiqa*, 72. Apparently the above cited article *mafhum al-tarikhiya al muftara alaih* ("Historizität. Der missverstandene Begriff") from 1995 is part of his *al-Tafkir fi zaman al-takfir. Didd al-jahl wa-l-zaif wa-l-khurafa* (Denken im Zeitalter der Exkommunikation. Wider die Ignoranz, den Betrug und das falsche Gerede, Kairo/ Engl: Thinking in the age of ex-communication. Against ignorance, betrayal and false speech, Cairo). The article was reprinted in Abu Zayd's *al-Nass, al-sulta, al-haqiqa. Al-Fikr al-dini baina iradat al-ma'rifa wa-iradat al-haimana* (Text, Macht, Wirklichkeit. Das religioese Denken zwischen Streben nach Wissen und dem Streben nach Vorherrschaft/ Text, Power, Reality. Religious Thought between Striving for Knowledge and Striving for Dominance), Beirut and Casablanca 1995, 67–89. Y. Rahman refers to the reprinted version.

148   Abu Zayd means all primary sources that are available on the Quran and secondary literature. Arkoun calls the entire body of literature: the *interpretive corpora*. Abu Zayd demands the accessibility of all manuscripts that contain especially early Quranic writings, in order to provide all facets and possible versions of Quranic material. (From this could be inferred that Abu Zayd would have been approving of the *Corpus Coranicum* project led by Angelika Neuwirth and Michael Marx in Berlin, where they analyse material inherited from Bergsträsser and Pretzel. One agenda of this research as mentioned above is the accessibility of analyzed data.)

149   Abu Zayd, *Ein Leben mit dem Islam*, 23.

Although Abu Zayd does not discuss this option, he mentions that the term *muṣḥaf* has as root *shf*, which is the root for 'sheet' (*Blatt*) but also for the word 'distortion' (*Entstellung*).[150] With regard to the different readings (*qirā'āt*), Abu Zayd conceives that it is difficult to know today whether the different readings were permitted by Muhammad himself in order to enable other Arab tribes to understand the wording according to their use of language. However it might have been that we can today refer to plural versions of the *muṣḥaf* and the existence of variant readings, which means for Abu Zayd "that there is no final recitation of the Quran."[151] In Abu Zayd's view, to think that the compilations which are available today are identical with the original Quran puts it at genuine risk of manipulation and generalization of a particular meaning that suits worldly political, ideological and theological interests.[152]

Abu Zayd believed that engagement with the text must take place in the awareness that any investigation occurs from the relative, changeable and therefore human position.[153] If we asked Abu Zayd whether the relative Quran might in this scenario not be possibly different from the original Quran, more to say an only approximate version of the original, the communication between the Divine and Muhammad, he answers: "Es ist notwendig an dieser Stelle zu betonen, daß die Vorstellung von einem >Rohtext< eine metaphysische ist. Außer dem, was der Text selbst dazu aussagt, wissen wir nichts über sie. Wir müssen Text notwendigerweise vom relativen und veränderlichen Standpunkt des Menschen verstehen."[154] With 'raw text' (*Rohtext*) Abu Zayd probably refers to the idea of a text inscribed on a divine tablet (see concept of *al-lawḥ al-maḥfūẓ*, as mentioned above). It seems that for him the question about the original Quran cannot be answered. People must approach the text as it presents itself and not how it could have maybe been. Explicitly Abu Zayd speak against all who claim to know that the recitation of the Quran through Muhammad equals that of a raw text and would even go further to declare today's written version as image of that raw text.

> Der Text veränderte seinen Charakter vom ersten Augenblick seiner Sendung an – d.h. seitdem der Prophet ihn im Moment der Offenbarung rezitiert hat. Er verwandelte sich von einem göttlichen Text, wurde zu einer Vorstellung und somit zu einem menschlichen Text. Er wurde von einer Offenbarung zu einer Interpretation. Das Verständnis des Propheten vom Text stellt die erste Phase in der Bewegung des Textes in seiner Interaktion mit der menschlichen Vernunft dar. Hier muß man die Behauptungen des religiösen Diskurses außer acht lassen, dass das Verständnis des Propheten vom Text dem ihm innewohnenden Sinn entspricht, wenn wir überhaupt solch einen inhärenten Sinn annehmen können. Diese Behauptung führt zu einer Form der Vielgötterei, da sie eine Kongruenz zwischen dem Absoluten und dem Relativen, dem Unveränderlichen und dem Veränderlichen herstellt, wenn sie die göttliche Absicht mit der menschlichen Intepretation dieser Absicht in eins setzt,

---

150 Abu Zayd, *Ein Leben mit dem Islam*, 24. Abu Zayd mentions this not without pointing out that the scepticism towards the written word in Muslim societies often hinders a constructive engagement with the texts. With reference to the Quran, its memorization is often valued more than critical investigation of the text.

151 " [...] dass es keine endgültige Rezitation des Korans gibt." (Abu Zayd, *Ein Leben mit dem Islam*, 23.)

152 Abu Zayd, *Rethinking the Qur'an*, 10.

153 Abu Zayd, *Politik und Islam*, 86.

154 Abu Zayd, *Politik und Islam*, 87.

auch wenn es sich bei dem Interpreten um den Propheten handelt. Aus dieser Behauptung resultiert die Vergöttlichung oder die Heilsprechung des Propheten, und es wird vergessen, dass auch er nur ein Mensch war."[155]

5. *kalām* and *dalāla*

In this section I take up Abu Zayd's argument against the idea of the uncreatedness of the Quranic speech. For Abu Zayd the Quran is God's speech (*kalām Allāh makhlūq*),[156] created in time and space. This we can infer from his understanding of historicity. The speech is a deed attribute (*ṣifāt al-afʿāl*) of God,[157] which – like all speech and also the human speech – only comes into being via interaction;[158] which means the speech is in need of an addressee (*muhātab*). As mentioned above Abu Zayd holds that the idea of a pre-existent eternal speech without an addressee does not make sense. The term *al-lawḥ al-maḥfūẓ* like some other Quranic image terms (*Bildbegriffe*; such as 'the throne of God' or anthropomorphisms of God) must be understood as metaphors (*magāz*).[159] The speech of God is therefore not an essence attribute of God. Such would be "timeless and eternal" and uncreated as God itself.[160] The belief in the uncreatedness of God's speech as essential attribute (*Wesensattribut*; *al-dhāt al-illāhiyya*), or 'divine essence,' violates not only the communication model but also the concept of *tawhīd*, the oneness of God.[161] Abu Zayd follows here a Muʿtazila argument:

> Die Muʿtaziliten verstanden Gott als absolut transzendent, als einen, der nur in seiner Einheit, Einzigkeit und Ewigkeit der menschlichen Vernunft zugänglich sein könne. Wie könnte dann neben ihm etwas zweites Ewiges existieren? Daher bestanden sie darauf, dass der Koran in menschlicher Sprache ausgedrückt sei, in einer Sprache also, die von Menschen geprägt wurde und bereits existierte, bevor der Koran entstand.[162]

---

155 Abu Zayd, *Politik und Islam*, 87: "The text changed its character from the first moment of its sending – that is, since the Prophet recited it at the moment of revelation. It transformed from a divine text, become a concept and thus a human text. It transformed from being a revelation to an interpretation. The understanding of the text by the prophet represents the first phase in the movement of the text in its interaction with human reason. Here we have to disregard the religious discourse's assertions, that the understanding by the Prophet of the text is equivalent to the text's inherent meaning, if we can even assume such an inherent meaning. This assertion leads to a form of polytheism, because it establishes congruence between the absolute and the relative, the unchangeable and the changeable, if it equates the divine intention with the human interpretation, even in the interpreter is the Prophet. From this statement follows the deification or sanctification of the Prophet, and it is forgotten, that also he, too, was only a human."

156 Sukidi, "Naṣr Ḥāmid Abū Zayd," 184. He refers to Abū Zayd, *al-Tafkīr fī zaman al-takfīr*, 2rd ed. (Cairo: Maktaba Madbūlī, 2003), 200–202.

157 Rahman, Y. *The Hermeneutical Theory of Naṣr Ḥāmid Abū Zayd*, 131.

158 Abu Zayd, *Gottes Menschenwort*, 81.

159 Hildebrandt, *Neo-Muʿtazilismus?* 409–10. He refers to Abu Zayd, *mafhūm an-nās*, 68.

160 Abu Zayd, *Gottes Menschenwort*, 80.

161 Abu Zayd, *Gottes Menschenwort*, 82.

162 Abu Zayd, *Mohammed und die Zeichen Gottes*, 70: "The Muʿtazilites understood God as absolutely transcendent, as one who could only in His unity, uniqueness

Along this line Abu Zayd criticises those Muslims who refute the Christian idea of Jesus being God and 'a created human' (*makhlūq basharī*),[163] and at the same time believe that the Quran would be a part of God, eternal and uncreated like the Divine itself. This is, according to Abu Zayd, not only illogical and inconsistent but also bares specific complications for today's Muslim societies: „In beiden Fällen wird der Mensch verleugnet und aus seiner Realität verbannt, und zwar nicht zugunsten des Göttlichen und Absoluten, wie es an der Oberfläche scheint, sondern zugunsten der Klassen die die Stelle des Göttlichen und Absoluten einnimmt."[164] Abu Zayd goes on saying that if the Quran were not created, then Arabic would be a divine, non-human language and humans would not be able to understand it, at least not in all its different levels of *dalāla* (meaning).[165] This proclaimed inscrutability or obfuscation (*istiqlah al naṣ*) of the text's meaning will then be emphasized and the *'ulama'* will establish their monopoly on the 'right understanding of the Quran.' Abu Zayd seems to say that the *'ulama'* alienate the Quran so that its meaning can only be discerned by special agents like themselves. He suggests that this artificial and wilful eleva-tion of the Quran into a sacralized item goes along with the *'ulama's* claim to own exceptional interpretative authority that derives off a privileged access to the text. In Abu Zayd's eyes, by making this claim, they and also other participants in the contemporary discourse about Islam commit idolatry (*Götzendienst*).[166] However, he does not deny that interpretative engagement with the Quran requires skills. This is because the text emerged in a timely and historically era different from today's and it is difficult to understand the text within the scope of only contemporary horizons. As his interpretation method will reveal, much knowledge is required to analyse the Quranic text in a scholarly manner (which has to be distinguished from the individual spiritual engagement with the Quran).

We see that for Abu Zayd the Quran is a creation on mutliple fronts. One is Abu Zayd's understanding of the historicity (*tārīkhiya*) and referentiality of the (oral) Quran. Another is the process of redaction (*Redaktion*), the Quran (*muṣḥaf*) underwent after its revelation and compilation. Here one needs to keep again in mind that most of the Quran was memorized first and written down later. This is another aspect of human 'creation' that according to Abu Zayd needs to be considered while engaging

---

and eternity, be accessible by human reason. How then could alongside him exist something second eternal? Therefore, they insisted that the Qur'an is expressed in human language, a language that was shaped by people and already existed before the Qur'an emerged."

163   Sukidi, "Naṣr Ḥāmid Abū Zayd," 186–7, refers to Abū Zayd, *Naqd al-khiṭāb al-dīnī*, 205.

164   Abu Zayd, *Naqd al-khiṭāb al-dīnī*, 196–7, cited in Kermani, *Das Konzept* wahy, 63; also cited by Hildebrandt, *Neo-Mu'tazilsmus?* 412 in a slightly different translation: „Und in beiden Fällen ‚wird der Mensch negiert und seiner Realität entfremdet, und das nicht zugunsten des Göttlichen und Absoluten, wie es an der Oberfläche er-scheint, sondern zugunsten jener Klasse, die den Platz des Absoluten und Göttlichen einnimmt.'" Hildebrandt cites here from an article by Abu Zayd (1995): *al-Nass, al-sulta, al-haqiqa. Al-Fikr al-dini baina iradat al-ma'rifa wa-iradat al-haimana*, Beirut/ Casablanca, here cited from the 2nd edition, 1997, 204f. (cf. footnote above: 148)

165   Cf. Abu Zayd's article "Spricht Gott nur Arabisch?"

166   Hildebrandt, *Neo-Mu'tazilsmus?* 412, refers to Abu Zayd (1995): *al-Nass, al-sulta, al-haqiqa.* 72+74.

with the text today.[167] A third front might be the meaning production, which takes place according to Abu Zayd in the interaction between reader horizon and text horizon (Abu Zayd follows Gadamer's understanding). Here the meaning of the Quran is a creation (a co-production) and not a given.

Examining the use of the various derivations of the terms related to 'recite' and 'recitation' *qa'ra* and *qur'ān* in the Quran, Abu Zayd concludes that *Quran*, understood as the revealed word, is not the only speech of God (*kalām Allah*). God's speech is not limited to the Quran as restrictively represented in the *muṣḥaf*. Abu Zayd wants to show that the 'speech of God' is only an umbrella category. He refers to those Quranic passages that describe the word of God as never ending. Thus, he concludes the word of God then can be found in many other creations.

> Nicht allein der Koran ist das Wort Gottes oder die Rede Gottes, er ist vielmehr *eine* Manifestation vom Wort Gottes. Ausdrücklich spricht der Koran von der Thora, den Evangelien, den Psalmen und anderen heiligen Schriften als früheren Manifestationen des Wortes Gottes. Auch die Bezeichnung 'Volk des Buches', *ahl al-kitab*, für all diejenigen, die göttliches Wissen erlangen oder erlangten, zeigt, dass der Koran den Begriff 'Wort Gottes' als übergeordnete Kategorie verwendet.[168]

By showing that the Quran and its language is a product of history in time and space, Abu Zayd does not want to reject the idea of the Quran's universal power of expression ('universale Aussagekraft'; *'umūm ad-dalāla*).[169] In his understanding of *waḥy* (cf. chapter III) it will become clearer how he hopes to reconcile historicity and the divinity of the Quran. Hildebrandt explains that Abu Zayd accuses those who uncritically deny the thought of the historicity of the Quran "to have no idea of the laws of the linguistic *dalāla*, which hold over centuries, because even under changed circumstance texts are able to address humans and to step into a process of exchange of meaning with them."[170] This also means that today it is not sufficient trying to restate the alleged understanding of the Quran of the 7th century's audience. The text speaks today and in order to have an audience, humankind needs to engage with it: „Wenn die Botschaften des Korans nur vor dem Kontext ihrer Zeit ihren Sinn besäßen und darüber hinaus nichts zu sagen hätten, hätten weder dieser Text noch die islamische Religion bis heute überlebt."[171]

---

167 Hildebrandt, *Neo-Mu'tazilismus?* 417.

168 Abu Zayd, *Mohammed und die Zeichen Gottes*, 68–9: "Not only the Quran is the word of God or the speech of God, it is rather *a* manifestation of God's Word. Specifically, the Quran speaks of the Torah, the Gospels, the Psalms and other holy scriptures as earlier manifestations of the God's word. Even the term 'People of the Book', *ahl al-kitab*, denouncing all those, who gain or obtained the divine knowledge, shows that the Quran uses the term 'Word of God' as overarching category."

169 Hildebrandt, *Neo-Mu'tazilismus?* 410.

170 Hildebrandt, *Neo-Mu'tazilismus?* 411. ("[...] wirft der Autor vor, keine Ahnung von den Gesetzmäßigkeiten der sprachlichen *dalāla* zu haben, die sich über die Jahrhunderte erhalte, da Texte auch unter veränderten Umständen noch dazu in der Lage seien, den Menschen anzusprechen und in einen Prozeß des Bedeutungsaustausches mit ihm zu treten.")

171 Abu Zayd, *Mohammed und die Zeichen Gottes*, 60: "If the messages of the Quran possess their meaning only in the context of their time, and if they had nothing to

6. Access through Language and Reason

The question of how far the Quranic text is intelligible for human reasoning, in other words, how accessible the Quran is, can be answered by considering the complexity of the Quran. As we have learned, the Quran's complexity consists of its dialectical character, its historicity, and its createdness. As Sukidi points out, for Abu Zayd the speech of God manifests itself in "a linguistic text in a human language (*lugha bashariyya*)."[172] Hence it is accessible for human reasoning. Abu Zayd wants to avoid a situation in which the content of the Quran, because of its religious impetus, is withdrawn from the process of rational reflection). His definition of 'thinking' contains the claim that it must necessarily engage with the non-ostensible (*Nichtaugenscheinlichem*) e.g. with the message of the Quran. Relating to religious thinking he cautions that it does gain "[...] on grounds of its object, namely faith, [...] neither holiness nor absoluteness."[173] Hence it can be assumed that Abu Zayd believed there should occur a constant and dynamic conversation between the reasonable human and God expressed in multiple Quranic interpretations. It remains open, in how far Abu Zayd might consider some parts of the Quran ambiguous, hard or impossible to understand. This will be investigated in the analysis of his hermeneutics.

Comparison

Abu Zayd and Arkoun recognize the history of the Quranic text as an originally oral event, collected into a *mushaf* and later sacralised through tradition. Rahman does not discuss the history of the text but refers occasionally to Western scholarship attending to it. He does not seem to embrace one or another account and in practice assumes a traditional understanding of the Quran's emergence. However, he confirms that the layers of interpretations must be studied in a critical spirit in order to enable a fresh look at the Quran's meaning for today's Muslims. Only if the Quran is freed from the artefact of past understandings, it regains its capability of guiding humankind towards the divine principle of justice. All three accounts admit that the Quran is a product which comprises modes of expression common to its environment of emergence.

All three accounts allow for the createdness of the Quran. Rahman and Abu Zayd reject literal interpretations of *the preserved tablet* (and both reject the idea of determinism). Rahman locates the tablet in the heart of the Prophet or abstracts it into the divine command (*amr*). Abu Zayd understands it as preservation of God's words in the believers' hearts. Rahman holds that the Quran emerged in connection to the Prophet's mind. Both, Abu Zayd and Arkoun distinguish between the oral and the written Quran which leaves the question as to which degree written accounts today depict the original discourse. However, Arkoun leaves out any attribution to a divine agent, while Rahman and Abu Zayd openly believe in God as the source for revelation. Although Abu Zayd does not discuss the possibility of whether the Quran contains

---

say beyond that, neither this text nor the Islamic religion would have survived until today."

172   Sukidi, "Naṣr Ḥāmid Abū Zayd," 186–7, refers to Abu Zayd, *Naqd al-khiṭāb al-dīnī*, 205.

173   Abu Zayd, *Politik und Islam*, 153: "durch seinen Gegenstand, den Glauben, [...] weder Heiligkeit noch Absolutheit."

all of the original discourse, he treats it as if it did. Arkoun is clear on that the written Quran only represents one of various possible versions of the discourse.

Rahman and Abu Zayd find that the Quran is doing a service to humankind, since it 'guides' (Rahman) and 'inspires' (Abu Zayd) humankind. For Rahman humankind still has to develop towards the ideal society and therefore needs re-appropriation of the Quran. In a slightly different way, Abu Zayd believes that the interpretation of the Quran ideally carries on God's creation, by setting free creative energies amongst humankind.

Abu Zayd regards the Quran more as a spiritual text, not as an answer giver to all questions. On the other hand, Arkoun does not reflect on whether the Quran is giving answers or guidelines, but rather points out its socially powerful language mechanisms. For Rahman the Quran entails the coherent guidance towards justice and hence potentially delivers sufficient material for conducting an Islamic society.

Chapter III – Prophecy and Revelation

Many aspects entailed in the three thinkers' views on the Quran (chapter II) depend on how they understand revelation and prophecy. In this chapter I will explore how the three thinkers envisage revelation. I also investigate how Rahman, Arkoun and Abu Zayd understand the role of Muhammad in the process of revelation and his tasks as Prophet.

Rahman

1. Divine Source & Muhammad's Mind

Rahman believes in the divine source of the Quran and at the same time he proclaims a dual character of the Quran which incorporates both a divine and a human aspect. The twofold nature of revelation emerges from the way revelation proceeds. To consider the revelation process is hence crucial for understanding the double aspect of the Quran. From our investigation of Rahman's views on the Quran (chapter II) we are already familiar with Rahman's efforts to avoid an emphasis on the Quran's externality. This means that he denies that Muhammad was a merely passive receiver and transmitter of the divine messages. He suggests that some internal process must have taken place. Rahman considers an active participation of Muhammad in the revelation process, and – looking at the data – I am inclined to say that he goes even further, namely portraying Muhammad as having made contributions to the process. Therefore it will be worth asking in how far Rahman thinks of Muhammad having participated in or even contributed to revelation.

The controversies about Rahman's views on Islam and the Quran need to be understood against the background of an emerging Pakistani state which was striving for political and ideological unity. In league with religious leaders the authorities tried to achieve such unity, and at the same time embracing a unifying Islam. As minister of education Rahman expressed ideas for an Islamic education system and state modernization, though Rahman's allegedly unorthodox and polarizing views on the Quran were seen to endanger the aim of unity. In addition, Rahman in this representative status and with his controversial views on Islam seemed to have been perceived as a rival for the established religious authorities. Amongst other issues Rahman's views were perceived as a violation of the theological teaching of the externality of revelation.

The main reason for his critics to reject Rahman as a person and Muslim is specifically his vision of the dual character of revelation. Rahman writes: "I defended the idea of the verbal revelation of the Quran, which is the universal belief." However, it seems that the standard orthodox accounts of revelation give a mechanical and externalist picture of the relationship between Muhammad and the Quran – "Gabriel coming and delivering God's messages to him almost like a postman delivering letters." Rahman does not deny the divine origin but takes into consideration that the message "'comes down to the heart' of Muhammad." In addition he "stated that the Qur'ān is entirely the Word of God insofar as it is infallible and absolutely free from falsehood, but, insofar as it comes to the Prophet's heart and then his tongue, it was entirely his word."[174] In all that, Rahman renders Muhammad as a fallible being.[175] Fallibility implies the potential for error, although Rahman does not say whether there is a possibility of falsehood in Muhammad's words. His overall philosophy suggests that Rahman believes Muhammad to be infallible in the moment of revelation and afterwards in the act of prophecy. A passage will illustrate Rahman's understanding of Muhammad's influence on the revelation process:

> At times this situation naturally affected the Prophet's own inner life and made him pause to think whether the whole effort was worthwhile, or had any real prospects of success. On the one hand was the utter conviction that the message was from God and that he must execute it—otherwise his own society was doomed to perish; on the other, the actual situation was so distressing and prospects of success so problematic that if a dilemma had real horns, this one surely did. We must remember that Muḥammad (PBUH) was not by temperament an aggressive or obtrusive man—indeed, a close study of his character reveals a naturally pensive, introverted, shy, and withdrawn personality who had been impelled by an inner urge born of an acute perception of the existential human situation to enter the arena of historic action. This explains why the Qur'ānic revelations, particularly in the early stages, are characterized by a staccato-like abruptness and consist of very short expressions like sudden volcanic outbursts or the passage of a huge river through a gorge. The Angel of Revelation spoke directly through Muḥammad's (PBUH) heart.[176]

This quote illustrates how Rahman bases much of his understanding of the revelation process on Muhammad's experiences. Since the Quran contains very little information on the Prophet, Rahman must have considered Muhammad-biographies and other supplementary material, while trying to comprehend the Prophet's mental changes during revelation. However, this quote does not help us understand the details of Rahman's view on the occurrence of the revelation. At this stage Rahman only asserts the interconnectivity between Muhammad's heart and the divine revelations which were delivered by an angel or spirit.

Let us keep in mind that any assumption of Muhammad's active participation or slightest contribution to the divine revelation poses theological problems. One could ask whether the word is divine or human and this leads to questions of how much authority the Quran ought to receive. In Rahman's quest for explaining the nature of revelation he reflects on the most explicit Quranic verses stating three ways of revelation to humankind:

> It does not belong to any human that God should speak to him [directly] except by Revelation [i.e., infusion of the Spirit] or from behind a veil [i.e., by a voice whose source is invisible] or that he should send a [spiritual] Messenger who reveals [to the Prophet] by God's permission what He wills-and He is exalted and Wise. And

---

174   Rahman, "Some Islamic Issues in the Ayyub Khan Era," 299. Cf. Rahman, *Islam*, 31: "But orthodoxy…lacked the intellectual capacity to say both that the Qur'ān is entirely the Word of God and, in an ordinary sense, also entirely the word of Muhammad." Cf. Berry, "A Life in Review," 45 & Berry, *Islam and Modernity*, 48.

175   Rahman, *Major Themes*, 13. Rahman refers to Q. 7:100 and 41:36 from which he concludes that Muhammad was not immune against the devil's temptations, just as any other fallible human.

176   Rahman, *Major Themes*, 59.

even so have We revealed unto you [i.e. infused in your mind] the Spirit of Our Command-you did not know before what the Book is nor what Faith is, but We have made it a light whereby We guide whomsoever We will of our servants, and you, indeed, guide [people] to the straight path. (42:51–52)[177]

However, here the Quran is not specific about the method by which its own revelation took place, which is therefore open to speculation. This has allowed Islamic tradition to develop diverse ideas about this process. As the Quran offers no explanation to the events of its own revelation, numerous secondary sources are often consulted for a reconstruction of the occurrence. These sources however are not without contradictions and themselves subject to interpretation.

2. Emanation

I will now investigate how Rahman understands the revelation process. As I have shown, Rahman clearly opposed the traditional view which understood "Muhammad as a wholly passive recipient."[178] Both, the human state of mind and the divine message contributed during revelation; in other words, it was neither pure dictation nor pure imagination. Rahman rejects the idea that revelation took place by letting Muhammad feel revelation (or its content, for example the divine moral law) and thus expressing those feelings in his own words. Rahman asserts: "[...] it is a mistaken notion that ideas and feelings float about in it [revelation] and can be mechanically 'clothed' in words. There exists indeed, an organic relationship between feelings, ideas and words. In inspiration, even in poetic inspiration, this relationship is so complete that feeling-idea-word is a total complex with a life of its own."[179] So how must we understand this complex of feeling and words? Rahman believes that Muhammad received something from outside him, words which then became part of Muhammad's own inner state (heart). So either Muhammad received words or he received inspiration that he formulated into words. The case seems difficult given that Rahman rejects the idea of clothing feelings and ideas into words and also rejects the idea that Muhammad simple received formulated words and repeated those. Still, we will follow Rahman's thoughts on these matters and see which scenario – either one of the two described above or a third– he is more inclined to put forward.

First of all Rahman does not seem satisfied with the idea that Muhammad received words in the ordinary sense. He writes: "the words heard were mental and not acoustic, since the Spirit and the Voice were internal to him" and although "revelation emanated from God, on the other it was also intimately connected with his deeper personality. Thus the popular traditional accounts of the utter externality of the agency of Revelation cannot be accepted as correct."[180] Rahman reveals here

---

177   Rahman, *Major Themes*, 69. Rahman uses Arberry's translation, which he finds is the best English version.

178   Cragg, *The Pen and the Faith*, 97.

179   Rahman, *Islam*, 33. cf. Kermani, "Revelation in its Aesthetic Dimension." Kermani writes: "The Platonic theory of enthusiasm, [...] describes the artist as kindred to the Prophet, [...]," 222. Kermani mentions that in Islam the Prophet Muhammad was integrated in the Greek idea of inspiration (by i.e. Farabi, Rushd, Ibn Sina) which can be found in Plato's Phaidros (244a-256d).

180   Rahman, *Major Themes*, 100.

what he thinks was the nature of the 'words' the Prophet obtained. Transmitted were non-acoustic, mental idea-word sounds.[181] This is admittedly a difficult idea to comprehend. It also poses the question how these mental words finally transformed into human utterances specifically in the Arabic language. We could ask whether Muhammad formulated the words by himself or was he guided by a divine agent and if he was guided how much of a contribution did the personality of Muhammad make? Although Rahman does not answer these questions, from what we know by now, the 'contribution' (not to the revelation process itself but to the wording of the revelations) of Muhammad seems in Rahman's mind to go further than simply formulating idea-words into Arabic language.

Rahman usually distinguishes between the divine and the human sphere, but when it comes to revelation he seems to mediate both. While the Quran was revealed to Muhammad, his psychological state still played its part in imaging these words. There emerges a tension between Rahman believing that Muhammad received words and at the same time holding that Muhammad's mind took part in imagining them. However I attribute this tension to the way Rahman understands the nature of these 'words' which I therefore set out to clarify. Kenneth Cragg sees Rahman generally acknowledging problems arising here which had wide ranging consequences:

> He has known personally the tensions involved in Qur'ānic studies, especially in respect of how the role of the Prophet should be understood in the incidence of *Tanzil*, and *Waḥy* – the interplay (if any) between the mind and spirit of Muhammad in recipience [sic!] and the action of the mediating agency. There is intelligibility in the language medium, when revealed. How is that intelligibility related to the intelligence of the Prophet in its receiving? Fazlur Rahman was both sound and courageous in insisting that the answer given here has vital consequences for the whole approach, not to say the decisions, of *Tafsīr*, or commentary.[182]

I also find that Rahman's writings on the idea of Muhammad's contribution to the revelation are scarce and often unclear. Rather he offered a scheme of thought posing numerous possibilities without embracing one or another. In addition I assume that he was inspired by Ibn Sina's (Avicenna) understanding of *imagination* or *intellectualization*. Given that, by considering Ibn Sina's influence on Rahman it may be possible to construct at least one of the possible models of revelation that Rahman's thinking allows for. Before I continue it needs to be emphasized that Rahman does not claim to embrace Ibn Sina's theory of imagination. I am merely trying to find an explanation for Rahman's view on revelation as being both, divine and human. I will mention few of Ibn Sina's ideas that seem to have influenced Rahman's account of revelation.

Ibn Sina's theory of the transfer of knowledge from God to humans is explained in the manner of neo-Platonic speculation.[183] Hence he thinks of such transfer as a process of emanation. Not only Ibn Sina, but also other neo-Platonic Muslim thinkers incorporated the (also Gnostic) idea of *logos* (Greek for *ratio*, Engl. *reason* or

---

181 Rahman, *Major Themes*, 99.
182 Cragg, *The Pen and the Faith*, 91–2.
183 The theory of emanation was expressed in the *Enneads* by Plotinus (ca. AD 204/5–270), who is understood to be co-founder of Neo-Platonism.

rationality) in their philosophy of knowledge.[184] The Arabic term best to describe the idea of logos is *'aql*. Rahman mentions that according to a *hadith*, *'aql* was believed to be the first creation by God (some *'aḥādith* mention other first creations).[185] Muslim philosophers and theologians developed different ideas about *'aql* and its functions. Rahman writes: "'Aql is broadly divided into the theoretical (al-nazari) and the practical intellect (al-'amali); the former apprehends the quiddities or universals, while the latter deliberates about the future actions and through the appetitive faculty moves the body to the attainment of the good."[186] Alexander of Aphrodisias, who interpreted Aristotle's' thought on *logos* (*'aql*) had most influence on Islamic thought on this topic. He believed that reason could be divided into the *potential intellect* and the *active intellect*. The equivalent Greek word for intellect is *nous*. The *active intellect* can be divided into *intellectus habitu* and *intellectus actu*. Ibn Sina incorporates these terms in his theory of emanation and gives his own understanding of how such intellects are actually acquired. Rahman explains:

> According to Ibn Sina (al-Shifa', De anima) the potential intellect ('aql bi 'l-quwwa, or 'aql hayulani = intellectus potentialis or materialis) reaches the first stage of its actualization when it acquires the axiomatic truths (this is called 'aql bi 'l-malaka = intellectus in habitu), the second stage (called 'aql bi 'l-fi'l = intellectus in actu) when it acquires the secondary intelligibles from the primary intelligibles or axioms, the final stage ('aql mustafad = intellectus acquisitus) when it actually contemplates these intelligibles and becomes similar to the active intellect. Ibn Sina, inspired by Neo-platonism, affirms that the universal cannot be acquired by abstraction from the particulars, but by direct intuition from the active intelligence. The final stage of human bliss comes when the human intellect becomes one with the active intellect, which happens, according to al-Farabi and Ibn Sina, only after death, although Ibn Rushd allows such a union during earthly life.[187]

The merging of the human soul (Greek, *psychē*/ Arab., *nafs*) with the divine intellect is a common idea within *Sufism*, Islamic mysticism. Some Muslim thinkers held that *'aql* is God himself, some said it would be part of the human soul. However, for Muslim mystics – generally speaking – the merging of the human soul and the Divine is the aim of all human souls and different schools of thought and practice were founded to provide training in order to learn to 'walk' the path of gaining knowledge towards this final merging. Many of these paths teach that the human soul, which has its origin in the divine creation, wants to return to the origin, hence merge with the Divine.

Rahman comments on Avicenna's "detailed account of the nature of the action of the active intelligence on the potential intellect in order to render it actual,"[188] which roughly says the following: A human mind prepares its potential intellect for

---

184 Knowledge in the sense of cognition (German: *Erkenntnis*).

185 Rahman, "Aql." He refers to Goldziher, 'Neuplatonische und Gnostische Elemente im Hadit', ZA, 1908, 317–9.

186 Rahman, "Aql."

187 Rahman, "Aql."

188 Rahman, *Avicenna's Psychology*, 116–7. Rahman's early work was directed towards the analysis of Ibn Sina's writings on *psychē* and its acquiring of knowledge. This work was the focus of Rahman's PhD, which he gained in Oxford under supervision of Simon van den Bergh in 1949. Two years later his thesis was published with an English translation of chapter six, book two of Ibn Sina's *Kitāb al-Najāt* (Lat.: *Liberatio/*

the emanation of the active intellect through comparing images, which comprise material objects.[189] Comparing images is aimed at finding the universal in all of them and not the cause for the understanding but the necessary premise for it. Understanding happens through the "intellectual intuition coming directly from the active intelligence."[190] The *active intellect*, Rahman points out, was identified by medieval Muslim philosophers as the lowest intellect of ten intellect spheres. He also lets us know that this 10th intellect was occasionally identified as the spirit or angel Jibreel who is also described as "the ruling 'aql of the sublunar sphere."[191] Ibn Sina, whose influence on Rahman I assume, believed that there takes place an emanation process of knowledge from the *active intellect* to humankind.[192] Ibn Sina gives a detailed account of this process,[193] for which is no place in this thesis. Though, it is essential to know that Ibn Sina speaks of gaining knowledge in general, whereas Rahman discusses the reception of revelations by a Prophet. One idea that Ibn Sina and Rahman have in common is an active participation of the human mind in the process of gaining knowledge (Ibn Sina) or Prophetic revelations (Rahman). According to Ibn Sina the human mind has to prepare to gain knowledge.[194] Here we are reminded that Rahman emphasizes that the revelation to Muhammad was an active act from both sides – a semi-mutual process.[195]

Rahman's account of how the Prophet received emanation from the 'ultimate source of all being' is not as detailed as that given by Ibn Sina. But it suggests a conception at least similar to Ibn Sina's:

> [...]: what the Qur'ān is essentially saying is that God's Prophets or human Messengers are recipients of some special or extraordinary power which emanates from the ultimate source of all being and which fills the hearts of these Prophets with something which is light whereby they see and know things the way others are not able to. At the same time, this power determines them upon a course of action that changes the lives of whole peoples. This undying and ever renewed Spirit is nothing

---

Engl.: *Book of Salvation* or *Book of Deliverance*), parts of which and other works by Sina comprise the book known in Latin scholarship as *De Anima* (Engl.: *About the Soul*).

189 See Avicenna's use of words (*'aql manā, 'aql fa'āl*) in Rahman, *Avicenna's Psychology*, 116. *'aql* is a frequently applied term in rational Islamic thought and can be found in the above mentioned translations: Engl. *reason*, Latin *ratio*, and Greek *logos*. Further terminology and translation in Latin and Arabic are 'potential intellect' (Lat.: intellectus potentialis/materialis. Arab.: *'aql bi'l-quwwa/'aql hayulani*), 'active intellect' (Arab.: *'aql fa'āl*)). *Fa'āl* is derived from the Arabic verb for 'doing.'

190 Rahman, *Avicenna's Psychology*, 116–7.

191 Rahman, "Aql."

192 Strohmaier, *Avicenna*, 65.

193 Strohmaier, *Avicenna*, 72–3.

194 Such preparation is the comparison of images in order to receive the categorical terms, which reveal the truth of things. This preparation could be called a necessary (not self-sufficient) contribution of the human mind to the intellection act. The human potential intellect is activated by the divine intellect and therefore the intellection is divine in origin but also conditioned by the human intellect's preparation.

195 Cf. chapter III 3.1+2. Abu Zayd understands the Divine to be in need of the thinking and language ability. Otherwise the Divine would be void of tools of communicating its message to the people. Abu Zayd sees parallels to this dependency in Hegel's *weltgeist*, which relies on humankind to know itself.

other than the Agency of all being and life. It is the guarantee that whenever the human race sinks into the moral morass of its own follies, there is always hope for its rescue and renewal.[196]

If we combine Rahman's thoughts on revelation and Avicenna's thoughts on intellection, we find the following: Let us recall that for Rahman the concept of God is justice, which is as concrete as the Word of God.[197] The universal in all images, which is to be recognized by the illuminated Muhammad, would hence be the divine law and concept of God: Justice. The universal message Muhammad shared with his followers was for this reason that God is just and all creation is aimed at justice. Hence all deeds should be righteous and represent this concept of justice and lead towards its establishment in society. This universal message was expressed in particular words concerning historical events during the life time of Muhammad. Therefore the message itself is an object of the past act but it is as particular as the act of intellection itself, hence intelligible, leading towards knowing the universal and initiated by the Divine.[198]

From linking Avicenna's notion of intellectualisation and Rahman's views on revelation we can speculate about what Rahman understood as Muhammad's contribution to the revelation process. Considering Ibn Sina's scheme of emanation, a contribution by Muhammad could have been his preparation of the human potential intellect onto which follows the intellectualisation via the emanation of the active intellect. Ibn Sina and his contemporaries thought that Prophets were not in need of such preparation, but Rahman's writings leave this option open. Still what will remain a bit of a puzzle is in how far the personality of Muhammad added any specifics to the process of revelation or as Rahman says: "the Revelation emanated from God, [...] it was also intimately connected with his deeper personality."[199] It is likely that Rahman has in mind the *sīra* literature, the biographies of Muhammad, which try to show at what points in Muhammad's life, thoughts and deeds, revelations occurred.

Rahman also reflects on the traditional notion of revelation. In this notion revelation is received by Muhammad from the angel Jibreel. Rahman's reflections do not shed light on the internal processes within Muhammad during revelation. Instead they speculate about the nature of the spirit as mediator between God and Muhammad. The belief in a mediator indicates that Muhammad did not receive messages directly through inspiration from the Divine but that this inspiration was channelled through a medium, or as Fazlur Rahman formulates, through an "agent of Revelation."[200] We remember that the 10th intellect was sometimes associated with the angel Jibreel in medieval Islamic thought. In her entry in the encyclopaedia of the Quran Gisela Webb (2010) explores the concept of angels and Islamic beliefs related to them. With reference to Rahman's *Major Themes* she says that Rahman showed how the spirit of revelation is in the Quran not identified as the angel Jibreel, indicating that the spirit is probably of a nature higher than the angelic one.[201] Rahman works out that "the Qur'ān describes the agent of Revelation, at least to Muhammad, never as an angel,

---

196   Rahman, *Major Themes*, 98–9.
197   Rahman, *Major Themes*, 15–6.
198   Rahman, *Avicenna's Psychology*, 119.
199   Rahman, *Major Themes*, 100–3.
200   Rahman, *Major Themes*, 93.
201   Webb, "Angel," EI.

but always as Spirit or spiritual Messenger. [...] the Qur'ān does not mention them [the angels] as agents of Revelation [...]."[202] Rahman goes on to say: "It is probable that the Spirit is the highest form of the angelic nature and the closest to God (cf. 81:19–21 [...])."[203] That Rahman recognizes the medium of a spirit between God and Muhammad does not diminish the internal character of revelation within Muhammad. Rahman cites passages from the Quran which state that revelation comes down to the heart of the Prophet (Rahman refers to 2:92, 26:193, 42:24).[204] He reads from these passages that God sends this spirit to the heart of Muhammad, and in support of the indirect revelation to Muhammad he emphasizes that the Quran denies any direct conversation between God and humankind.[205] Furthermore he considers an interesting interpretation of how the *spirit* could be understood to mean something distinct from mediator:

> There is also a suggestion that the Spirit is the actual content of Revelation: "Even so have We revealed to you a Spirit of Our Command" (42:52; cf. Also 40:50: "He casts the Spirit of His Command upon whomsoever He wills"). Perhaps the Spirit is a power or a faculty or an agency which develops in the Prophet's heart and which comes into actual revelatory operation when needed, but it originally does "descend" from "above." This is in perfect harmony with a well-known Islamic tradition according to which the entire Qur'ān was first "brought down" to the lowest heaven (i.e., the Prophet's heart, as thinkers like al-Ghazālī and Shāh Walī Allāh al-Dihlawi would rightly say) and then relevant verbal passages produced when needed.[206]

This interpretation could support the idea of Rahman that the Quran has a certain spirit, which is – as we have observed in chapter II – geared towards the good and just of humankind. If Muhammad also achieves a certain spirit of such kind then he channels the revealed contents literally in this spirit's spirit. Muhammad's heart in this scenario serves as an intermediate station, possessing the entire Quran and releasing its content in applicable situations. The idea of storing information on one level and releasing it as piecemeal has already been mentioned. There the idea is that the active intellect serves as storage for all forms (mental and materialistic). In the scenario of Muhammad's prophecy it is Muhammad's heart that becomes the storage. The whole idea puts some constraints to the notion that the Quran was occasionally revealed as reaction to specific situations. If the entire Quran was already within the earthly realm of Muhammad's heart, then it predicted all situations that triggered the revelations beforehand. This would strengthen the idea of determinism, which Rahman rejects as we have seen in chapter II. But we can speculate that Rahman might have had in mind that Muhammad received the divine message which entails the concept of justice, and that Muhammad then expressed this general sense of justice in certain circumstances. Against the background of what I have so far depicted, namely that Rahman's understanding of the actual revelation process is not clear, I believe Tamara Sonn's (1991) statement that "Fazlur Rahman offered a comprehensive and systematic methodology for understanding revelation, [...]" needs to be re-considered.[207]

---

202 Rahman, *Major Themes*, 95.
203 Rahman, *Major Themes*, 96.
204 Rahman, *Major Themes*, 97.
205 Rahman, *Major Themes*, 97.
206 Rahman, *Major Themes*, 97.
207 Sonn, "Fazlur Rahman's Islamic Methodology," 213.

By subtracting the ambiguities in Rahman's thought on this topic we summarize Rahman's understanding of revelation as follows: Revelation is of divine origin. However, God never communicated with Muhammad directly but through a medium, a spirit close to God. This spirit the Quran (unlike secondary literature) does not identify as angel Jibreel. The spirit infused messages into the heart of the Prophet. This was an internal process in which Muhammad perceived these messages as non-acoustic idea-words (perhaps one could call them 'verbal thoughts'). Muhammad was inspired to use specific words in the Arab language to utter the messages. It might have been that Muhammad received a kind of spirit, in reaction to which he formulated the given messages when needed. Rahman does not exclude and even suggests that Muhammad's heart was in possession of the entire Quranic messages before he released them on specific occasions spread over 22 years of prophecy. All wording uttered by Muhammad were issued by the Divine and in the divine spirit. There cannot be any falsehood in it. Of course, this infallibility seems hard to be reconciled with the idea of Muhammad as a fallible human. In the end we can only say, that the human contribution to the revelation was Muhammad's mind, which was gifted by the Divine to receive and understand all content (mainly concepts of justice) of the revelations. Although, Muhammad's initial struggles with his task as Prophet, show his fallibility and prove his humanity and individuality, there is however no fallibility in the Quranic wording.

3. Muhammad's Inner Struggle

Having tried to comprehend Rahman's understanding of the revelation process from the divine sphere to Muhammad, we now turn towards the horizontal level on which Muhammad communicates the Quranic wording to the first audience. Here Rahman is interested in Muhammad's personal response to the given tasks of a Prophet. Rahman believes that Muhammad initially struggled with his role as mediator, since he was shy and did not like to get involved with other people's lives. On the other hand – through his growing experience with the divine revelation – he became increasingly determined to secure the fundamentals of the ethico-legal purpose of the Quran. I assume Rahman's portrait of Muhammad's personality relies on *sīra* and *hadith* material although Rahman mostly does not explicitly refer to these.

As we know from Rahman's views on the Quran, it is also the purpose of revelation to install *taqwā*, the conscious obedience of divine laws (cf. Rahman's specific understanding of *taqwā*). One could then also say Muhammad accepted that he should be obedient to the revelation and slowly took on the task to be its utterer. Growing into his role as a Prophet Muhammad was "with this mixture of opposing mental traits and conscious of a 'heavy mission,' as the Qur'ān says [...] engaged in a constant inner dialectic-the ideal moral state for man to be in, according to the Qur'ān." Rahman illustrates this mental struggle in his explanation of sura 53: "The verses in sura 53, where the Prophet had reportedly made concessions to the goddesses of the Meccan pagans that were subsequently 'abrogated,' are along with other Qur'ānic evidence, direct proof of this phenomenon. The second side of the Prophet, his determination, finally won over his other side."[208] It is not clear from this sura whether a concession

---

208   Rahman, *Islam and Modernity*, 16–7.

was made by Muhammad towards the Goddesses, so perhaps Rahman has *hadith*-material on this matter in mind. And indeed well known works on the biography of Muhammad such as Ibn Ishaq's *Life of Muhammad* mention that the Prophet made concessions to worshipping the three Goddesses. Muir termed these inputs to Muhammad 'satanic verses.' However, the Quran text itself does not talk about making concessions but rather asks about recognizing the beliefs in the Goddesses and criticizes the practices regarding those Goddesses. Practices and beliefs towards the Goddesses are questioned with regard to their authority, since they were not installed by (the true) God. Rahman asserts that Muhammad was not immune to the devil's temptations, just as any other fallible human.[209]

However, Rahman incurs from this verse a gradual change in Muhammad's attitude throughout the time of revelation. Here Rahman opposes the orthodox view, which as Cragg (1985) describes "sharply rejects the implication that Muhammad was in any way liable to even temporary 'parleying' with adversaries in the struggle the witness entailed."[210] This view does not allow the idea that Muhammad at all questioned or resisted taking on his role as a Prophet. In contrast Rahman believed that Muhammad's determination for fixing the fundamentals had to win over his humble and shy side. Through overcoming his personal constraint he could finally take back compromises he had to make in the beginning of his Prophethood. One of these compromises seems to be in Rahman's view a concession towards the pagan worshippers. Rahman indicates that is was the eternal psychological state which resulted in Muhammad's behaviour. However through this account Rahman seems to give an alternative interpretation of traditional accounts, which mention that the concessions made towards paganism originated in satanic verses. According to this narrative, the false verses were later abrogated by God (cf. chapter V 1.1).

Rahman is firm in his belief in divine revelation and that each verse bears potentially universal implications. At the same time he grants Muhammad's personality an influential position within his Prophetic enterprise. I have already enquired what this influence might entail. What becomes apparent in the end is that Rahman ascribes a functional and very practical role to Muhammad and his prophecy. He confirms that "Muhammad's Prophetic career was likewise geared toward the moral improvement of man in a concrete and communal sense, rather than toward the private and metaphysical."[211] Kenneth Cragg, who explores Rahman's views in his book *The Pen and the Faith* formulates his observation as follows: "Muhammad's significance lies not in inaugurating ecstasy but in definitive public action and institutional

---

209 Rahman, *Major Themes*, 13. Rahman refers to Q. 7:100 and 41:36. cf. also *Major Themes*: "For the Qur'ān, it is neither strange nor out of tune nor blameworthy for a Prophet that he is not always consistent as a human. It is nevertheless as a human that he becomes an example for mankind, for his *average* level of conduct is still so high that it is a worthy model for mankind. Prophets are humans who must constantly struggle inwardly, but in this inward struggle truth and righteousness prevail; if Prophets did not struggle and suffer inner travail, they could not become examples for other humans [...]," 62.
210 Cragg, *The Pen and the Faith*, 99. See also Rahman, *Islam and Modernity*, 16–7, and Cragg's *The event of the Qur'ān* about 'the struggle to mean' in 141–3.
211 Rahman, *Islam and Modernity*, 2.

achievement."[212] Muhammad's role was that of an exemplary human being. Given that Muhammad's impact ought to be seen specifically in the practices of the new society, one would think that the understanding of the messages as perceived by the first audience is paramount. However, Rahman (in contrast to Arkoun and Abu Zayd) does not examine how complex the initial understanding of the revelations was. But since Rahman pleaded that historical settings of the revelation event should be considered, we assume that he must have paid tribute to their knowledge, when picturing the first reception of the messages.

Rahman's idea that Muhammad's policies were over time corrected support the two notions, that Muhammad was fallible and that there was progression of events in which revelation took place. Especially Rahman's view on Muhammad as a fallible person brought much controversy about his thinking. But why does this seem such a controversial thought? Islam is known for its proclamation that no human acquires Godhood. This rejection often appears in anti-Christian polemics. However, there still existed the idea in Islam that Muhammad was closer to God and in the moment of revelation he elevated into a higher being. This idea finds expression within Islam as the 'Muhammadan Light' (*nūr Muhammed*) which is according to some *'ahādith* the first creation of God.[213] I mention this idea in order to illustrate how Rahman's notion of the fallible Muhammad could have been received as an insult against the Prophet's infallibility. We know that Rahman particularly emphasized the inner struggle and progression of Muhammad's mind towards accepting and fulfilling his Prophethood. Hence Rahman's understanding avoids such elevation of Muhammad to a superhuman entity. His interpretation of Muhammad's ascension (*mi'rāj*), as a mental instead of a physical journey supports this avoidance. Muhammad, as understood by Rahman, can actually be followed by humans, since he was a human himself. Rahman must therefore refute *hadith*-literature and Quran exegesis that lead to such ideas like that of the 'Muhammadan Light'. We must assume, since Rahman does not express this explicitly, that Muhammad had at least an emblematic role as human, because he was chosen by God. Hence his *sunna* (habits), which are recorded in *hadith*-literature, need to be considered as a role model for living a God-willed life. At least such secondary literature must have been of some worth for Rahman. In example, he does not refute the use of *hadith*-literature for highlighting Muhammad's personal involvement in the process of establishing the first Muslim society. For Rahman *hadith* is a valuable source for reconstructing Muhammad's further *ijtihād* on the basis of the revealed messages. On the other hand Rahman is much aware that secondary literature needs

---

212   Cragg, *The Pen and the Faith*, 91–2.

213   Cf. Rubin, "Nūr Muhammadī," EI. Körner explains this concept with reference to Ömer Özsoy's mentioning of this Islamic idea, which renders Muhammad as pre-existent: „die Vorstellung, dass Muhammad vor Adam erschaffen wurde. Bereits einige frühe Hadîthe zeigen Muhammad als präexistent: Der Glanz seiner Existenz durchstrahlt die Schöpfung von Anbeginn. Der Begründer der westlichen Islamwissenschaft, Ignaz Goldziher, bezeichnete solche Vorstellungen vor einem Jahrhundert als ‚Neuplatonische und gnostische Elemente im Hadit[h].'" (Körner, *Alter Text-neuer Kontext*, 80. Körner refers to *Zeitschrift für Assyrologie* 22 (1909), 317.)

to be treated with caution and suspicion, since it is liable to human corruption.[214] In all cases. for Rahman the Quran remains highest authority.[215]

Hence, Rahman thinks that *sunna* and *hadith* are only partially reliable sources. The collection of *'aḥādith* is a product of mankind and may be penetrated by political, personal interests and contradictions,[216] which lie outside the Quranic message. These assumptions lead to Rahman's claim that *hadith* literature can be corrupted, whereas the Quran cannot.[217] However, as we have shown above, Rahman relies on some secondary material. Here we ought to ask, what are the criteria for Rahman's judgement on whether a secondary source sheds light or oblivion on the Quran's meaning? I assume, first of all the *hadith* should not contradict the Quran's principle of justice and secondly Rahman might follow the traditional categorization of reliability according to the chain of transmission (*isnad*).

In Rahman's interpretation of the Quran he seldom explicitly refers to *hadith* but some of his conclusions seem to be derived from the *hadith*. In the following I will refer to *hadith* as such material that comprises the sayings of Muhammad as well descriptions of his *sunna*. Rahman demands an interpretation of the Quran, which is supported by *hadith* as a source for gaining insight to *asbāb an-nuzūl*.[218] *As we mentioned above, he also trusts sunna* in addition to the Qur'ān to gain insight to Muhammad's state of mind and personality.[219] According to Rahman *hadith* needs to be studied historically and systematically in order to distinguish reliable content from unreliable content.[220] But even if a *hadith*'s content is found unreliable according to historical and systematic standards, Rahman pleads for the search within this *hadith* for a good principle, that if found "should be adopted."[221] Rahman points out the importance of *hadith* as a whole when he calls it the "basis for the historicity of the Qur'ān."[222]

---

214 Cf. The above discussion on the nature of the agent of revelation: "Those Hadīth stories, then, where the angel Gabriel is depicted as a public figure conversing with the Prophet whose companions say him, must be regarded as later fictions." (Rahman, *Major Themes*, 97)

215 "[...] Fazlur Rahman defined *sunna* as the *idjmā* of the early Muslims, reflected in *ḥadīth*, not derived from it [...]. *Ḥadīth*, while not strictly historical, represents "the interpreted spirit of the Prophetic teaching" [...]. Later generations of Muslims must duplicate this interpretive process, not by a literal application of *ḥadīth*, but by discovering the spirit of the Prophetic example for themselves. While such revisionist views have not gained a wide following, they have nevertheless exerted enormous influence on modern Muslim discussions of religious authority, giving rise to a plurality of definitions of *sunna* reminiscent of the formative period of Islamic thought." (Brown, "Sunna," EI)

216 Sonn, "Fazlur Rahman's Islamic Methodology," 218.

217 Rahman, *Islam and Modernity*, 147.

218 Rahman, *Islam and Modernity*, 143.

219 Rahman, *Islam and Modernity*, 15.

220 Berry, *Islam and Modernity*, 36, refers to Fazlur Rahman, 'The Impact of Modernity on Islam', Religious Pluralism and World community, Edward J.Juri, ed. Leiden E.J. Brill, 1969, 248–262.

221 Rahman, *Islam and Modernity*, 147.

222 Rahman, *Islam*, 66–7.

Arkoun

1. Revelation – An Anthropological Approach

Arkoun does not mention whether revelation is a fact or not, but demands the researcher takes seriously Muslims' belief in the divine source of revelation. The recognition of the importance of this belief permits what Arkoun regards as an adequate approach to Prophetic religions such as Judaism, Christianity and Islam. In his written works Arkoun remains silent on his own belief in revelation and prophecy, although he recognizes that so called Prophets are said by religious traditions to have experienced revelations. More concrete within the three monotheistic religions Judaism, Christianity and Islam the event of revelation is associated with the establishment of a covenant (*mīthāq*) "between God humankind." Arkoun sets out to approach revelation from the anthropological and philosophical perspective:

> Revelation is not normative speech, which fell from heaven, to force humankind to repeat forever the same rituals of obedience and action; it is a suggestion to dedicate meaning to existence, which can be revised and interpreted in the frame of the covenant freely sealed between God and humankind (see the verses in the Quran which abrogate others and which were abrogated).[223]

What was in these events in the first instance a personal experience, will be subsequently communicated within groups of people and eventually incorporated into entire societies. Arkoun is not much concerned about how or even whether events like actual revelations took place. Indeed he proclaims their scientific study impossible. He is more interested in how to study the beliefs in them and their effects. The effects of the belief in revelations are ultimately linked to the accounts of meaning and truth that are generated through this belief. Two ideas follow: firstly revelation according to Arkoun needs to be psychologically explained as a subjective experience of an individual. Hence it can only – if at all – be explained with reference to information given by the subject of that experience. It cannot be assessed whether such experience was initiated by a metaphysical source. Secondly, and this is the realm in which most historical research can take place, revelation must be understood in terms of social effects of belief in its actuality and potential to deliver meanings and truths.

What makes Arkoun's approach challenging for researchers of religions is its demand for sensitivity towards beliefs and their objects (revelations, God etc.). This goes beyond the basic fair judgement employed by religious studies approaches. Much more he demands an inner recognition of the belief under scrutiny and an overcoming of what appears in Arkoun's thinking to be a sort of a spiritually 'blind objectivism.' Although Arkoun does not assert the factuality of any metaphysical beings or

---

223 Translated into German by Günther: 'Offenbarung ist keine normative Rede, die vom Himmel fiel, um die Menschen dazu zu zwingen, auf ewig dieselben Rituale von Gehorsam und Handlung zu wiederholen; es ist ein Angebot, der Existenz Sinn zu verleihen, das revidiert und im Rahmen des aus freien Stücken geschlossenen Bundes zwischen Gott und Mensch interpretiert werden kann (siehe die Verse im Koran, die andere außer Kraft setzen und außer Kraft gesetzt wurden)' (Arkoun 1992, 217, meine Übersetzung)." (Günther, „Zum Potenzial von Mohammed Arkouns Ansatz für Dialogkonzepte," 219)

happenings, he wishes the researcher of religion to be open to the thought of their possible existence.[224]

Ursula Günther who offers the first systematization of his thought, sees that Arkoun understands revelation as "manifestations of the divine consciousness in history." However, I could not find proof to support this statement and she does not refer to a written statement by Arkoun. Maybe she received this impression from interviews with him, hence through privileged access. For sure, Arkoun consistently reminds us of the power of revelation, or the belief therein. He emphasizes that the content of what is believed to have been revelations offers existential meanings that can be determined through constant interpretations and their social (re-)appropriations. Therein lays the power of the concept of revelation. It offers numerous existential meanings which are transported via language mechanisms. He leaves unanswered whether the language mechanisms have divine or human origin. This question of course comes down to whether he accepts what is believed to be revelation, in our case the text of the Quran, entails only divine wording or, rather, human formulations. My study of his understanding of the composition of the Quranic text in chapter II helps us to realize what he might imply. We remember that for him the Quran is a product of discourses that consist of Muhammad's utterances and the reactions of the first audience; in addition the Quranic texts were mostly written later by people with fallible memories; and the texts were selected and compiled in an artificial order. Hence we can conclude that the language mechanisms in the Quran, as powerful they may be, are likely to be partially products of humans other than the Prophet (cf. polyphony of the Quran).

This said, Arkoun proclaims the significance of the language mechanisms in the Quranic texts, that have the power to develop certain dynamics of beliefs within cultures.[225] One can study the beliefs, the cultures that emerged from these beliefs,

---

224 Given that the portrait of Arkoun's stance here is correct, his approach to religions reminds of that developed of one father of religious studies, namely Friedrich Heiler. He anticipated an essence (Wesen) inherent in all religions. Religions are then just different phenomena of this essence. Like Arkoun, Heiler thought that the purely rational study of religion that ignored the existential meaning of religious truth was insufficient. And even if Heiler and Arkoun are not explicit about it, it seems to me that they both wanted researchers of religion to approach religions as potentially originating in a divine force. Since I enter speculative grounds, this short reflection ought to suffice. However, another parallel between Arkoun and Heiler is that they stressed the Prophetic character which is common amongst many religions. Arkoun almost exclusively speaks about revelation in the context of the three monotheistic religions (Judaism, Christianity and Islam).

225 The language mechanisms that still fuel the understanding of Muslims today is the repeated opposition of believers (*mu'minun*) and non-believers in the Quranic stories. One religious signal that can be understood as a product of society that operates according to these oppositions are the different dress codes for Muslim females. Arkoun writes: "Women, actually, are treated just like the beard and the moustache. They are no more than signals used to separate the "true believers" from the "infidels", meaning those militants seeking a new political order and those who monopolize an illegitimate power and impose it on the *Umma* (community). These signals are internationalised by the believers/militants as symbols related to the Revelation, which in turn illustrates the continuous ambiguity of symbols, signs,

and also the culture of the time in which the alleged revelations took place. For example, the concepts within Hijazi culture can be studied, as can their familiarity with the idea of inspirations. According to Arkoun, only in such environment could a revelation, as the one Muhammad proclaimed, have had the chance to be comprehended and its message implemented. The medium of revelation was in this way a successful tool for motivating people into a certain direction of societal development and actions. This development of a new religious community gained a special drive from the narratives within revelations of gaining salvation and eternal life. Revelation established what Arkoun calls a 'sacred force,' a power that makes the belief in Muhammad's utterances as divine revelations to appear as existential necessity. At the same time revelation was meant to establish a new social rule within the profane realm. It infused dynamics inside the minds of the first audience and led to reshaping the social landscape.

The Prophetic function shows the interweaving of revelation with social settings. These show themselves in the portrayed reactions to revelation, which are reflected on in the Quranic texts. They could be approving, critical, disapproving or rejecting as numerous verses indicate.[226] According to Arkoun this interaction of the Divine via Muhammad with reality makes the Quranic Reality (QR) a space and time that can be studied in all its historicity, as is typical for the human sphere. Of course the study relies on the materials available from these times. Arkoun acknowledges the scarcity of this material. For him, the historicity of events and facts is the basis for anything that can be subject to research. He wants to widen the notion of historicity not only to mean the nature of an event or fact which had actually taken place but also to include ideas like the *imaginaire* of revelation that affected society.[227]

To believe in the truth of historical accounts is a matter of trust, and – by definition – that of belief. It is not a proof of the factuality of an event. The study of revelation then exposes the scholar to common problems of historical studies. In addition, the Islamic tradition has its own accounts of historicity. A variety of such accounts appear, and they are disputable. Within Islamic scholarship the notion of historicity, which was subject to discussions about, for example, the nature of the Quranic speech and the circumstances of the occasions of revelation (*asbāb an-nuzūl*), is well established. This treatment was ongoing until one side or the other tried to establish their doctrines in connection with politics. Arkoun detects a decline in consideration of historicity within Islamic thought since the 10th century. This decline can be traced back to labelling the Quran as uncreated (*ghayr makhlūq*).[228] This idea was initiated by Ibn Hanbal after ending of *miḥna*, the inquisition of Muʿtazila against unbelievers in the doctrine of the createdness of the Quran. We already mentioned the Muʿtazila in connection with Abu Zayd's views on the Quran. To recall: The Muʿtazila were an

---

and signals in all societies. There is no way to convince a believer/militant that he is actually destroying the values for which he fights. This can only be done when social imaginaire is touched either by a generalized scientific education or by a violent revolution, which would develop new systems of representation." Arkoun, "Algeria," 9.

226   See Martin's article on *iʿjāz*, which displays some of the challenges that Muhammad was exposed to in justifying the divine origin of revelation. Martin, "Inimitability," EQ.

227   Arkoun, "Revelation Revisited," 20.

228   Cf. Arkoun, *Rethinking Islam*, 36.

intellectual and political group supporting the idea of the createdness of the Quran. They promoted a critical assessment of the history and descent of the Quranic text, although I believe the term *historical criticism*, as understood today, cannot be applied to their approach.

While Arkoun reflects on past scholarship on the historicity of the Quran he not only refers to the Mu'tazila, but also to Western philosophers. In the context of discussing Quranic studies and the history of the Quran's reception Arkoun refers to Vico, Herder, Dilthey, Heidegger, Sartre, Aron, and Ricœur and pleads for a re-introduction of the notion of historicity in the (social) study of religious thought. Repeatedly Arkoun calls for an enrichment of Quranic studies through the approaches of different scholars and schools of philosophy. Here Arkoun is not blind to the difficulties arising from such integration. He critiques

> Mere mention of this line of thought and of so many European thinkers in the context of a discussion of the Qur'ân as revelation, suffices to raise the spectre of blasphemy for many Muslims. They are apparently unable to grasp the idea that historicity is not a mere intellectual game invented by Westerners for Westerners. Rather, it has been part of the human condition since the appearance of man on earth.[229]

Yet Arkoun must not be understood as speaking of the actuality of revelation. In fact by 'revelation' he refers to the beliefs in it and their impact on human history. As we have discovered, he explicitly exempts the moment in which divinity and humanity meet from historical study. However his insistence on the importance of the concept of revelation and its impact on human history leads me to assume that he does not treat 'revelation' as a sheer assumption but as a real possibility. He writes: "There is no way of interpreting what we call revelation outside the historicity of its emergence, its development through history and its changing functions under the impact of history."[230]

If Arkoun hopes to introduce historical scholarship into Quranic studies, how far he regards revelation as a historical happening becomes important, as does how much justice he does to the theological notion of a divine origin of revelation. Would such historical study of the Quran and Islam be satisfying for Muslim scholars if the divine aspect is left out? It might help to understand how Arkoun views historicity:

> In its most basic sense, the historicity of an event means that it happened in actuality, rather than existing merely in collective memory, or *imaginaire*, as is the case with legends, mythological narratives and ideological constructs. Philosophically, this definition points towards two different scientific outcomes, positivist historicism on one hand, and on the other, the concept of the **radical historicity** of the human mind which is inseparable from its socio-historical embodiment. This is the concrete meaning and effect of what I allude to when I mentioned above *the social institution of mind.* Historicism regards only those events, facts and individuals as real, hence as valid subjects for historical study, for which there is available evidence in authentic documents. It thus excludes the beliefs and representations which animate the collective *imaginaire* and which have a determining influence on the historical dynamic. Positivism thus ignores or misconceives the reality of the imagination as a creative faculty at work in artistic activities and political visions. The latter expand as ideologies structuring the social *imaginaire* furiously solicited by the managers

---

229   Arkoun, "Revelation Revisted," 20.
230   Arkoun, "Revelation Revisted," 20.

of the sacred, the media and all types and levels of political discourse. What is called the return of religion in the conflicting ideologies of contemporary societies adds more confusions and violent clashes between imagined national, religious, cultural "identities" or "differences" claimed by individuals as well as competing ethno-confessional communities.[231]

Arkoun bases his critique of historicity on a perception that seems specific to Arkoun, but not necessarily to the actual practice of historians. Basically he identifies historicity as positivism of history, regarding those events which have taken place in actuality and of which we have written or any other 'hard evidence' as scientifically researchable. With revelation this is of course quite difficult, given that its source comes from the non-physical realm, although it then manifests itself in the earthly sphere. For Arkoun human consciousness and imagination do have 'hard' influence on the course of history because for him reality is also made of these mental formations such as consciousness and the imagination. In addition, he sees great dangers in ignoring these mental capacities as reality-transformative powers. However, he criticises positivist historicity for ignoring such powers and hence enhancing the dangers of ignoring their impact. The role of the concept of revelation in this line of thought is that of an initiator of mental transformations, which manifest themselves in concrete history.

2. Quranic and Prophetic Discourse

On what I call the horizontal level, Arkoun is mostly concerned with studying the effects of revelation in terms of reception of its messages by the first audience; the function of the messages within society; installation of Muhammad's Prophethood and its social impact; the role of Muhammad as Messianic figure until today as exemplary model of humanhood and the relationship between God and humankind. The horizontal level produced the first material which can be subject to scientific enquiry, in contrast to the vertical level of which only the effects of the beliefs in it can be studied.

Two aspects of the horizontal level are a) the role of the Messiah and b) the teachings of salvation. The hopes of salvation which are installed by the revelations and communicated by the Prophet evoke respect from the people towards Muhammad. In some sense Muhammad brings the tools for salvation into the world and hence becomes regarded as a saviour, re-installer of the true faith. The Prophet's authority is also nurtured by the belief in a Messiah who will inaugurate transformation and shift in current power hierarchies, hence bring justice, salvation and "a joining with God – the *ittisâl* according to the sûfî experience."[232] While studying Rahman's ideas of revelation, we were already introduced to this mystic idea of the joining of the human and the Divine. It is the Prophet who enables the people to build upon such hopes and to strive for the goal of terrestrial transformation and eternal salvation. Arkoun writes that the Messiah

> is more a constituent force of the whole communal, national and ethno-cultural conscience striving for the appropriation of values of justice, security, knowledge and salvation. Messianism is a power for the transformation of the entire history of

---

231　Arkoun, "Revelation Revisited," 20. The expression "manager of the sacred" is used by Arkoun in variations, e.g "managers of faith" and "managers of religion."
232　Arkoun, "Revelation Revisited," 43.

the world through an irrepressible wait that implies a radical reorganization of the current unjust order in the name of the Just order that will institute the Messiah (the Mahdî, or the Imâm in Islam).[233]

When Arkoun speaks of the function of revelation and prophecy he mostly means their sociological function. He stresses that it could develop its influence on the people only because they were living in a culture penetrated by mythological narratives and beliefs.

The most difficult term in the context of the horizontal level is 'Quranic discourse.' The exchange of knowledge of the Quranic message took place in a period which Arkoun calls Quranic Reality (QR), which I introduced in chapter II. The Quranic discourse takes place within this reality. We will enquire now what Arkoun might understand this to be. 'Discourse' is a term which was used and developed within Western thought in which it has specific and variant meanings. Most generally discourse means debate and exchange of knowledge and opinions about a certain topic. In this regard it does not have a strong existential character, in the sense that it actually shapes lives. Since Arkoun comes from the French school of thought and employs terms common in Francophone philosophy one can assume he employs the term 'discourse' in a way specific to such philosophy.[234] For example Michel Foucault, to whom Arkoun frequently refers, understands discourse as the linguistic attempts within human history to describe reality, or simply what is held to be truth. The discourse entails rules which regulate who says what, when, where, and how. The rules also regulate whether something is allowed to be said or not. This regulation of expression correlates with the regulations Arkoun detects in Islamic thought. Discourse in that regard influences how a society expresses knowledge about reality and also which knowledge about it is oppressed. Also, within Islamic discourse, rules tell what is thinkable, unthought and unthinkable; key concepts in Arkoun's deconstructivist approach to the history of Islamic thought.

We know already from Arkoun's views on the Quran and its transformation from orality to writing that he consciously distinguishes between the oral announcements (*l'énonciation orale*) and the written accounts (*énoncés écrits*).[235] Thus the Quranic

---

233   Arkoun, "Revelation Revisited," 42.

234   I assume the term implies more than a mere 'discussion.' Felix Körner shows that the term 'discourse' is applied to the Quran also by the Turkish *Ankara School*. He comments though that the German term, as understood let's say by Habermas and Ricœur is not suitable for applying to the Quran: „Im Deutschen wird 'Diskurs' entweder als 'kritische Kommunikation über Geltungsansprüche' (Habermas) verstanden; oder als einem bestimmten Wissensgebiet zugeordneter und dessen Regeln unterworfener sprachlicher Austausch (Ricoeur). Zur Wiedergabe des 'koranischen [...] discours' eignet sich 'Diskurs' daher nicht." Körner, *Alter Text-neuer Kontext*, 85.

235   Arkoun, "Contemporary Critical Practices and the Qur'an," EQ. What is more, Arkoun emphasizes that the Quran was originally an oral event, expressed in human language (French: *langage*), in a specific language (French: *langue*), Arabic. The Quran's initial orality carries certain implications. The text expressed in Arabic was carried by spoken words, or what de Saussure calls *parole*. The term 'discourse' was introduced by Ricœur and combined with de Saussure's terms *langage*, *langue* and *parole* in a system of linguistic that could be applied to Scripture.

discourse needs to be understood as such oral proclamations by Muhammad to the first audience.[236] Arkoun writes: "The principle idea is that of a recitation conforming to a discourse that's heard, not read. That is why I prefer to speak of Qur'anic discourse and not of text in the initial phase of enunciation by the Prophet."[237] So the Quran read today is a recitation of an oral discourse. Obviously today, only the written accounts can be explored but Arkoun demands that we have to keep in mind the original oral nature of the Quranic text. The Quranic discourse is only this oral event, which is different from what believers think as speech being embodied in written text. The text, as we will see, cannot capture the speech itself. There are two distinctions between the written and the oral accounts: the difference between the spoken world (*parole*) and speech (*discourse*), and that between oral and written accounts. The difference between spoken word and speech is that speech is the meaningful combination of spoken words in a particular moment. The spoken words in this combination produce a particular meaning whereas the same spoken words in a different combination at a different time would result in a different meaning. The other difference is that speech takes place in a specific moment, whereas the written accounts are abstracted from this specific moment. The written account of speech is static, timeless. The writing fixes the words, the literal *parole*, which was used in the speech. It does not reflect the speech, the discourse itself. The shift from orality to writings, which we have discussed already in chapter II with regard to the shift from orality to *muṣḥaf*, influences also how one understands the meaning of the speech. Reading the written speech words, does not guarantee that the intention of the speaker is transmitted successfully. This is because the chances that the intention is transmitted successfully are higher when the speech is carried via voice, intonation and mimic expressions of the speaker.[238] This is of course a general problem for the interpretation of all written thoughts and speech.

---

236   A definition of the Quranic Discourse: „Verkündigung der Offenbarungen durch den Propheten zu dessen Lebzeiten. Der koranische Diskurs ist mit dem Tod Muhammads beendet, weil er sich nur auf die unmittelbare Äußerungen, d.h. linguistisch gesehen den Sprechakt (*énonciation*) bezieht und nicht auf die als Text fixierte Rede (énoncé). Er ist außerdem als ein ausgefeiltes System semantischer Beziehungen wie Assoziationen, Gegensatzpaare, Implikationen zu verstehen. Das bedeutet, dass sich einzelne Textteile in einem großen Zusammenhang des Gesamttextes erschließen, wie z.B. über Wortfelder (LC: 41, besonders Anmerkung 11.)." "Proclamation of the revelations by the prophet in his lifetime. The Quranic discourse has ended with the death of Muhammad, because it only relates to the immediate expressions, this means linguistically, the speech act (énonciation), and not the speech (énoncé) which is fixed as text. It is moreover to be understood as a sophisticated system of semantic relationships such as associations, contrastive pairs, implications. This means, that individual parts of the text are revealed in the great context of the whole text, as for example through lexical fields." (Günther, *Mohammed Arkoun*, 269)

237   Arkoun, *Rethinking Islam*, 30.

238   cf. Öszoy in Körner, *Alter Text-neuer Kontext*, 85.

Abu Zayd

1. Divine Source & Human Word

For Abu Zayd there is no doubt about the divine source of revelation.[239] But like Rahman he emphasises its context-related sending and the need to study the social conditions of the Hijaz at the time of revelation. Such historical and sociological knowledge enables us to subtract the contingent parts of revelation, and by interpretation we will find a way of understanding what he perceived as the code of the message.[240] We will see in chapter 5 which disciplines Abu Zayd wishes to be employed in interpretation. For our enquiry now it suffices to see Abu Zayd shifts his concern away from speculations about the divine source and is more concerned about current applications of text-understanding. In this endeavour he always grants divine origin to the Quran, but simultaneously – just as Arkoun – removes it from the field of scientific investigation. Abu Zayd says:

> Jedes Gespräch über den Koran vor dem Augenblick seiner Verkündigung ist ein metaphysisches Gespräch, kein wissenschaftliches. Der wissenschaftliche Diskurs muß mit dem Augenblick seiner Verkündigung beginnen. [...] Er ist ein göttlicher Text, insofern er einen Ursprung hat, den wir nicht kennen und den wir nicht studieren können.[241]

Although Abu Zayd exempts the Quranic divine origin from scientific examination, he still employs certain ideas regarding the revelation process. We consider in the coming paragraphs how Abu Zayd views the communication between God and Muhammad and between Muhammad and his audience. Hermeneutic, which is for Abu Zayd the 'other side of the text,' is a tool for today's' Muslims to engage with the divine message.[242] Here we attempt to understand Abu Zayd's accounts of the first two steps of the message's journey: revelation and its communication via Muhammad's prophecy. Since Abu Zayd acknowledges that the communication between Muhammad and God cannot be investigated, it is especially interesting what ideas Abu Zayd has of this process and which are still relevant for today's exegesis because these ideas could also influence his understanding of the subsequent processes, the communication between Muhammad and the people, and later the understanding of the message by the people through history until today.

2. *waḥy* and *shifra*

In this paragraph I will explore how Abu Zayd understands revelation and, in particular, the revelations from God to Muhammad. *Waḥy* is the Arabic word which is often translated in English to 'revelation'. In *mafhūm an-nās* Abu Zayd analyses the concept *waḥy*, how it was understood in pre-Islamic times and during the time of the Quranic

---

239   Abu Zayd, "The Dilemma of the Literary Approach to the Qur'an," 34.
240   Abu Zayd, "The Dilemma of the Literary Approach to the Qur'an," 39.
241   Abu Zayd, in and interview cited in Kermani, *Das Konzept* wahy, 63: "Every conversation about the Quran, [in its state] before the moment of its pronouncement, is a metaphysical discussion, not a scientific one. The scientific discourse must begin with the moment of its [the text's] proclamation. [...] It is a divine text, insofar as it has an origin, which we do not know and that we cannot study."
242   Abu Zayd, "The Dilemma of the Literary Approach to the Qur'an," 39.

revelations, and how it is used in the Quran itself. The Quran uses *waḥy* (six times) and its related verb (seventy times). By examination of pre-Islamic understanding, Abu Zayd hopes to shed light on how the Quranic use of the term ought to be understood, especially against the background of the first audience's comprehension. Historical conditions and their influences on language conception and comprehension are incorporated in the idea of reconstructing the first audience's understanding. Abu Zayd concludes that *waḥy* within the Quranic usage refers to multiple different communication processes, just as the term does within pre-Islamic times. *Waḥy*, Abu Zayd points out, referred in pre-Islamic time to poetry, prophecy (*nubuwwa*), and soothsaying (*kahāna*),[243] which could include communication between humans and *jinn*. Therefore *waḥy* indicated contact and communication between humans and superhuman beings.[244] Abu Zayd claims, the speciality of *waḥy* is that only the person directly addressed can understand the "mysterious and hidden information (*iʿlāman khafiyyan sirriyyanit*)."[245] For the observer (*al-murāqib*) of this process *waḥy* remains silent and inexplicable.[246] *Waḥy* can mean „jeden Kommunikationsvorgang, der eine Art von 'Verkündigung' (*iʿlām* – in diesem Kontext auch zu übersetzen mit 'Informationsübermittlung') enthält', und zwar 'eine Verkündigung im Verborgenen'."[247] If we consider again the example of *waḥy* meaning communication between human and *jinn*, Abu Zayd concludes that *waḥy* was generally understood as communication between the super-human sender (*mursil*) and the human receiver (*mustaqbil*), to whom both the code (*shifra*) is known. A pre-requisite for successful transmission of information is the intelligibility of the code, a common platform of understanding. With reference to the Islamic understanding of *waḥy*, Abu Zayd says:

> Der Islam ist eine „Botschaft", die Gott dem Menschen durch den Propheten Muhammad, seinen „Gesandten", der selbst ein Mensch ist, geoffenbart hat. Was das betrifft, ist der Koran eindeutig. Eine Botschaft stellt eine kommunikative Verbindung zwischen einem „Sender" und einem „Empfänger" durch einen bestimmten „Code" bzw. ein bestimmtes Sprachensystem dar.[248]

This notion of the *shifra* or *code* as part of the communication process is inspired by the Russian semiotician Yuri M. Lotmann,[249] who employed the mathematical theory of communication as developed by the American theoretician of information Claude

---

243 Kermani, *Das Konzept* wahy, 39; Sukidi, "Naṣr Ḥāmid Abū Zayd," 194, refers to *mafhūm an-nās* 32.

244 Wild, "Die andere Seite des Textes," 258. (see Abu Zayd, *mafhūm an-nās*, 38+44)/ Kermani, *Das Konzept* wahy, 42. cf. Sukidi, "Naṣr Ḥāmid Abū Zayd," 195. Sukidi refers to *mafhūm an-nās*, 34.

245 Sukidi, "Naṣr Ḥāmid Abū Zayd," 193. Sukidi refers to *mafhūm an-nās*, 32f/ cf. Kermani, *Das Konzept* wahy, 39.

246 Wild, *"Die andere Seite des Textes,"* 258.

247 Abu Zayd, (1999), *mafhūm an-nās*, 35–6, cited in Kermani, *Das Konzept* wahy, 39. From Sukidi, "Naṣr Ḥāmid Abū Zayd," 193 we learn the Arabic term for communication, *ʿamaliyyat ittiʿāl*, used in *mafhūm an-nās*, 32.

248 Abu Zayd, *Gottes Menschenwort*, 87–8: "Islam is a "message," which God revealed to man through the Prophet Muhammad, his "missioner" who himself is a human. As far as that, the Quran is unambiguous. A message represents a communicative link between a "sender" and a "receiver" by a certain "code" or a specific language system."

249 Works of Yuri M. Lotmann are amongst others: "Analysis of the Poetic Texts", "Universe of the Mind", and "Semiotics of Cinema."

Elwood Shannon (1949).[250] Shannon uses a model of encoded broadcasting which can be understood only when the sender uses a code that the addressee knows and is able to decode.[251] The communication is first mute for the third party, which might only be aware that communication takes place,[252] without understanding its content. Within this definition of *wahy* the nature of superhuman and Divine are distinct, however the Divine is by definition included in the category of 'super-human'. *Shifra* becomes the medium (*wasīla*) to communicate the message (*risāla*). Hildebrandt here suggests that Abu Zayd understands *shifra* itself as being based on human convention,[253] whereas from Kermani and Wild the impression arises that this code is only known to the sender and the receiver. One might argue that there is no obvious contradiction or exclusion. Hildebrandt evokes in his presentation the impression that Abu Zayd thinks of *shifra* as a product of the human language and therefore it would entail all forms of expressions (*Ausdrucksformen*) of human language. These forms are for example the semantic relation between *dāll* (*Deuten*) and *madlūl* (*Bedeutung*) and the principal of *magāz* (metaphors). Here *shifra* does not seem to be exclusively understandable for sender and addressee, since these expressions are found in the Arabic texts of the Quran. Maybe Abu Zayd means that the code itself is not exclusive but the message is. This notion can be supported by Abu Zayd's claim that the revelations to Muhammad were first of all non-verbal. It also explains why the message is initially mute for the third party. However I sense that Abu Zayd deems the code as decipherable since he believes in the potential of the Quranic text also to address people today. I believe it might be helpful if Hildebrand, Kermani and Wild distinguished between saying that 'the code is exclusively understandable to Muhammad and the divine sphere' and saying 'the message is meant to be addressing Muhammad exclusively first' but using a code, that is understandable by the entire addressee, people of the first audience. And it is of assistance to discern whether one speaks of the text that has been already been decoded by Muhammad for the final audience, and the initial meaning production through Muhammad. According to Abu Zayd's understanding of language as human convention, the code itself is known to Muhammad and subsequently also to the people who are part of his culture and language community. Zayd says: „Die Botschaft des Islam hätte also keinerlei Wirkung gehabt, wenn sie die Menschen, die sie zuerst empfingen, nicht hätten verstehen können."[254] In this exploration of the possible understanding of the function of *shifra* I recognize that it mainly focuses on literal *wahy*. But as we will find out, for Abu Zayd *wahy* between the divine sphere and Muhammad was first of all a non-verbal process. We will see later what this notion entails.

The Quran mentions three types of revelation: through inspiration (*al-ilhām*), from behind a veil (*min wara'i hijāb*), or through a messenger (cf. Quran, 42:51–52).[255] An example of *wahy* through inspiration is "*wahy* to Moses' mother (al-Qaṣaṣ/28:7). The notion of *wahy* here is to signify 'speech without word' (*kalām bidūni qawl*), or 'code-speech without sound' (*kalām bi-shifra ghayr ṣawtiyya*)."[256] The second, 'from behind

---

250   Shannon, C.E, Weaver, W., *The Mathematical Theory of Communication*, 1949.

251   Wielandt, "Wurzeln der Schwierigkeit innerislamischen Gesprächs," 260.

252   Kermani, *Das Konzept* wahy, 39.

253   Hildebrandt, *Neo-Mu'tazilismus?* 400.

254   Abu Zayd, *Gottes Menschenwort*, 89. cf. Abu Zayd, "The Dilemma of the Literary Approach to the Qur'an," 38.

255   Abu Zayd describes the three ways in *Gottes Menschenwort*, 128.

256   Sukidi "Naṣr Ḥāmid Abū Zayd," 195. He refers to *mafhūm an-nās*, 41.

a veil' is illustrated in the story of God speaking to Moses from behind a mountain. A different verse (4:164) indicates direct speech of God to Moses. Sukidi shows how Abu Zayd tries to reconcile the idea of speaking from behind the mountain with direct communication. Abu Zayd "argues that God's direct speech to Moses represents 'speech with language' (*kalām bi-lugha*) so that Moses could easily comprehend His speech." It did not mean speech uttered face to face, nevertheless directness is found in the comprehension of the spoken language.[257] For Abu Zayd it becomes clear that this third sense means first of all 'speech with language' not merely 'God's speech.' This is also reminiscent of Abu Zayd's understanding that God's speech is described in the Quran as infinite (see below).[258] Still, in the context of this specific verse which displays the communication of God with Moses, *wahy* does indicate 'God's speech.' Abu Zayd wants to make clear that this indication does not come naturally with each Quranic use of the term *wahy* or its related verbs. He describes the third sense of revelation:

> Der dritte Kanal gilt als der Kanal der Offenbarung des Koran, wobei der vermittelnde Bote, der Engel Gabriel, die Aufgabe hatte, Gottes Rede auf dem Wege der nonverbalen Kommunikation an Muhammad zu übermitteln. Daraus ist zu schließen, dass der Begriff *wahy* in seiner koranischen Verwendung semantisch mit dem Begriff der 'Rede Gottes' nicht übereinstimmt.[259]

Abu Zayd asserts further: „Offensichtlich sind Gottes Worte nicht nur diejenigen Worte, die im Koran geschrieben stehen. Der Koran selbst erklärt uns in Sure 31, dass das Wort Gottes schier unbegrenzt ist[...]."[260] As we have seen above, when verbs rooted in *w-h-y* appear in the Quran they relate to communication between superhuman and human. However, it also refers to sign language between humans. Abu Zayd cites here the non-verbal communication, which, as the Quran claims, took place between Zacharias and his people (19:10–11/3:41).[261] It becomes lucid from this that *wahy* as a communication process does not necessarily require a divine or super-human agent, but can refer to non-verbal communication between humans. Still, the use of the term *wahy* and its derivative verb in this context is of less interest for our enquiry. For us it is essential to examine Abu Zayd's understanding of *wahy* relating to two acts of communication between agents of two different ontological levels, firstly – which concerns us here – that between Allah and Muhammad and secondly that within the interpretation process of individuals, namely between believers and the Divine (cf. chapter V).

Abu Zayd points out that the use of *wahy* in its non-verbal nature also appears in the Quran, in order to show that the term can refer to non-verbal communication. In an interview he even suggests more strongly, that *wahy* in all its appearances in

---

257   Sukidi "Naṣr Ḥāmid Abū Zayd," 196. He refers to *mafhūm an-nās*, 41.
258   cf. Abu Zayd, *Gottes Menschenwort*, 126.
259   Abu Zayd, *Gottes Menschenwort*, 129. ("The Quran. God and Man in Communication"): "The third channel is the channel of the Quran's revelation, in which the mediating messenger, the angel Gabriel, had the task to transmit God's speech in the way of non-verbal communication to Muhammad. One can conclude from this, that the term *wahy*, in its Quranic application, does not identify the concept of 'God's speech.'"
260   Abu Zayd, *Mohammed und die Zeichen Gottes*, 69: "Obviously God's words are not only those words that are written in the Quran. The Quran itself tells us in Sura 31 that the word of God is entirely unlimited." Abu Zayd cites Q. 18:109.
261   Kermani, *Das Konzept* wahy, 40 and Sukidi, "Naṣr Ḥāmid Abū Zayd," 194 refer to *mafhūm an-nās*, 32.

the Quran refers to non-verbal communication.[262] Hence Muhammad's first audience was familiar with the term's meaning as non-verbal process. This might not serve as a good argument for the non-verbal communication between the divine sphere and Muhammad. But Abu Zayd also draws on *hadith*-literature in order to argue for *waḥy* being a non-verbal event.[263] I attempt to enquire why this seems important for Abu Zayd. In our interview Abu Zayd states:

> Generally speaking, Muslims believe that *waḥy* in case of Islam, in case of Quran, was through a mediator: Jibreel. So God sent Jibreel, the angel and Jibreel transmitted the divine message to Muhammad. How, we don't know. We have no clue. We have only the reports by Muhammad about this process, in the *sīra*. As the reports of Muhammad, if we study them, he would say at the beginning it was very, very hard. It was like ringing bell, or like the sound of so many [ants? (unclear)]. Whether it is a bell ring or the wind, it is not verbal. And we have his description of his wife Aisha, when he was under *waḥy* they have to cover his face. Because he would feel very hot, even in a cold day. He was sweating and his face changed. When it is over, I mean this *waḥy*, then he could come out with the verbal expression of *waḥy*. So it is obvious from this description that *waḥy* through the mediator according to the Islamic belief, was not verbal communication. We have Quranic evidence. In Quranic evidence, there is a passage in the Quran [...], God would never communicate with humans but only with three channels. By *waḥy*, which means non-verbal communication, or from behind a veil, and this has been understood as the way of God communicating with Moses from behind the mountain, Sinai, or from behind the [am]bush. From behind the fire [am]bush or from the Sinai Moses just heard the voices, he did not see God [unclear:of course this is impossible]. There was a voice here. [unclear: the third mean that] God sent the messenger [...] reveal, which means, by *waḥy*. So we have in the third case, which was taken by Muslim theologians as this is how Muhammad received the message. The word *waḥy* is used, that God sent a messenger [by his message]. But the messenger, *yuḥy*, which means inspired, Muhammad. Again, the Quran is using the word *waḥy*, which means non verbal communication.[264]

Abu Zayd holds on to the idea, that even the communication between the medium and Muhammad was a non-verbal inspiration. Abu Zayd says: „Und gemäß dem Koran hat auch der Überbringer eine Inspiration gebracht, keine wörtliche Offenbarung."[265]

According to this view Muhammad was non-verbally inspired and exited the revelation process in a state of verbalising these inspirations. With reference to Ibn Haldūn's understanding of revelation, Abu Zayd assumes that the inspirations to Muhammad took place via *ru'yā* (*Traumgesicht*) or *ḥulm* (*Traum*/dream).[266] Here Abu Zayd deviates from Rahman who denies that Muhammad clothed whatever message he received into words. We remember that Rahman believed that the feeling-word-complex is complete and did not require Muhammad's active choice of words. Still, Abu Zayd holds an understanding of the verbalisation process that seems to resemble some characteristic of what Rahman called the complete *feeling-word-complex*. I detect this resemblance in what Abu Zayd calls the synchronicity of the sending of the

---

262   Cf. Abu Zayd, "Interview 2009." (3:76 min.)
263   Abu Zayd, *Mohammed und die Zeichen Gottes*, 73. Abu Zayd refers to al-Buchari.
264   Abu Zayd, "Interview 2009."
265   Abu Zayd, *Mohammed und die Zeichen Gottes*, 74.
266   Cf. Hildebrandt, *Neo-Muʿtazilismus?* 417.

message and the comprehension of its meaning by the receiver. What does he mean by this? Navid Kermani lets us know that Abu Zayd refers to Ibn Haldūn's comment on the character of *wahy*, in which Ibn Haldūn understands *wahy* to take place outside of time.[267] Abu Zayd claims that sending and decoding take place simultaneously and he asserts that this simultaneousness is reminiscent of what is understood as timelessness by modern linguistics. In our context, synchronicity excludes the anteriority of Quranic revelation with ex post facto coming into effect (*nachträglicher Inkrafttretung*) of the entailed message. This means the revelation has instant meaning for the Prophet. Kermani comments on Abu Zayd's understanding of prophecy that „[...] ein Text ohne Bedeutung ist kein Text."[268] This means the communicative character of the message to Muhammad entails the necessary comprehension of its message.

One way of understanding the communication between God and creation is revolving around the idea of divine signs. Such signs should be witnesses for the divine origin of God's creation. Abu Zayd understands the inspirations to Muhammad also as signs of God. With reference to Ibn Arabi, Abu Zayd understands the Quran and the entire creation as sign (*ayat*) of God.[269] While natural signs are visible for all humans who wish to understand creation, revelation as oral text is in need of a *nabī* (Messenger), who receives the signs and communicates them with an audience. Basically, Abu Zayd maintains, all people should be able to understand the Quranic signs (*ayāt*).

God chose a human as Prophet and hence human language to communicate a verbalised message with the people. This verbalised message is accessible for all humans through their rationality. If I understand Abu Zayd correctly, the *shifra* mentioned above was known to Muhammad who could instantly decode the inspiration and reveal its meaning. The *shifra* here is commonly known by God and Muhammad. Later – when the verbalised message is spread – people have to apply their rational abilities to understand the codes that remain in the text, especially in the ambiguous parts. Decoding and recoding then takes place in human terms where the *shifra* is known to every human. In the aftermath of the actual revelation to Muhammad, Abu Zayd wants to understand the Quran not only as the verbalised will of God but also as God's speech in order to emphasise the communicative character of the divine message. God speaks to the people and his speech is an *ayāt* to them, which can be understood in human terms and whose meanings can be explored and expressed in human language.

Let's consider how Abu Zayd believes the sending of the Quran to have taken place. Abu Zayd embraces the traditional notion of the chain of transmission as put forward by Islamic theology. It distinguishes between the three steps of communication within the Quranic revelation process. The first communication is that between God and Jibreel (*tanzīl*),[270] secondly between Jibreel and Muhammad (*wahy, risāla*),[271] thirdly between Muhammad and humans (*balāg, indar*). The following graph shows this chain.

---

267   Kermani cites a passage from Ibn Haldun's *Al-Muqaddima*, 98.

268   Kermani, *Das Konzept* wahy, 40.

269   e.g. Quran 2:118/187/221/230/242/266; 3:103; 5:89; 24:58f; 57:17.

270   See Y. Rahman, *The Hermeneutical Theory of Naṣr Ḥāmid Abu Zayd*, for use of *inzal* in the Arabic language. 128–9.

271   A slight distinction of these terms is that *wahy* means inspiration (as discussed above according to its different accounts), and *risāla* refers to 'sending a message.' From the term *risāla* the honor title *rasul* is derived which indicates Muhammad as 'The Messenger.'

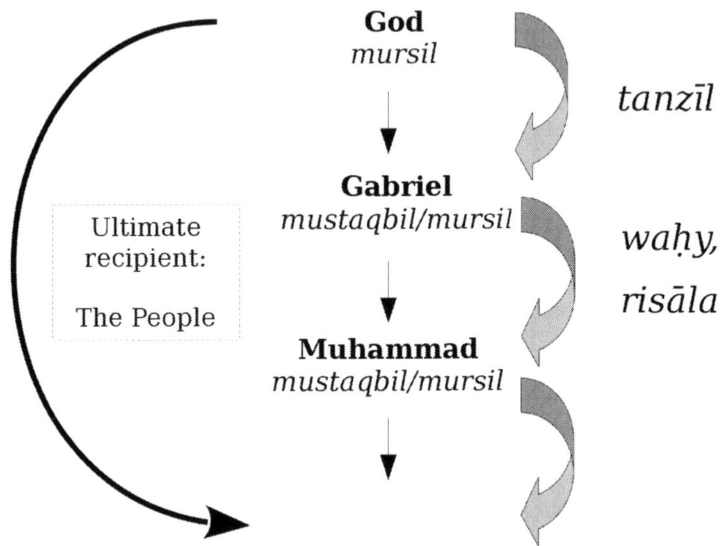

We remember that Abu Zayd explicitly holds that *tanzīl* and *waḥy* are not possible subjects for scientific analysis. The only process researchers can examine is the way "God reveals himself in the world."[272] For humans in the aftermath of Muhammad's first reception of revelation this worldly realm is first apparent in the narratives about Muhammad's experiences as Prophet and the writings about the first Islamic community. Islamic philosophy also puts forward notions of Muhammad's state of mind during revelation. Here I will not examine these notions, but we know from our discussion of the theory of imagination by Ibn Sina, the enquiry into Fazlur Rahman's understanding of revelation, that the only possible contribution by Muhammad to the revelation process might have been the preparation of his mind for receiving the universal messages. Without finding enough evidence that Rahman took over exactly Ibn Sina's view, I assumed that this idea of the preparation of the mind had inspired Rahman to think of Muhammad's mind taking actively part in the revelation. Also, Abu Zayd embraces the idea that Muhammad was in a state of transformation during revelation. Yusuf Rahman who like Kermani and Hildebrandt explores Abu Zayd's *mafhūm an-nās* finds Abu Zayd to embrace the idea that Muhammad evolved during revelation to a higher mental level:

> The transformation of Muhammad to the level of angel, according to Abū Zayd, however, was not a literal physical transformation [...], but rather occurred through imagination [...]. This is where Abū Zayd introduces the philosophers' and Sufis' discussion of prophecy. According to them, a Prophet can grasp the revelation through his imaginative faculty [...]. This faculty is greater in the Prophet than in philosophers, mystics or ordinary people. Compared to philosophers and mystics,

---

272   Kermani, *Das Konzept* wahy, 87.

the Prophet does not need training to increase the power of his imaginative faculty but has this granted to him by God. In ordinary people, by contrast, this faculty can only be performed in a limited time, especially during sleep.[273]

Yusuf Rahman now considers a slightly different understanding of the mind of Prophets, as it was developed within Islamic philosophy. This account states that Prophets are not in need of preparation of the mind but are gifted by God to understand instantly the messages being sent. I cannot find evidence in Abu Zayd's writing that he embraces either of the two ideas. And I do not see how far Abu Zayd understood Muhammad preparing or not preparing his mind before revelation to be important because Abu Zayd wants to concentrate on the earthly realm, in which the divine message got understood and spread via Muhammad. It is more crucial to take from Abu Zayd's ideas on revelation and prophecy that Muhammad received the messages non-verbally and hence had to use his fallible and limited human language abilities to clothe the messages into human words, which could be understood by the first audience. This account of Muhammad's experience is vital for Abu Zayd's proposals of interpretation. This finding will be of importance for the further discussion of whether Abu Zayd believed in verbal inspiration and how he must have understood this process.

Here I would like to offer two critical remarks. First, I see a similarity between Fazlur Rahman's and Abu Zayd's understandings of Muhammad's experiences. In the context of discussing these, Rahman refers to the Night Journey (*al-isrā'* and *mi'rāj*) of the Prophet. Various Islamic accounts state that Muhammad physically experienced the journey. In contrast Rahman understands it as a mental journey, not a physical one.[274] Abu Zayd denies that Muhammad was physically elevated to the spheres of angels in the moment of receiving revelations. He also believes such experience has been a spiritual one. These events are located by Rahman and Abu Zayd in the rational and imaginational faculties of Muhammad, who as a Prophet might have been granted a special gift of grasping the divine messages instantly.

Secondly, in his interviews, Abu Zayd points toward an understanding of the message delivery from God to Muhammad that is different from how Kermani and Hildebrandt depict Abu Zayd's ideas. Hildebrandt sees Abu Zayd refuting the idea that only the transmission of the message's meaning (*ma'nā*) took place between God and Jibreel; and that the transmission into language or word-sound (*lafẓ*) would have taken place subsequently. Hildebrandt creates the impression that Abu Zayd believes this idea would contradict what he extracts from the text-understanding that he finds in the Quran. Abu Zayd himself refers in his article 'Dilemma' to the Mu'tazila thought of al-Nazzam's student and Abu 'Amr b. Bakr al-Jāḥiẓ (d. December 868/January 869) who believed that the meaning (*ma'nā*) is delivered with the word (*lafẓ*). This means the signifier (*al-dalala*) comes along with the signified (*al-madlūl*).[275] But despite Abu Zayd's adherence to some of the Mu'tazila ideas, he does not explicate whether he follows al-Jāḥiẓ in this regard. However, he also does not reject this idea. Hildebrandt assumes Abu Zayd believed in the transmission of *lafẓ* from God

---

273 Rahman, Y. *The Hermeneutical Theory of Naṣr Ḥāmid Abu Zayd*, 37. Y. Rahman refers to *mafhūm an-nās*, 49.
274 Rahman, *Major Themes*, 92–4.
275 Abu Zayd, "The Dilemma of the Literary Approach to the Qur'an," 12.

to Jibreel and Muhammad without "noch so subtilen Beitrag Muhammads oder des Engels Gabriel zur Formulierung des koranischen Wortlauts" anzunehmen.[276] Similar to my attempt to discover how Fazlur Rahman thought about a possible contribution by Muhammad of the revelation and its wording, Hildebrandt also scrutinizes Abu Zayd's stance on this matter. He comes to the conclusion that Abu Zayd envisages contributions, by Muhammad and humans in general, only in terms of their participation and presence in history and conditions in which revelation occurred. For Abu Zayd, Hildebrandt remarks, the wording is entirely divine, without any human contribution. Kermani seems to take the same line and concludes that Abu Zayd believes in the "inverbation of God in the Quran."[277] But my previous findings contest this stance. Abu Zayd's strong emphasis on the nature of revelation as non-verbal inspiration, and his explanation of the concept of *wahy* as the transmission of codes known to sender and receiver and mute for others, suggest that he viewed verbal inspiration as follows: Muhammad received non-verbal inspirations which he then uttered in the Arabic language, the only human language he had known. That this language was not the language of the revelation is clear to Abu Zayd who believes that in this situation neither God not Jibreel spoke Arabic. Hence the code known between Jibreel /God and Muhammad must have been one that is different from the Arabic language. This account is also supported by Abu Zayd's assertion that the orally expressed Quran is the first interpretation by Muhammad.

The idea of verbal inspiration is problematic for exegesis. If the wording is already determined by God, then the human contribution of the Prophets in formulating the proclamations is only that of the receiver and giver. Hildebrandt and Kermani seem to argue that Abu Zayd believes Muhammad to have received words and meaning simultaneously. One consequence of this is that the text, which is believed to capture the wording, is entirely God's speech. It might be too harsh a critique or conclusion, but it seems to me that this supports the idea of the *istiqlah ma'nā al naṣ*, the inscrutability of the text's meaning. And Abu Zayd argues that this *istiqlah* is a crucial obstacle for modern Muslim societies to approach the Quran. From the citation of the interview above I am inclined to cautiously state that Abu Zayd believes (in the way I have concluded above in contrast to Hildebrandt and Kermani) in verbal inspiration, without discussing his understanding in more detail. Maybe he does not follow up what could result from his stances on the Quran and revelation, because of the scarcity of material available to reconstruct the actual act of revelation. What also seems difficult is that Kermani holds that Abu Zayd never questioned that Muhammad received *wahy* via the angel Jibreel: "Nicht in Frage gestellt wird von Abu Zayd, daß Mohammed sein wahy nur indirekt über einen Boten, den Engel Gabriel, empfangen habe. Dabei ist dies keineswegs so eindeutig [...]."[278] Kermani admits that it is ambiguous to think that Muhammad received all revelation via Jibreel. And we know from the interview that Abu Zayd definitely believed that Muhammad received revelation via inspiration and most probably through a mediator. Abu Zayd though does not go into detail.

---

276   Hildebrandt, *Neo-Mu'tazilismus?* 417.
277   Kermani, *Das Konzept* wahy, 63.
278   Kermani, *Das Konzept* wahy, 57: "It is not called into question by Abu Zayd, that Mohammed had received his wahy only indirectly through a messenger, the angel Gabriel. Yet this is by no means so clear."

One question that seems to remain unanswered is that if *tanzīl*, the revelation process between Jibreel and Muhammad was non-verbal, then how did Jibreel inspire Muhammad? In other words, which role did Jibreel have in the inspiration process? We were previously exposed to this problem while discussing Rahman's understanding of revelation. Here we refer to Abu Zayd who was aware of this problem: "So God sent Gabriel, the angel and Gabriel transmitted the divine message to Muhammad. How, we don't know. We have no clue." It does not seem too much of a problem for Abu Zayd to simply take Jibreel as a given in the process. For Abu Zayd it was more important to understand Muhammad as a fallible human in the process of revelation which took place as non-verbal inspiration. What we can be sure of is that Abu Zayd understood revelation as an interaction between Muhammad and the metaphysical sphere, and not as dictation.

3. Muhammad's Legacy

Abu Zayd, similar to Arkoun, rejects the possibility of researching the actual event of revelation.[279] Nevertheless we have seen that he refers to secondary literature that depicts the Prophet to have received revelation non-verbally.

The recognition of the cultural and timely conditioning of revelation and its messages is reflected in Abu Zayd's distinction between two different roles of Muhammad. During the first half of the period of revelation the Prophet acted as alerter, and in the latter part he acted to a greater degree as messenger. In this context Yusuf Rahman explores once more Abu Zayd's *mafhūm an-nās* and finds Abu Zayd asserting that "during the first phase, Muhammad's role was to warn people *(indhir)*, to fight against the past traditions and to draw attention to the new belief, while in the second phase his mission was to build a new society."[280]

With reference to the study of different periods of revelation and prophecy Abu Zayd emphasizes the importance of *asbāb an-nuzūl* literature which contains information about the background of the revealed messages. The process of revelation over many years slowly but steady transformed the *jāhiliyya* culture into an Islamic society. As it is the aim of the Divine to address the people, it was also the aim to transform their lives, not only the life of the Prophet. Muhammad's struggle for acceptance as a Prophet mirrors the slow transformation of the minds of the people and the connection of the message to the people's pre-knowledge. Such knowledge included a particular understanding of communication between the metaphysical and the physical spheres. From Abu Zayd's discussion on the use of *waḥy* in Arab culture he concludes that the pre-Islamic understanding of soothsaying, poetry and the communication between humans and *jinn* "was the cultural basis for the phenomenon of religious revelation itself."[281] If the people had no knowledge of such a communication concept, God must have chosen a different way of delivering the messages. The assumption that the Arabs were familiar with the concept *waḥy* is supported by those Quranic verses that refute

---

279 Navid Kermani sees a 'Copernican Turn' of Islamic thought in Abu Zayd's rejection of scientific access to the revelation process.

280 Rahman Y. *The Hermeneutical Theory of Naṣr Ḥāmid Abu Zayd*, 137. refers to Abu Zayd's *mafhūm an-nās*.

281 Abu Zayd, (1999) *mafhūm an-nās*, 38, cited in Kermani, *Das Konzept* wahy, 43.

accusations against Muhammad by his contemporaries, saying Muhammad would not be a Prophet but a soothsayer or poet.

Muhammad and his biography do not play a significant role in Abu Zayd's approach to the Quran as a literary text (as we will see in chapter V). The most important aspects the person of the Prophet and his experience deliver for the subsequent approach to the Quran are first that Muhammad received the revelations non-verbally and hence his utterances are the first human interpreted accounts of the Quran; secondly the revelations took place at specific times and circumstances which might be revealed through looking at biographies of the Prophet or the *sunna*;[282] thirdly the text needs not only to be understood as a manifestation of oral utterances but also as comprising different voices which represent for example reactions to Muhammad's prophecies. All the knowledge about Muhammad's and the first audience's comprehension of the revelation must not lead to the claim of absolute authority of these accounts. Every individual today needs to engage anew with the text, as did Muhammad in his initial experience of the revelations.

Comparison

In this chapter I wanted to shed light on how the three thinkers understand revelation. The importance of this enquiry lies within its capacity of showing how the thinkers believe the Quran came into being and which are the human aspects that they believe to be entailed in the available text today. Rahman's and Abu Zayd's account of revelation could be discussed in more detail than Arkoun's. This is because Arkoun generally refrains from speculations about the revelation process. At the same time Rahman's and Abu Zayd's accounts remain mostly speculative whereas Rahman's ideas are more detailed with regard to the actual revelation process and Abu Zayd delivers a more concrete understanding of the nature of what has been revealed to Muhammad.[283] Overall most parallels in their account of revelation are found between Rahman and Abu Zayd who both admit to the historical factuality of revelation and prophecy. Most prevalent is that both believe in the double character of the Quran as human and divine, which comes down to their perception of the nature of revelation. More precisely, the double character originates in the role of Muhammad in the process of receiving and mediating the revelations. Rahman believes that non-acoustic idea-words were revealed to Muhammad's heart and mind, without specifying how Muhammad formulated those into clear Arabic. Abu Zayd takes it that the Prophet received non-verbal inspirations which he then clothed into Arabic and language expressions which were common at that time and place of revelation. Abu Zayd's account is more concrete than Rahman's.

Both stress the fallibility and humanity of Muhammad, but they do not raise the possibility of errors made by Muhammad in the hinge between receiving revelation

---

282   Abu Zayd asserts that material on *sunna* was "canonized as a revelation equal to the Quran in its legal authority." (Abu Zayd, *Reformation of Islamic Thought*, 94). Abu Zayd is of course critical with the heavy reliance on *hadith* material in Islamic scholarship.

283   For a comparison see my article "Two Accounts of Quranic Revelation – Fazlur Rahman and N.H. Abu Zayd on Muhammad's *Contribution*." *Journal of Islam and Christian-Muslim Relations*. 2015: 271–286.

and formulating the prophetic speech. Still, Rahman admits that the mental stage of the Prophet had immediate influence on the Quranic formulations. For example it manifested in the "staccato-like abruptness" of the early verses. Rahman in fact offers different possible scenarios of how revelation took place and some of his ideas are reminiscent of the neo-platonic speculations as put forward by Ibn Sina, who I believe influenced Rahman's view on revelation as an event taking place within the human. I hope to have shown how Rahman's controversial statement of the double nature of the Quran might rest on this specific notion of revelation. Arkoun, although he does not confirm the divine origin of the revelations, also puts forward a similar 'human' aspect of the revelations. For Arkoun revelations are oral suggestions of meaning of existence. In the case of the Quran these suggestions were immediately discussed or reacted to by the first audience (*Quranic reality/Prophetic discourse*). Arkoun's Quran account then allows for the idea that the Quranic written texts incorporate these discourses. Arkoun, then similar to Rahman and Abu Zayd regards the event of 'revelation' as a complex that incorporates human contributions. If a scale depicted the level of these contributions as allowed for in the three different accounts it would probably appear to be as follows: With his recognition of Muhammad's contribution in the revelation process and his consideration of the sociological environment Rahman achieves the third place. Abu Zayd who asserts divine origin but detects numerous voices in the Quran which are not all divine; and who in addition allows for Muhammad's contribution in the interpretation or translation process from non-verbal messages into Arabic, achieves the second rank. Then, Arkoun who pictures revelation as a powerful religious notion with profound social impacts (terrestrial transformation) must rank first, since his account leaves open many doors for human involvement.

Chapter IV – Reform

Rahman

Rahman holds that the conduct of society requires practical instructions whose justification and application must be grounded in an ideology that delivers the theoretical framework.[284] In the scope of Rahman's overall ideology, the main goal is to reformulate agendas and solutions for Muslim life today. I will give a brief summary of Rahman's ideas on society (education, state, law, family) which he hoped would lead to a reformation.

Rahman believed that reform efforts must be geared towards installing a social system that allows society to live up to the demand for justice, which, he reckons, is the main principle entailed in the Quran. Here is how Rahman envisions the link between Quranic interpretation and social reform:

> In Islam, [...,] reinterpretation primarily means a reworking and restructuring of sociomoral principles that will form the basis for a viable social Islamic fabric in the twentieth and twenty-first centuries. This will certainly imply an interpretation of the Muslim *weltanschauung*, picking up the threads from the Qur'ān itself and making the cosmic symbols relevant to the sociomoral principles- a task that has really not been achieved in medieval Islam, but that contemporary Islam requires much [...].[285]

Reformation requires two components: first, the awareness of the Quran's main purpose, namely its ethico-legal content which is embodied in the principle of divine justice; secondly, the consciousness of its contextual revelation and the interpretation method of a double movement (see chapter V). Reformation that delivers solutions for modern Muslim societies involves the rethinking and re-organization of various disciplines and institutions of social relevance. 'Reworking' within the frame of Islam is the basis for an all aspects of life surrounding reformation. The aim is to formulate the ideal to which the Quran wants to lead. To strive towards this ideal is the aim of society. In chapter V we will find how Rahman hopes to achieve this extracting of the Quranic ideals. After having found the ideal it will lead to finding the most appropriate (Islamic) answer to contemporary social dilemmas.

Rahman's proposals for encountering modernity show how he tries to find unique answers within Islam to challenges of a contemporary life. Donald Berry (2003) has in detail worked out Rahman's responses to modernity.[286] In order not to be repetitive I will focus only on Rahman's most significant proposals for change and try to show which of them result from his interpretation of the Quran.

According to Rahman, rethinking Islam involves a rethinking of the role of the three crucial components of an Islamic people, namely the *'ulama'*, government administration and populace. Defining their roles must be based, like all re-working,

---

284   I intend to call Rahman's theological and philosophical thinking the 'ideology' that underlies his draft for a change of society and life conduct. By ideology I mean the set of ideas that lead to a certain system of thought. In that regard ideology as a value-neutral term meaning a set of ideas that make in this case the relationship and approach to Islam.

285   Rahman, *Islam and Modernity*, 124.

286   Berry, *Islam and Modernity*.

upon Quranic principles, primarily those of *justice*. This can be achieved through intellectual *jihad* (*ijtihād*) and moral *jihad*, which Rahman cites as internal struggles of each individual.[287] As long as these struggles are carried out, Islamic law and theology remain dynamic, socially applicable, and morally necessary. Obstacles for these struggles are a static *ijmā'* (consensus as found in orthodox Islam) and a closed door of *ijtihād*, abolition of (according to Rahman) original *shūrā* practice, and the lack of connection of law with theology and ethics.[288] Such impediments, he asserts, are responsible for the 'suicide of the Islamic development.'[289]

We can see how Rahman stresses that a viable Islamic society evolves on the basis of a genuine Islamic *weltanschauung* which can only be achieved by constant struggle for formulating ethics in the light of the Quranic principle of justice. Social norms and values borne from these ethics should be suggested by the *'ulama'* via *shari'a* weaved into a viable and constantly evolving social fabric.[290]

That, in a nutshell, is the underlying ideology which, in Rahman's view, leads to a reworking of Islam. It must permeate all efforts of restructuring political hierarchies and systems in order to improve the conditions of Muslim life in Muslim countries. Rahman deliberates in particular on the fields of education, state, law, family and society.

1. Education and Islamic Metaphysics

Rahman – before living in the USA – was the 'central education minister' of Pakistan in 1947,[291] and concerned with how to educate generations of Muslims in the newly emerging state. Rahman thought that in order to implement Quranic guidance towards justice in society, Islamic metaphysics must guide the educational system. For this reason he called for an 'Islamization of education.'[292] Nothing less, than the enlightenment of Muslim minds was the endeavour.[293] This attempt is predicated upon Quranic ethical ideals and by the careful study of Islamic history and other, non-Islamic disciplines which add to the body of knowledge but do not contradict the Quranic spirit.[294] The underlying principle of freedom of thought must be guaranteed at all times and all levels of education.

But what does Rahman mean by an Islamic metaphysics? For him a mutual relationship exists between metaphysics and knowledge. This means that metaphysics is not mere speculation but leads, in Rahman's view, to knowledge equal to that gained through physics. Metaphysics is grounded in knowledge and knowledge is the result of the applied metaphysics. The teaching of the seen (or physical) and unseen (or

---

287 Rahman, *Islam and Modernity*, 7.

288 Armajani, *Liberal Islam*, 87.

289 Rahman cited from his article "Islamic Concept of State," 270. (Hendrich, *Islam und Aufklärung*, 255)

290 "In any case, universal ethical values are the crux of the being of a society: [...]." (Rahman, *Islam and Modernity*, 160)

291 Karlekar, *Bangladesh: The Next Afghanistan?* 42.

292 Rahman was not the only thinker of his time to take on the task of rethinking education inspired by Islamic principles. His well known contemporary in the USA Ismail al-Faruqi for example is known for his project of 'Islamization of knowledge' and Seyyed Hossein Nasr is known for his 'Islamization of science' endeavour.

293 Rahman, *Islam*, 250, cited in Hendrich, *Islam und Aufklärung*, 254.

294 Rahman, *Islam and Modernity*, 133.

metaphysical) causes and effects within the world must be informed by the Quran's spirit, which points towards the establishment of justice and equality on earth. Rahman writes: "[...] it [metaphysics] is consciously or unconsciously the source of all values and of the meaning we attach to life itself. It is therefore all-important that this very ground of formation of our attitudes be as much informed as possible [...]."[295] Metaphysical knowledge seems, in Rahman's view, to lead to the formulation of ethical values. He understands metaphysics as a synthesis of knowledge and ethics.

A successful pedagogic system will integrate both aspects.[296] It will inform current social affairs so that the student is oriented in their social environment. Learning ought to widen "the horizons of one's vision and action," hence it should not only influence thought development but also one's behaviour. A reformulation of Muslim thought and action requires the application of Islamic ethics. Only through education, based upon an authentic Islamic *weltanschauung*, can God's message enter body and soul in order to guide people. The education system will train the youth of society, but the fruits of this education will show later in an educated, responsible and reflective civil society. In other words, education is the gateway for divine guidance into the *umma*. This is how Rahman envisions the benefits of Islamic metaphysics for education.

When reading Rahman it becomes clear that he was dissatisfied with the current education systems in Islamic countries. In his analysis of education schemes he describes two directions in which reform has occurred. The first reform simplified traditional curricula by shifting focus from medieval theology, philosophy, logic and Islamic law to *hadith*-science, Arabic philology, literature and the principles of Quranic exegesis. These trends are not always faithful to the Quranic spirit and often try to accommodate current religio-political ideologies. In addition, especially in modern times, this so called 'purification of Islam' relies heavily on selective reading of Quranic content (this is often the case in revivalist literature). The second education strategy combined modern ways of learning with old ones. Rahman gives the example of the educational system at the al-Azhar University in Egypt, which, in his eyes, was strongly influenced by medieval learning and for a long time not impacted by subjects like modern philosophy, sociology, and psychology. Still, he saw a slight integration of modern learning in theology and law into the al-Azhar schedule.[297] He also recognized attempts by Indonesia to change the education system and integrate modern subjects.[298]

After criticizing the predominantly unsuccessful attempts of education reform in the past, Rahman writes "This vicious circle can be broken only at the first point – if there come into being some first-class minds that can interpret the old in terms of the new as regards substance and turn the new into the service of the old as regards ideals. This, then, must be followed by writing of new textbooks on theology, ethics, and so forth."[299] For a start, the curriculum of religious leaders needs to be updated.[300]

---

295   Rahman, *Islam and Modernity*, 132.

296   Rahman, *Islam and Modernity*, 130.

297   The al-Azhar university was a place of reformists of the late 19th until the mid-20th century, embodied by scholars such as Jamal al-Din al-Afghani, Muhammad Abduh and Rashid Rida.

298   Rahman, *Islam and Modernity*, 138f. In addition he speaks hopefully of Turkey's chance of reshaping its intellectual heritage.

299   Rahman, *Islam and Modernity*, 139.

300   Rahman, "The Islamic Concept of State," 269.

In Rahman's view the fundamentalists over-simplified the curriculum by leaving out essential teachings and disciplines like medieval philosophy, especially Avicenna and Alfarabius, who were influenced by Hellenistic thought and were therefore considered to be impure and corrupted.[301] In contrast, Rahman believes that it ought to be the task of theology to offer an education which does justice to all knowledge (traditional-religious and modern-secular).[302] What is more, theology should even be informed by this body of knowledge.[303] As Rahman points out, a genuine combination of secular and religious branches within education could have prevented the strengthening of neo-fundamentalism, which in Rahman's eyes was mainly led by professionals lacking proper education.[304] Theology and education based on his ideas take into consideration other disciplines, like psychology and history, with the caveat that their application is in accordance with the Qur'ānic spirit and under its guidance.

Rahman's ideas for a reformation of education are not derived from the Quran per se. More than that, it is this general goal of developing a fair society that, in Rahman's mind, must be the driving force for shaping Muslim life today. He concludes, not so much with reference to the Quran, that education is at the root of this reshaping. He proposed to reform the education system to install the inner mindset for a life-long erudition. The more general demand for thinking and hence for education can be derived from the Quran and Rahman plead that scepticism and independent reasoning (*ijtihād*) must replace blind adherence.[305] Still, one cannot find a concrete role for the Quran in the development of Rahman's education scheme.

Rahman calls for the study of past and current social affairs as a prerequisite for understanding contemporary needs. This demand for sociological awareness does not derive from Quranic narratives but from his views on the nature of the Quran. For responding to specific circumstances, the knowledge about historic circumstances is crucial, as is the knowledge about current affairs in the application of Quranic principles to contemporary Muslim societies.

---

301 Rahman, "Roots of Islamic Neo-Fundamentalism," 29.

302 Rahman, "Roots of Islamic Neo-Fundamentalism," 30.

303 Cragg, *The Pen and the Faith*, 92.

304 Rahman, "Roots of Islamic Neo-Fundamentalism," 30.

305 It became clear in the previous chapter that Rahman is partly influenced by the medieval philosopher Ibn Sina. Also here it is my assumption that some of Rahman's ideas on education could have been inspired by this thinker. Ibn Sina declared that it is necessary that teaching children morality must go hand in hand with training them in intellectual thinking. Sina advocated "the usefulness of group discussions and debates" at schools. "In his curriculum for children between the ages of 6 and 14, Ibn Sina included study of the Qur'an, metaphysics, language, *adab* (belles-lettres), ethics and manual skills." (Mirbabaev, "The Islamic Lands and Their Culture," 34) *Adab* is here referred to as artistic writings of the *adab* culture. *Adab* is also referred to as a culture of certain spirit that emerged within Islamic society through its intense engagement with Greek literature and thinking. *Adab* in that sense is considered an equivalent to the Greek *paideia*, a culture or stream of mind based on holistic education (see chapter IV 2.1). At this stage, I cannot confirm that Rahman anywhere explicitly refers to Ibn Sina's education scheme as a role model. He might have also been influenced by his father, who was trained by the Deobandi School in free expression of critical thought. Rahman throughout his life promoted "open-ended" thinking, which he assumed was practised by the first original *umma*. (Armajani, *Liberal Islam*, 85–6.)

Some of Rahman's ideas for education can be traced back to his understanding of certain Quranic terms like *qadar*, *taqwā*, and *amr*.[306] *Qadar* is the quality of everything to 'be measured out,' which means to balance emotions and convictions towards a golden mean. Reflection, relativization, criticism encouraged by teaching and learning, will support the development of balanced personalities. *Taqwā* is the state of mind, in which the person remembers God in making decisions and carrying out actions. This remembrance helps to stabilize the personality. Hence, an education system that teaches religious knowledge, will contribute to this stabilization. Stable individual personalities will be the basis for lasting families which make up an important part of the social structure. *Amr* was already explained as the divine command which is mirrored in the preserved tablet. It leads towards justice and equality on earth. Underlying his proposed concepts for education are the premises regarding freedom of the person and the constant divine guidance as provided through the Quran. It becomes obvious that, for Rahman, religious guidance leads to a sort of liberation of the person. Where others might see a contradiction or at least a tension, when religion guides a society, for Rahman this is a necessity for enfolding one's humanhood.

One crucial element in reforming knowledge and teaching is what Rahman calls 'the ideal state of mind,' which comprises constant self assessment and comparison of personal action and thought with the Quranic spirit. Teachers must be of this 'ideal state of mind' and they must install in students this critical self assessment. Although Rahman emphasises a critical state of mind, he still wants to give the student assurances that living a Quran-inspired Islam is the best way to leading a morally just life. This assurance reflects what Rahman believes to be the becoming of a whole personality through remembering God.[307] In this respect Rahman is concerned with the establishment of an authentic Muslim identity, which might have been lost in the past. To secure this newly established identity it is important to embrace a firm social system. This social system must be reflected by a state government that does not allow political trouble making, just for the sake of opposition, as Rahman assumes is often practised in Western democratic systems. Despite Rahman's call for democracy, he also demands a strong leader with charisma and religious affirmation to initially head the state.[308]

2. Islamic State and Popular Sovereignty

To find a way of maturing a state, Rahman tried to discover an alternative to Islamic orthodoxy, fundamentalism and (non-Islamic) modernism. He did not see the adoption of a system like communism or capitalism as a solution for Pakistan. His ideas for an Islamic state were developed mostly with reference to Pakistan, for which he hoped to find ways of formulating a constitution on the basis of Quranic values. As mentioned in the introduction to this chapter, he started with rethinking the roles of three crucial components of Islamic society: religious authorities (*'ulama'*), state administration and community (*umma*). Hendrich describes Rahman's state system:

---

306   For a discussion of these three terms, see Rahman's *Major Themes*, 16–20.

307   Rahman, *Major Themes*, 19.

308   "The Qur'ān will tolerate strongman rule only as a temporary arrangement if a people are immature, for how can societies whose people remain immature produce mature leaders?" (Rahman, *Major Themes*, 29.)

[Der moderne islamische Staat] soll auf drei zentralen Elementen aufgebaut sein: Auf der Gemeinschaft der Gläubigen (*umma*) als gesetzgebender Souverän, der durch eine Ratsversammlung als Legislative repräsentiert wird; auf der Ulama als „religiöse Führerschaft für die Gemeinschaft" [...]; und auf der „administrativen" Führung des Staates durch eine einzelne Persönlichkeit, die bis zu einer möglichen Abwahl durch die *umma* regieren soll.[309]

Most crucially, the *umma*, the Muslim community and base of the Islamic state, is formed by the attempt "to implement the will of God as revealed in the Qur'ān and whose model in history was created by the Prophet." The leader of the *umma* should be driven by the "genuine spirit of service rather than rule."[310] The *'ibāda*, service to God, is necessary to implement the divine *amr* (command) of justice.[311] By practising *shūrā*, mutual consultation, the *umma* decides how the representative of the state should operate.[312] According to Rahman the Quran democratized the Arabic terms *nādī* (assembly) and *shūrā* (mutual consultation), which already existed in pre-Islamic Arabia. The term *shūrā* (as understood by Rahman)[313] reveals the inmost dedication of Islam to democracy.[314]

However, Rahman's view of democracy does not necessarily match Western accounts of democracy. For example he found a multiple party system unsuitable for emerging Islamic states, because it causes confusion. The one party system is, according to Rahman, in itself democratic, since it can be formulated in accordance with *shūrā*. A multiple political party system might be possible in the future when the young state has become more stable. Rahman finds the need for an Islamic state supported by the Quran: "That is why, with all its concern for a liberal pluralism of institutions and basic individual

---

309   Hendrich, *Islam und Aufklärung*, 254: "[The modern Islamic state] must be built on three central elements: The community of believers (*umma*) as a legislative sovereign, who is represented by a council as a legislative power; on the ulama as a "religious leadership to the community" [...], and on the "administrative" leadership of the state by a single personality, who is to govern until a possible recall by the *umma*."

310   Rahman, "The Islamic Concept of State," 261–2. This understanding of the character of the Muslim Prophetic leader is probably influenced by Rahman's view on the character of Muhammad, who did not choose himself to carry the burden of reforming society through preaching God's words and installing a new social and political order. See also Cragg, *The Pen and the Faith*, 97.

311   Rahman, *Major Themes*, 20. The 'goal of man' to bring good into the world does not incorporate explicit reference to the Quran and seems applicable to all humankind, 'all creation' (not only Muslims). See Rahman's *Islam and Modernity* for "the struggle for the cause of the good," 14.

312   Berry refers to an article by Fazlur Rahman: "The Principle of Shura and the Role of the Ummah in Islam," in *State Politics and Islam*, Indianapolis, American Trust Publications, 1986, Mumtaz Ahmad (Ed.), 91 (Berry, *Islam and Modernity*, 121.)/ See also Rahman, "Roots of Islamic Neo-Fundamentalism," 29.

313   "Fazlur Rahman's usage of Shura differed from the traditional usage of the term, which referred to a council of advisers who consulted the Khaliph. [ibid., pp. 92–93] The practice of 'mutual consultation' never took root because the doctrine of 'absolute obedience' insisted that the Khaliph held the keys to the Qur'ān and the Sunnah of the Prophet." Berry refers to Rahman, *Islam*, 239 and *Islam in Pakistan*, 36–7. (Berry, *Islam and Modernity*, 122.)

314   Rahman believes that *shūrā* is "Muhammad's exemplary practice of consulting several people in his decision making." (Armajani, *Dynamic Islam*, 87)

freedom, the Qur'ān, under certain conditions, admits that the state, when representing society, is paramount."[315] However, were multiple political parties are permitted, they must operate by the principle of *shūrā*. Any party system needs to "fully represent the masses. It must be a mass movement as Islam was in its early days."[316] As we see, Rahman's idea of an Islamic state is derived from both his interpretation of the history of Islam and the usage of Quranic terms in historical context. Hence he often refers to the Quranic élan or spirit and to examples from the Islamic history to back up his opinion.[317]

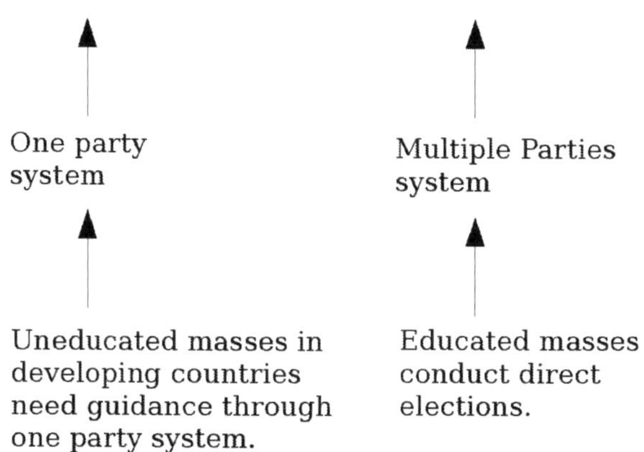

Where politics was concerned Rahman clearly distinguished between the divine and the human sphere. In his view only humans can be sovereign within politics. Of course God's sovereignty is stated in the Quran as being ultimate, but "it is equally true that this has no reference to political sovereignty whatever. It does not refer to legal sovereignty." He goes on saying: "What the Qur'ān is saying is that God has bestowed a certain constitution both to this universe and to man...The Qur'ān sometimes asks Muslims that when they decide matters, they should do so in accordance with the Qur'ān, and at other times that Muslims should decide matters in accordance with justice and equity."[318] The Quran then became one of several sources for the guidance of mankind but all justice derived from outside sources needs to be in accordance with the Quranic

---

315   Rahman, *Major Themes*, 29.

316   Rahman, "The Islamic Concept of State," 262.

317   An example from Islamic historiography helps Rahman to support his plea for democracy and the power of the people of voting about the head of state: "Abū-Bakr categorically stated that he had received his mandate from the people who had asked him to implement the Qur'ān and the Sunna, that so long as he did their behest he should be retained but that when they found that he was going grievously wrong, he should be deposed." (Rahman, "The Islamic Concept of State," 263)

318   Rahman, "The Islamic Concept of State," 264.

ethics. Rahman concludes from this Quranic statement: "What follows from this is that the Muslims should allow the dictates of justice, whose principles have been enunciated and illustrated in the Holy Book and the practice of the Prophet."[319] This means Rahman does not exclude the possibility of deriving principles from sources other than the Quran. For instance, to follow the Prophet's example means also to consider *sīra* and *sunna*-literature for the formulation of principles. Outside data needs to be always checked on its accordance to the Quranic élan. This is because the infallible Quran contains in its wisdom all that there is to know about justice. Therefore all other statements about life and society must never contradict Quranic principles.

God's words are put into operation in the Quran to guide toward justice. To help the *umma* live according to this concept, the Muslim state's duty is to promote justice. Rahman concludes: "[]...all human rights, universally recognized are automatically vouchsafed and guaranteed by a Government based on shūrā, i.e., mutual confidence."[320] A state's task is hence geared towards the promotion of justice and must, in Rahman's opinion, be composed of certain Quranic concepts, informed by values derived from Islamic sources and include all human rights that are declared universal. At the same time, the Islamic state shall never be secular:

> Many Muslim societies, in general, and Pakistan, in particular, have inherited this dichotomy of society into religious and the political authority, which, in the case of a country like Pakistan, has been accentuated by over a century of foreign rule. This ugly un-Islamic legacy of medieval-cum-foreign rule has to be eliminated and the Head of the State, i.e., government machinery, must take over full reins of total, indivisible, rule.[321]

Head of State: Concentration of civil, military and 'religious' executive powers, ultimate control and direction of practical religious life.	Council of Ministers advices Head of State: Men of sound judgement and good character, in whose hearts the interest of the nation lies supreme.
History of Islamic Community has shown that: Head of State needs to act in accordance with council of advisers (except in emergency case, when security of state is in danger, he assumes total powers of legislation ('Islamic Concept of State', 267). For the sake of the common good of society, the Head of State can be deposed by votes against him in cases of major breaches between him and the council.	

The unity, strength and determination of an Islamic state need to be reflected in effectively securing the frontiers of the country and guaranteeing the integrity of the territories. An effective armed force, equipped with the most modern and powerful weapons, has always to be kept as a stand-by.

---

319 Rahman, "The Islamic Concept of State," 264.
320 Rahman, "The Islamic Concept of State," 265.
321 Rahman, "The Islamic Concept of State," 266.

Rahman interprets from the Quran that the *zakat* system ought to have more holistic implications than having been previously applied. It can be understood as the basis for a Islamic state tax system that secures a just wealth distribution. In the past the *zakat* system degenerated, due to a poor religio-legal understanding. Against the background of the injustice in wealth distribution in Mecca Rahman finds that the Quran introduces the *zakat* to hamper wealth inequality.

Rahman also reads from the Quran that to live by the rules of God is ultimately more important than to obey the authority of human leaders. Similarly the fate of the broader community is ultimately more important than the internal interests of families.[322] In addition, the stability of the state must not be disturbed by rebellion from within. We already saw before that Rahman puts much emphasis on state stability. The Quran clearly calls for severe punishment of rebels against God's rule. Since Rahman refers to a particular Quran text in the context of addressing state stability, his rhetoric seems to level God's rule with state government to a certain degree. He cites sura 5:33–4:

> The punishment of those who take up arms against God and His Messenger and devote themselves to [corruption], creating discord on the earth, is that they should be killed or hung on the cross or their hands and feet should be severed from the opposite sides or they should be exiled—such should be their disgrace in this life, and in the hereafter there is greater chastisement for them, except those who repent before you lay your hands upon them. (5.al-Mā'idah:33–34).[323]

3. *shari'a* Law – System of *ijtihād, shūrā, ijmā'*

Law in this section is understood as *shari'a* law, which means the religious interpretation of social rules, derived from religious scriptures. For Rahman *shari'a* is an essential organ in the body of the state. The interpretation of *shari'a* is carried out by the *'ulama'*, the religious clerics, who communicate suggestions for religio-social conduct amongst the people. The populace can vote on the acceptance or rejection of laws that would result from the *'ulama'*'s suggestions.

The recipe for a religious law system sounds similar to that for the education system. It calls for development of an authentic Islamic *weltanschauung* by systematic deduction of Quranic principles, promotion of free will and thinking (*ijtihād*), constant scrutinizing of *ijmā'* (consensus) under changing social circumstances. *Shari'a* is based on scholarly opinions which may differ in their conclusions about what the Quranic text means today; hence it cannot be treated as a catalogue of set regulations.

> In theory, therefore, this body [of opinions], even though it became rigid and inflexible as actually applied, presents a bewildering richness of legal opinions and hence a great range and flexibility in the interpretation and actual formulation of the Sacred Law (the *shari'a*). In other words, a system of law or even a variety of legal systems can be created on the basis of this body of opinions, even though these opinions themselves do not strictly speaking constitute law.[324]

Rahman denies the immediate applicability of Islamic law in court decisions. Islamic law, in fact, is not law in a modern sense; it is a treasure of legal materials thrown

---

322 Rahman, *Major Themes*, 28.
323 Rahman, *Major Themes*, 30.
324 Rahman, *Islam and Modernity*, 32.

up during long centuries of sempiternal discussions, upon which modern Islamic legal systems can certainly be built, but only a part of which could ever be enforced in court.[325] As Rahman points out, *shari'a*, the body of opinions cannot be used as material for unanimous thought. It is likely to provide material for a 'variety' of legal systems and therefore the basis for a plurality of social governances. The body of opinions, its plurality and processes of discourses can help crystallize the underlying moral laws of the Quran and distinguish them from their contingency. *Shari'a* is the tool for identifying the principles relevant for the contemporary *umma*. For Rahman *shari'a* becomes "the most important and comprehensive concept for describing Islam."[326] *Shari'a* provides adaptable guidelines for a dynamic Muslim life, and furnishes the essence of Islam, the goodness and justice of God's creation. It rests on resolving disputes and exchanging opinions, which lead to manifold accounts of how the Quranic message should be formulated as a practical guidance for mankind.

In the context of Quranic scholarship Rahman hopes to see a growing awareness of the link between law and ethics, which he perceives as mostly lacking in Muslim thought. This consciousness is of great importance, especially since it should save Islamic law from becoming a secular endeavour. Islamic law and ethics are so closely linked that they should be studied within one common academic field.[327]. Essentially, Islamic law is the primary tool to set the values to which the society lives up to in order to implement social justice.

After having explained Rahman's understanding of *shari'a* and the role of Islamic law, we shall now see how he views the standing of the *'ulama'*. He refers to his understanding of the historical development of Muslim law, to argue against the exclusive control of *'ulama'* over *shari'a*. The *'ulama'*'s function is not synonymous with formulating *shari'a* since history showed Rahman, that "ijmā' was regarded as the ijmā' of the community and not of the *'ulamā'* alone until well after the second century of the Hijrah when the concept of the *ijmā'* of the *'ulamā'* replaced that of the community."[328] The representatives of the people are those who create law through practicing *ijtihād* and not the *'ulama'* who claim to have absolute monopoly over *ijtihād*, which "is really an attempt at thinking and nobody ever either 'gave' any one the right to think or 'confiscated' this right from him."[329] Rahman saw that within Islamic history the *'ulama'* were increasingly supportive of politicians and the state's interests and hence they elevated *shari'a* opinions into an objectified "body of knowledge." Hence, a consolidation took place of what was originally a personal understanding of God's will, always acknowledging the possibility of multiple interpretation, since 'only God knows best'. This consolidated view and the collusion of clerics to maintaining the political power of statesmen led to a neglect of ethics and Quranic spirit of justice.[330] Actually, *shari'a* must be exercised with the awareness of its duty to ethically develop the *umma*. *Shari'a*, understood as the office of the *'ulama'* offers a platform for discussing ethical duties and practices under the expertise of clerics who are trained in religious matters. Still, sovereign individuals then practice *ijmā'* and decide about the implementation of the suggestions made in the

---

325   Cf. Berry, *Islam and Modernity*, 145.
326   Rahman, *Islam*, 100. (Referred to by Berry, *Islam and Modernity*, 107)
327   Rahman, *Islam and Modernity*, 154.
328   Rahman, "The Islamic Concept of State," 269.
329   Rahman, "The Islamic Concept of State," 269.
330   Armajani, *Liberal Islam*, 86–7.

104

frame of *shari'a*. Rahman's account of the role of the *'ulama'* challenges their previous status as authoritative power over laws generated from religious sources. Below is a diagram of Rahman's idea of an ideal Islamic legislation (see chart below) as informed but not solely ruled by *shari'a*:[331]

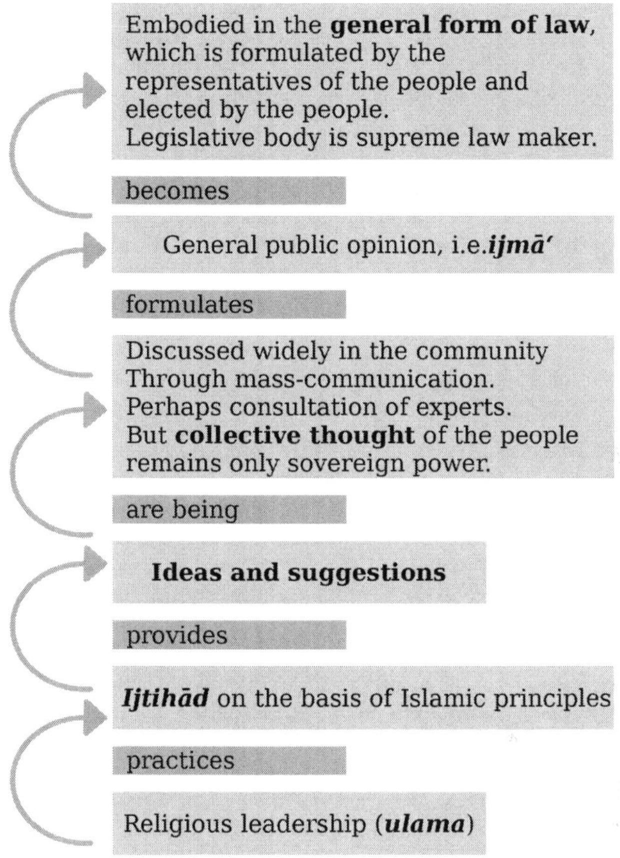

Rahman made concrete reform suggestions for the legislations of the newly constituted Pakistan. For example they addressed: banking interest through discussing the Quranic use of *riba*, which means usury; polygamy as allowed in the Quran but abrogated through higher principles of justice; family laws concerning heritage and birth control via contraception. Berry (1998) gives a detailed account of Rahman's reform ideas. In the next chapter I will show how Rahman hoped to justify his interpretations of selected matters. Here I will mention some of Rahman's major reform ideas in the context of legislation for Pakistan, especially concerning marriage, heritage, gender rights and equality, and family planning. Rahman's interpretation of Quranic passages on, for example, polygamy leads him to conclude that for contemporary

---

331   Cf. Rahman, "The Islamic Concept of State," 262–3.

Muslim societies monogamy is the ideal form of marriage. Rahman also calls for moderate interest in banking, and the mechanical slaughter of animals for food production, and "large scale introduction of modern technology" to fight poverty (with reference to Pakistan).

Within this line of thought, he also approved and even recommended the use of contraception in order to lower the birth rate, with which developing countries struggle.[332] For human civilization, beyond Muslim societies, Rahman constituted universal equality: "The essence of all human rights is the equality of the entire human race, which the Qur'ān assumed, affirmed, and confirmed. It obliterated all distinctions among men except goodness and virtue (*taqwā*): [...]."[333] In other words the only difference between humans could be found in different values and ethical practices. For Rahman, ethics must exceed the dichotomous thinking in categories of the forbidden and allowed, because the Quran "is a document that primarily exhorts to virtue and a strong sense of moral responsibility, suggesting that a comprehensive sense of responsibility can very well take care of all human rights; but the converse is not so true—indeed, a society that begins to understand 'rights' in terms of permissiveness and lawlessness spells its own inevitable doom."[334]

Arkoun

Problematic in analysing Arkoun's thought with regard to reform is that his few explicit statements are scattered through his writings in need to be filtered out. Those parts then have to be pieced together into a coherent picture. I try to concentrate on issues he addresses more explicitly and which seem important for the current discourse on society. In this chapter I also enquire into his more general outlook on a global ethic and holistic education and his specific proposals about state system, the civil person, the role of intellectuals and religious leaders in the discourse about Islam.

Arkoun was sceptical about the instrumentalization of Islam "used as an ideological lever, a tool of offensive or defensive justification" which "is rarely a subject of study or a source of value certainty in the fight against aspects of underdevelopment such as ignorance, eruptions of violence, corruption, and intolerance."[335] Since he does not want to support ideologizations of Islam he does not deliver a ready-made idea about Islam which immediately seeks followers and application.[336] Arkoun was more inclined to trust in the power of education, and a steady shift of awareness through patient

---

332 Berry, *Islam and Modernity*, 45–6.

333 Rahman, *Major Themes*, 30.

334 Rahman supports a traditional account of reading human rights from the Quran: "With perfect justification have the lawyers of Islam emphasized four fundamental freedoms or rights—life, religion, earning and owning property, and personal human honor and dignity ('*ird*), all of which it is the duty of the state to protect[...]." (Rahman, *Major Themes*, 31.)

335 Arkoun, *Rethinking Islam*, 86.

336 His scepticism towards *ideology* seems reminiscent of Marx's concept of ideology as a set of thought and ideas that strive to justify hegemonies while at the same time hiding true facts of reality. In this way ideologies are forged and spurious justifications of power.

pedagogy. Arkoun's ideas cannot be pressed into programmatic theory about society or religion, because his reform suggestions are not systematic enough.

1. Source of Inspiration: *adab*

A source for inspiration for much of Arkoun's reform ideas seems to be a holistic approach to education called *adab*.[337] Education in general, so Arkoun hopes, ought to be a holistic project which ultimately leads to the emergence of a 'new ethos' within a solidarity project between cultures. He refers to the tradition of *adab* as an Islamic example of holistic learning, which had the potential to reach this goal.

Adab belongs to knowledge, which was according to Arkoun oppressed or silenced by the dominating orthodoxies or what Arkoun calls the hegemonic reason. Such marginalized knowledge needs to be brought to light and examined as to which degree and in which way it could and did contribute to human knowledge about the world and our being in it.[338] It is a tradition of writings on human ethics, education and behaviour and sometimes also identified as Islamic *humanism* or Islamic humanist *culture* itself.[339] Within Islamic history of the most famous representative of this tradition is Ibn Miskawayh (932–1030 AD), a Persian neo-Platonist, humanist and ethicist, on whose work Arkoun wrote his doctoral thesis.[340] Günther suggests that it is this initial study on Islamic humanism, as presented by Miskawayh that lay the foundation of Arkoun's "long-term project of a critique of Islamic reason embedded in the generic context of religious thought."[341] And indeed there are parallels between elements of Miskawayh's *adab* and Arkoun's approach. Commonalities include the openness towards various, also non-Islamic sources of knowledge, the belief that it is necessary to overcome borders of religious doctrines, and the liberalization of thinking,[342] which

---

337   Greek counterpart: *paideia*. In 'ancient Greek' *paideia* meant "a system of broad cultural education" or formally "the culture of a society." *The Oxford Dictionary of English*. Groff, Islamic Philosophy, 6: Adab "comprises knowledge of poetry, rhetoric, oratory, grammar and history, as well as familiarity with the literary and philosophical achievements, the practical-ethical wisdom and the exemplary individuals of the pre-Islamic Arabs, Indians, Persians and Greeks. It can be said to encompass the natural sciences as well, although its primary focus is always on the human. [...] at its apex, the adab tradition – at least as interpreted by Islamic humanists such as Abu Suleyman Muhammad al-Sijistani, al-Tawhidi and Miskawayh – gave rise to the cosmopolitan ideal that wisdom and moral exemplars could be drawn from many cultures, and that their insights were the collective birthright of humankind."

338   Arkoun, *Rethinking Islam*, 76.

339   Still the term *adab* existed in similar use in pre-Islamic time. *Adab* in its oldest meaning "implies a habit, a practical norm of conduct, with the double connotation of being praiseworthy and being inherited from one's ancestors." (Gabrieli, "Adab," EI)

340   Arkoun's PhD thesis on Miskawayh from 1970 is discussed in detail by Günther in her PhD thesis *Mohammad Arkoun*, 161–7. Arkoun also wrote an entry on 'Miskawayh' in EI², vol.7, 143–4.

341   Günther, "Mohammad Arkoun: Towards a Radical Rethinking of Islamic Thought," 129.

342   Arkoun, "Auf den Spuren," 148. Arkoun on the other hand writes, "[...] in dem, was ich den philosophischen *adab* (*paidaia*) des 4. bzw. 10 Jahrhunderts bezeichnet habe, können wir eine Liberalisierung der kognitiven Aktivitäten ähnlich derjenigen in der europäischen Renaissance sehen [...]." He asserts though that Renaissance as well as enlightenment was not free from theological influences.

should result in "renewal and creativity."[343] Arkoun throughout his work consequently attempts to unravel and deconstruct cultural and religious restraints and promotes the communication and sharing of knowledge ('collective birthright of humankind') and the application of numerous disciplines to a more inclusivist approach to religion.[344] Another parallel between *adab* and Arkoun's approach is the hope that through enhancing human sciences one arrives at a formulation of ethics, which incorporates the practical instruction of people towards moral thinking and behaviour. Goodman (2006) formulates Miskawayh's views on humanity: "Society, Miskawayh argues, is our means to this end: Each of us is necessary to someone else's perfection, and all of us must cooperate to provide the material base necessary to humanize our existence." This incorporated the idea that humankind ought to be developed into an educated and hence moral culture as part of the "fulfilment as individuals and as a species" and to seek "inner sustenance [...] in the clarity and learning of the mind, the rule of reason, nourished not by the sunna of the Prophet but by *paideia*, the *adab* of humanity."[345] Here we can glimpse a tension between the philosophical approach to life and knowledge as opposed to the traditional theological advance. As I mentioned earlier, much of the hopes for the modern Muslim world Arkoun rests on the rethinking of the Greek heritage, specifically the sciences and philosophy. Referring to the prosperous times for these disciplines within the Islamic ruled societies of the medieval ages he writes: "neither the Qur'an nor the Prophet encouraged the study of these subjects; quite to the contrary [...]."[346] These subjects experience strong opposition by the established orthodoxies. We see then that also Arkoun's notion of education and how to formulate ethics might challenge the purely religious accounts. In addition "Miskawayh's philosophical interests centred mainly upon ethics and political thought. He presents philosophy as the sole 'true education' (*adab haqiqa/alethine paideia*), and as the way to salvation (*najah/soteria*)."[347] Arkoun agrees with Miskawayh's idea that philosophy is the main deliverer of such education and he hopes Islamic thought will review its

---

343 Arkoun, *Rethinking Islam*, 77. In fact, all three thinkers of this study propose the openness towards all sources of knowledge. This is to mention in contrast to the rejection (as practised by Ghazali) of the Greek heritage of rationalism, or sources from outside the Islamic realm (as excluded by Ibn Taymiyya).

344 Arkoun often mentions the necessity and usefulness of a range of disciplines which he would like to link through a general sense of philosophical scrutiny. Those disciplines are linguistics, philology, semiology, literary studies, anthropology, psychology, history, philosophy, archaeology and sociology. Since he regards religion as one of the most succinct expressions of human existence, the disciplines of researching this element of the complexity of humankind must be versatile. Arkoun takes up positively from *adab* two aspects which are worth being carried over into present academia: "Intellectualizing scientific disciplines (*al-ulum*) [...]" and "liberalization of cognitive activities." („[...] Intellektualisierung der wissenschaftlichen Disziplinen (*al-ulum*) [...]" and „Liberalisierung der kognitiven Aktivitäten." Arkoun, "Auf den Spuren," 148.)

345 Goodman, *Islamic Humanism*, 109.

346 Arkoun, *Rethinking Islam*, 74.

347 Kraemer, *Humanism in the Renaissance of Islam*, 231. Kraemer refers to Miskawayh, *Tahdhīb al-akhlāq*, 49–50. See also how Walzer reflects on translations from philosophical works in Greek into Arabic, "Some Aspects of Miskawayh's Tahdīb al-Akhlāq," cited in Kraemer 232–3.

often marginalized Greek heritage and generate autonomously a genuine way of formulating values for today's' societies.

2. Ethos, Islamic Studies and Philosophy

Arkoun promotes the development of an ethos which goes beyond principles of Western enlightenment and renaissance and also develops beyond Islamic traditions like the *adab*.[348] Europe tries to define values in various projects, amongst which is the *Weltethos* project formulated by the German scholar Hans Küng. Muhammad Arkoun is one of the representatives of religious denominations who were frequently addressed and asked for advice and support by Hans Küng for this project. Muhammad Arkoun amongst other scholars signed the "Universal declaration of global ethos" presented 1993 at the parliament of world religions.[349] The tenets of this declaration read as follows: 'Commitment to a culture of non-violence and respect for life, commitment to a culture of solidarity and a just economic order, commitment to a culture of tolerance and a life of truthfulness, commitment to a culture of equal rights and partnership between men and women.' I assume that with his support for the declaration comes necessarily along his reinforcement of the pronounced tenets. I take it that the establishment of these values is what lies at the heart of Arkoun's overall project.

Now having an idea of the higher aim of Arkoun's work, I take a look at his more specific proposals of reform, here with regard to scholarship of Islamic Studies. He wants both, Oriental and Western Islamic studies to be reformed. Günther (2003) delivers a thorough account of Arkoun's critique of both scholarships. Hence I will only mark what is important for our discussion. Overall, Arkoun says Oriental Islamic studies should open up for additional disciplines like social sciences and overcome the limits of thinking as set by orthodoxy. Western Islamic studies should give up their neutrality and become engaged in a dedicated discourse about current issues, cause and effects in the Islamic world. Both Western and Oriental scholarship must reach what Arkoun calls a meta-level on which both achieve autonomy and where it does not matter any more from which cultural or religious background the scholars come.[350] Arkoun addresses here the Islamic world which includes Muslim Diaspora communities and the new generations of Muslims born in non-Muslim countries. For the inner-Islamic debate as we know already he most strongly recommends a reassessment of *turāth* (heritage). Islamic historiography uses in Arkoun's eyes mechanisms of selection and distortion, e.g. apotheosis of heroic acts and mythologization of authorities.[351] Of these mechanisms one always needs to be aware when dealing with writings. In addition, he heavily criticizes the low intellectual quality of inner-Islamic religious discourses, speaking of what he calls the 'scandalous shortcomings of Islamic discourses.'[352] Apparently – and of course we know this from the case of the trial against Abu Zayd in Egypt – even if Muslim intellectuals aim to contribute

---

348   For this discussion compare also my article "The Humanistic Heritage of Muhammad Arkoun", in: *Philosophical Investigation*, No. 17, 2016, 203–227.
349   Küng. *A global Ethic*, 47. Cf. *Declaration Toward a Global Ethic* (http://www.urband harma.org/pdf/ethic.pdf)
350   Günther, *Mohammad Arkoun*, 107.
351   Günther, *Mohammad Arkoun*, 112.
352   Günther, *Mohammad Arkoun*, 108

to the religious discourse, they are often excluded from it.[353] The fate of being omitted from the religious discourse in core Islamic countries is that of several modern Muslim thinkers who then often need to spread their word in the non-Islamic realm.

Arkoun sees in some Western Orientalist accounts of Islam the tendency to support the exclusion of non-mainstream Islamic thought. Also Western scholarship should adopt a more critical and detailed perspective on Islam, since Islam is diverse and not represented solely by a dominant orthodoxy.[354] It must be the task of Western scholarship to inform students and the public about this diversity in order to shape awareness of the many facets of Islam.

In addition to reforms of Islamic studies on both sides (the confessional and non-confessional) he pleads to introduce philosophical learning and teaching in their curriculum and methods. Such he considers crucial for expanding the horizon of education since the 'philosophical attitude is the basis for the mental flexibility and openness.'[355] Hence philosophical studies will contribute to the holistic education, which is necessary for aiming at the new ethos. We see again that Arkoun closely links education with an emerging humanism. This becomes apparent in his critique of the history of philosophy in Oriental Islamic studies. He makes out a decline of culture of knowledge in Islamic culture since the 10th century, more specifically since the dominance of the theological thought of al-Ghazali. Arkoun acknowledges specifically the diminishing of *ijtihād*, individual thinking applied to Quran and *hadith* in order to derive legal opinions. Along this line Goodman mentions al-Ghazali's opposition to much of Miskawayh's humanistic and secular elements.[356] Here I assume that Arkoun adopts an assertive position towards *adab* and Miskawayh's draft of humanist thought while also taking on a critical stance on al-Ghazali's hostility to

353   Günther, *Mohammad Arkoun*, 109. Günther writes: „In den meisten Ländern des Nahen und Mittleren Ostens sind die sozio-politischen Bedingungen nicht gegeben, die notwendig sind, damit sich innovative Strömungen entfalten und etablieren können. Der Rahmen, innerhalb dessen Diskurse stattfinden können, ist weitgehend vorgegeben. Darum kritisieren Intellektuelle, die sich weigern, sich den herrschenden Konventionen anzupassen, d.h. der öffentlichen Meinung und der offiziellen Ideologie zu folgen, eine Isolierung der jeweiligen wissenschaftlichen Gemeinschaft, schlimmstenfalls müssen sie ein vergleichbares Schicksal wie Nasr Hamid Abu Zaid in Kauf nehmen [...]." "In most countries of the Near and Middle East, the socio-political conditions do not exist which are necessary for innovative trends to develop and establish themselves. The frame, in which its discourses can take place, is largely predetermined. That is why intellectuals, who refuse to follow the prevailing conventions, that are the public opinion and the official ideology, criticize the isolation of the scientific community, and must, in the worst cases, risk a similar fate as Nasr Hamid Abu Zaid."

354   Arkoun finds that Western scholarship promotes the dominance of orthodoxy when it considers it to be the only representative of Islam of worth to be studied and taught. He explicitly refers to van Ess as an example. Even further he writes "certain renowned Orientalists have helped to enrich the apologetic literature on Islam." (Arkoun, *Rethinking Islam*, 102.)

355   Günther, *Mohammad Arkoun*, 108.

356   Goodman, *Islamic Humanism*, 113.

elements of Miskawayh's thought.[357] Arkoun recognizes the negative influence of the line of thought established by al-Ghazali, on which Islamic orthodoxy heavily draws on. But he wants to make clear that Islam is not inherently anti-humanistic or anti-philosophical. He contends that it is a misconception that with al-Ghazali's critique of philosophy there was "put an end to the successes of Greek thought by contributing to the victory of orthodoxy."[358] What must occur is a recovery of the suppressed and marginalized streams of Islamic thought, especially those in the fashion of Averroism. Deconstruction of Islamic thought is the decisive tool for this archaeology.

Arkoun writes: "As for the fate of philosophy in the land of Islam after Averroes, we must undertake a double historical inquiry comparing sociological conditions for *failure* on the Muslim side with those promoting *success* on the Western, Christian side of what has been called Latin Averroism."[359] It needs to be remarked that Arkoun understands Islamic scholarship and philosophy in the form of Averroism as a starting point for current developments in Islamic thought towards modern philosophy of mind. Orthodox Islamic thought and other streams which ignore this Islamic heritage of Averroism ultimately miss out of this development.[360]

3. Mediterranean Realm and Project of Enlightenment

Next to reform ideas for Islamic studies and the proposal of reconsidering philosophical studies in all disciplines Arkoun frequently mentions the geographical common realm of countries surrounding the Mediterranean Sea. In this realm he sees a community of similar culture, history and thought, but understands that due to lack of education and study of their commonalities the cultures of the Mediterranean seem to be unnecessarily divided on multiple issues.[361] Arkoun detects two causes for the

---

357　I have discussed the 'Ghazali-Reception by Muslim Intellectuals in the West' in a presentation at Frank Griffel's workshop 'Aspects of al-Ghazali's Influence on Modern and Contemporary Islam', Dec. 9–10, 2011. Yale University.

358　Arkoun, *Rethinking Islam*, 75.

359　Arkoun, *Rethinking Islam*, 75.

360　Günther, *Muhammad Arkoun*, 113. For Arkoun philosophy is a means of education and training the mind to be open, reflective and critical. Hendrich formulates Arkoun's idea of the role of philosophy: "Angesichts der ‚faktischen Priorität'" dem ‚Primat der Gewalt als Antrieb der Geschichte' bleibt der Philosophie nur der vorsichtige Versuch eines pädagogischen Wirkens [...]." (Hendrich, *Islam und Aufklärung*, 307.)

361　Ursula Günther considers benefits of Arkoun thinking for the formulation of dialogue concepts in her essay "Zum Potential von Mohammed Arkouns Ansatz für Dialogkonzepte." She explains that Arkoun does not deliver a model or even detailed discussion of dialogue concepts, but his overall thinking delivers nevertheless numerous impulses for intercultural and interreligious dialogue. Paramount principles of Arkoun are to think freely, the broadening of horizons, and a meltdown of borders between allegedly established truths. Participants of a dialogue, especially the intellectuals who take part in an exchange of knowledge about values and histories, ought to step out of their dogmatic closure and engage with each other. Arkoun promotes a new way of thinking about religion, which roams outside theological frames. On the other hand he also approaches religion as a powerful social force. He refers particularly to the three book religions Judaism, Christianity and Islam (foremost in the frame of the Mediterranean realm) of which each claims to have received

chronic fragmentation in the Mediterranean realm: the split between philosophy and religious orthodoxy in Islam, and the artificial split between Western and so called Semitic religious thinking. So on one hand there is an inner-Islamic problematic and on the other hand there exists an opposition between Western (supposedly Christian) and the Jewish or Islamic religiously influenced cultures.[362] Arkoun hopes that a reform of instruction from primary teaching up to university learning can be intimately correlated to the transforming of awareness of a common heritage. We see here that similar to Rahman and Abu Zayd and other Islamic reformers, e.g. Muhammad Abdhu, Arkoun rests much hope on reform through education. However, Arkoun goes a step further, by addressing also Western education and not only teaching and learning in Islamic countries. With regret Arkoun mentions his perception that departments of philosophy in Western universities are not interested in teaching and engaging with Islamic philosophy. Therefore they do not shape the awareness of students of a shared or mutually influenced history of philosophy and values. Arkoun writes: "Beneath such disinterest there lies an old theological and ideological controversy between Islam and the West; an account of it will make a great chapter in psychological history."[363] From the arising awareness of a common heritage, Arkoun deduces a possible reunification of the cultures that are influenced by the three different books and religions of revelations within the Mediterranean area. Apparently all these efforts, and specifically the reformation of education, must be inspired by the aim of establishing universal ethical values. Through education humankind is enabled in its decision making and becomes an responsible and autonomous agent. Only then one can live up to the values as envisaged by Arkoun. Supposedly Arkoun's vision, although it starts from the geographic arena of the Mediterranean peoples, projects further into a kind of ethical value globalism.

---

through revelations the meaning of being. Arkoun does not discuss the truth claims of religions but regards each religion as one possible expression of truth. Revelations are in Arkoun's eyes the events that decode the meaning of life for the addressees of the messages. Any dialogue between religions should be aimed at understanding how the religions view the meaning of being. Such a dialogue would bring forth numerous similarities amongst the faiths and promote solidarity in the quest for establishing a tolerant civilization.

362   "The juxtaposition of these two historic splits explains why what we call 'Islam' and 'the West' stand opposed to each other as two poles of knowledge and civilization, even though they sit on the same philosophical-religious pedestal. A rediscovery of this pedestal would permit scholars to once again take up, in a critical way and with better evidence, all those problems repressed in the course of history and amidst the violence of conflict and the emotion of collective imaginaries. Such a path presupposes a thorough revision of curricula in the universities and in primary and secondary schools. This is what is at stake, it seems to me, in an exhaustive history of philosophy and of the religions of the Book in a reunited Western region." (Arkoun, *Rethinking Islam*, 77.)

363   Arkoun, *Rethinking Islam*, 77.

The traditional managers of belief with their monopoly on interpretation of scripture must be replaced by critical investigators. The pressing issue of defining an authentic Islamic identity within Islamic cultures seems to foster a "highly ritualized political Islam" which must be overcome,[364] or in Arkoun's terms, deconstructed (in Derrida's sense of the term *deconstruction*). He does not take on the task of formulating criteria for an authentic Muslimhood, but merely pursues liberation from the constraints of hegemonic Islamic thinking. We are reminded that orthodoxy tends at certain crucial points to ignore the historical character of the Quran and transcends it into the absolute. As we have discovered in chapters II and III the *Quranic event* is dissolved into the *Islamic event*. This dissolution results in the empowerment of orthodoxy. Reflective researchers must therefore be aware of the distinction between the two concepts or reality, in order to analyze the mechanisms that work behind the establishment of religion. Only through critical analysis, application of philosophical thought and patient pedagogy as proposed in Arkoun's thought on education might an Islamic enlightenment be possible. Hendrich in his analysis of Arkoun puts it this way: Arkoun prefers a "complex scientific discovery, a patient pedagogy, which disseminates proven knowledge, a politics of education, which allows every citizen to actually participate in the given civic rights and obligations"[365] The liberation from hegemonic thinking, whether Islamic or other, goes hand in hand with a liberation from the manipulation of society through religious symbolism. Such might even be active in its disguise as secularism, which borrows mechanisms of manipulation from religious systems. The liberation from the symbolic manipulations must be achieved by education toward critical-analytical thinking. But Arkoun still criticizes the insufficient liberty of educational institutions from the hegemonies of established thinking: "Current scientific culture permits us to glimpse opportunity for such a cognitive leap, which would serve to demystify many a murderous leader and 'revolution,' but schools and universities directly tied to the political viewpoint of these leaders are not yet ready to diffuse this new scientific spirit."[366]

4. Society beyond Education

I understand Arkoun's proposals for education to be ultimately geared at changing society, by means of evolving responsible, self reflective and critical citizens. In this endeavour solidarity of sciences must accord with solidarity of ethics. Politics should aim at building and preserving a civil society of tolerance (*Toleranzgesellschaft*). The system in use must be an institutionalized democracy which constitutes a society that is equally progressive and moral.[367] Arkoun criticizes governments of Islamic

---

364   I cite Arkoun here from the English (to my knowledge unpublished) essay "A Return to the Question of Humanism in Islamic Contexts," 2. This article was published in a German translation as "Auf den Spuren humanistischer Traditionen im Islam." The citation can be found on page 149 of the German version.

365   Hendrich, *Islam und Aufklärung*, 306. Original:… „komplexe wissenschaftliche Untersuchung vor, eine geduldige Pädagogik, die zuverlässig Kenntnisse zu verbreiten sucht, eine Bildungspolitik, die es jedem Bürger erlauben würde, seine bürgerlichen Rechte und Pflichten tatsächlich wahrzunehmen."

366   Arkoun, *Rethinking Islam*, 26.

367   Hendrich writes with reference to Arkoun that democracy is „Voraussetzung einer neuen Kultur der Kreativität und des moralischen Konsensus." See also Hendrich's

countries, which do not allow for freedom of thought, equal rights, education, and universal suffrage etc. He seems indeed quite sceptical towards the possibility of establishing democracy and civil societies in Islamic countries.[368] On the other hand he is also fault-finding with secular democracies. We will find that Arkoun often embraces certain outcomes of secularism, but at the same time also investigates them critically. One could call this a love-hate relationship of Arkoun towards liberalism and secularism. For example, France is in Arkoun's eyes not truly enlightened, since it actively and forcefully opposes public expressions of faith. He calls the French state system a "militant secularism" which attempts being a model of an enlightened secular state.[369] However, a truly enlightened state is aware of the religious fact and its mechanisms within society and does not on the contrary chose to ignore or even fight it. Religious reality is part of social reality and cannot be successfully denied. Ignoring the *fait religieux* leads in Arkoun's opinion to a gap within society from which one part will favour a religious leadership and the other support rational and secular leadership. We have already encountered that Arkoun anticipates that religion is an imminent factor of all societies, and we by now know that he takes this as a given and does not explain how he comes to believe this. Withal, it is certain that he pleads for an emancipated secularism that is aware of the dimension of religion. Arkoun seems to express that reality cannot be divided into that of belief and that of secular history, since both interact and penetrate each other.[370] Politics must lead towards an autonomous civil society under the guidance of solidarity of science and ethics. On such depends nothing less than a 'common future of all peoples.'[371] Discourse about this common future must take place in an atmosphere of freedom of will and thought. Ideologies (in Marx's sense of the term) will not be able to enhance the establishment of a responsible civil populace. Arkoun finds especially ridiculous the attempts of reading from the Quran that Muhammad was a socialist or a democrat; or in different contexts, reading newest scientific findings into the Quran.. These readings are reactions to modernity and only project human beliefs onto the text.

One such projection is the need of a theocratic society. He has in mind that some Muslim responses to modernity try to read the necessity of a unity of state and religion from Islamic history and Islamic scriptures (Quran, *sunna* and *sīra*). Arkoun admits that Muhammad reinvested the religious symbolic capital, in order to make the eschatology of the new religion relevant for the people at that time and place. Yes, the path to salvation must have been paved with new rules for society. But the actual "making of Islam into a state" took place due to the demand for a centralized administration

---

remarks on Arkoun's sceptic towards the capacity of Muslims to develop democratic structures, 306.

368   Hendrich, *Islam und Aufklärung*, 306.

369   Arkoun, *Rethinking Islam*, 77.

370   "Secularism with its juridical, philosophical underpinning continues to prevail in most Western, societies, but many churches, religious institutions, and civil organizations are making claims for articulating and encompassing theological-philosophical vision integrating the three concepts, person-individual-citizen, which they regard as inseparable." (Arkoun, "The State, the Individual, and Human Rights.")

371   Cf. Arkoun, "Auf den Spuren," 145.

of the fast expanding Islamic empire. Arkoun seems to say that neither Muhammad nor the Quranic text suggested such a unity, but that the demand for it was a later phenomenon. He writes, "since the death of the Prophet, Islam has never recovered the special circumstances permitting its double expression as symbol and politics [...]."[372] Although Arkoun is sceptical about French laicism, or 'militant secularism', he still was a member of the 'Committee for Laicism' in France.[373] Arkoun's view on secularism is mainly a critique of the idea that separating state and religion on legal and administrative levels is at all possible because religion still influences society. He is not denying the need for such artificial divisions, but calls for a secularism which is not blind to the religious fact as social fact. Further, in his remarks on nationalism Arkoun objects the feasibility of seeking a unity of the *umma* as long as the freedom of the individual is not guaranteed.

Arkoun believed that nationalism relies on a mythologized Islam, which in form of the *'ulama'* supports its interests. Nationalism is a political system favoured by numerous Islamic countries and the establishment of the Arab Islamic League is one of such attempts to unify Islamic peoples. The creation of unity must be understood as a reaction by Arabo-Islamic countries to Western dominance in an effort to cure Islamic cultures. But as long as an artificial unification is enforced onto a still illiberal people, democratic structures have no future. Arkoun notes: "[...] these people possess a wealth of resources still poorly understood, poorly interpreted, and insufficiently exploited. In vain they request means of democratic expression; explosions of anger are quickly repressed, dismissed as 'betrayal' of the national cause, [...]." Arkoun makes clear that "in the end, genuine unity must result from the freely expressed will of all citizens, but the path that leads there remains long, muddy, and disconcerting."[374] Again, Arkoun embraces the freedom of will and expression and human rights as declared by the global ethics project.

Intellectuals play a crucial part in sharpening the awareness of the need for these rights to be established. But Arkoun is sceptical about the intellectual and epistemological abilities of intellectuals who address issues of human rights like free choice of religion, freedom of thought and expression. This is because intellectuals are themselves often caught in a vicious circle. Their role is to critique and rethink conditions of society. They ought to contribute to shaping public opinion by making background information of political and social issues understandable and accessible to the public, and to communicate their critiques. But if they are not granted these rights of freedom in the first place, they can hardly contribute to form the consciousness for the necessity of such rights in the oppressed populace. How can deliverers liberate the conscience of the people, if they are not free themselves?

Despite Arkoun's apparent scepticism towards the religious and political structures in Muslim societies, he finds some positive impulses in Islamic history. For example, he believes that the original *umma*, during the lifetime of the Prophet, had the merits of an ideal community due to its "spiritual quality."[375] Such quality was determined through the immediate and intense link between God and the hearts of

---

372   Arkoun, *Rethinking Islam*, 21.
373   Cf. Arkoun's CV on the 'Ibn Rushd Fund for Freedom of Thought' webpage (www.ibn-rushd.org/English/CV-Arkoun.htm).
374   Arkoun, *Rethinking Islam*, 29.
375   Arkoun, *Rethinking Islam*, 53.

the people within the Quranic discourse. Arkoun does not think this original community is something today's Muslim communities could revive or imitate. Today's societies first need to rethink the claims of the three monotheistic religions (Judaism, Christianity and Islam) to possess truths. These truth claims are ultimately mutually exclusive and any thinking based on exclusivism cannot contribute to holistic and critical enquiry into the human condition. Here Arkoun pleads for a paradigm shift: "A reciprocity of consciousness as a base for an exchange of rights and duties on a level of legal equality would come only after there occurred an epistemological, hence mental, break with the concept of theological truth developed in the three revealed religions."[376] The mental break with exclusivist truth claims will enable intellectuals to enter a metalevel from which all strive to reveal mechanisms behind human phenomena, regardless, as said above, of their own backgrounds or affiliations. A common formulation of the values of an ideal society must occur outside religious exclusivist thinking. Although Arkoun did not compose a list of values (except those listed by Küng's global ethics project) he was concerned with finding a methodology to discover ways of maximising freedom from political, ideological, religious manipulative powers.

Intriguingly, even if Arkoun pleads for overcoming the borders of religious thinking and truth claims, he still finds inspiration for a model of the ideal community in divine revelation or as Arkoun calls them, the 'vistas of liberation.'[377] This stance illustrates Arkoun's internal conflict between Western modernity and the benefits of religious ideas. Arkoun believes that revelation and religious texts are potentially positive forces for the advancement of the person towards responsibility, which entails awareness of rights and duties.[378] He only refers though to the Quran as an example. Of course this material operates with narratives which speak of personal responsibility towards the will of God. Arkoun admits that the notion of citizen has no immediate foundation in the scriptures. But it seems scriptures lay down basic criteria for a kind of God-fearing citizenhood. The evolution of a person towards a responsible citizen is one of Arkoun's central issues that invoke the question of personhood and human rights. He admits that "Muslim theological thought has not committed itself to the kind of modern interpretation that would highlight" 'problems' "in contemporary discourse on human rights."[379] As we shall see, Arkoun's reading of sura 9 suggests that a discussion about human rights might have already been initiated by the Quranic discourse. The above quotation shows that the Quran contains the dynamic for forming a responsible and autonomous individual. Regarding sura 9 he writes "the fundamental message of sura 9 is not outmoded,"[380] and he says one efficacy of the Quranic discourse is the "deployment of the free person."[381]

---

376   Arkoun, *Rethinking Islam*, 54.
377   Arkoun, *Rethinking Islam*, 34.
378   "Revelation as collected in the sacred writings contains starting points, strong roots, and carrier concepts for the emergence of the person as a subject equipped with rights and as an agent responsible for the observance of obligations toward God and peers in the political community. The idea of peers does not coincide, of course, with the modern idea of citizen [...]." (Arkoun, *Rethinking Islam*, 55.)
379   Arkoun, *Rethinking Islam*, 56.
380   Arkoun, *Rethinking Islam*, 56.
381   Arkoun, *Rethinking Islam*, 57.

Hopefully, the analysis of Arkoun's reading of sura 9, as discussed in chapter V, clarifies how Arkoun detects such potentials for the development of responsible personhood in the Quran. Here is a glimpse at his account:

> The discourse of transcendence and of absoluteness opens an infinite space for the promotion of the individual beyond the constraints of fathers and brothers, clans and tribes, riches and tributes; the individual becomes an autonomous and free person, enjoying a liberty guaranteed by obedience and love lived within the alliance. The consciousness of the person thus liberated does not even require the mediation of another human consciousness, as it does in Christianity, which depends on the mediation of Jesus; the ontological access of a Muslim is direct, total, and irreversible. [...] Qur'anic discourse has broadly demonstrated its efficacy as a space for the emergence, training, and deployment of the free person, who enjoys guarantees of life, property, family, and private domicile not as "citizen" of a civil society managed by elected representatives or by universal suffrage (sovereign of the nation founded in 1789 by the French Revolution) but as God's partner in an eternal compact.[382]

Arkoun means here that Quranic revelation contributed to the liberation of the person from tribal codes. He also mentions that the new allegiance is based on obedience of the individual towards God. Surely there is a tension between such a model of personhood and that of the Western ideal of moral autonomy. Arkoun speaks explicitly of the "Muslim person", or the "person of Islam" who appeared first when the people of the former *jāhiliyya* committed "to the faith and to fighting (jihad) for the Prophet's cause, the small group of early believers (*mu'minūn*) [...]."[383] The growth and recurrence of this person he says comes down to the normative character and mythological structure of Quranic discourse, the force of ritual and the promise for salvation, the centralization of state "which took 'true religion' (orthodoxy) under its protection and drew legitimacy from it in return", and the image of original Islam and the narratives of "universal 'Islamic' history" as "initiated by the Prophet for individual and collective behaviour."[384] As Arkoun notices, "the emotional climate that predominates in Muslim societies today renders the scientific study of a large number of delicate problems impossible."[385] Still, he in contrast mentions the importance of the image of the initial Islam for the beliefs and developments in Islamic societies. He does not judge whether this widespread and traditional image of early Islam is erroneous or misleading, but emphasizes its impact:

> One can never overemphasize the role and recurrent power of the politico-religious imaginary put in place by what I have called the Medinan experience. All historical activity of any significance in the Islamic domain has been a result of this imaginary. These activities themselves presuppose the production of a type of person who has

---

382 Arkoun, *Rethinking Islam*, 57.
383 Arkoun, *Rethinking Islam*, 89.
384 Arkoun, *Rethinking Islam*, 89. As a remark: If one takes these criteria for the success of the Muslim person, it is understandable if researchers conclude a different image of early Islam, which then cannot serve anymore as this support for the constructed Muslim identity today. See studies on early Islam by the 'Saarland School', and research by Cook/Crone, and Kalisch.
385 Arkoun, *Rethinking Islam*, 93.

internalized all the representations, all the ideal symbolic images carries by traditional Islamic discourse. [...] The person should be studied as a haven of liberty;
choices are made, options eliminated, and combinations put together to make up
each *personality* and eventually to confirm the *selection* of the personage, the leader,
the imam at the level of local group, the nation, and the community of believers.
Such a study becomes indispensable to a reconstruction of the delicate mechanisms
that definitively order both individual destinies and the historical development of
societies.[386]

The basic personality receives, according to Arkoun, the meaning of the initial set up
of the Muslim person; in other words, what it means to belong to Islam according to
the context of the 'Medinan experience.' Arkoun is aware that this concept of person
is not the same as a modern notion of responsible individual with particular freedoms.
However he seems to attribute a positive effect to the notion of revelation and the
dynamics of the first Muslim *umma*.

Arkoun is especially interested in the notion of rights of the individual and he
was a vigorous supporter of secularism. Maybe this search into the roots of his own
culture and religion is inspired by his wish for the advancement of humankind.
With focus on this advancement Arkoun formulates the claim that the modern notion of tolerance ("the concept of tolerance is a modern achievement")[387] must be
strengthened. Even though Arkoun detects a few positive developments in Muslim
countries he still sees the need to overcome numerous obstacles and misdevelop-
ments. For example, with reference to nationalist movements in Egypt from 1952
onwards, Arkoun writes

> [...] the destruction of liberties, the negation of human rights, imperialist appetites,
> disorderly development, the ineffectiveness and often the destructiveness of tradi-
> tional values, unemployment, urban congestion, unequal distribution of resources,
> waste, and corruption. The progress achieved in public health, free schooling (but
> not education), security, transportation, and domestic comfort cannot compensate
> for the damages to the person caused by the destruction of ecological, sociological,

---

386   Arkoun, *Rethinking Islam*, 90. Arkoun's understanding of the Muslim person seems
      to resemble what he calls the 'basic personality'. He explicitly refers in this context to
      neo-Freudian psychoanalyst and ethnologist Abram Kardiner, who formulated that
      every culture brings forth a concept of personality, which then finds variation and
      development: "[...] with the help of the Islamic example, one could revive the concept
      of basic personality launched not long ago by the psychiatrist Abram Kardiner but
      left behind by anthropologists." Here a description by the sociologist Renner: „Die
      Basispersönlichkeit setzt sich zusammen aus denjenigen Persönlichkeitselementen,
      die die Mitglieder einer Gesellschaft aufgrund der gemeinsamen Erfahrungen in
      der frühen Kindheit miteinander teilen. Danach ist die Entstehung einer basalen
      Persönlichkeitsstruktur vor allem in den Sozialisierungspraktiken und – erfahrungen
      wie Stillen, Entwöhnen, Reinlichkeitstraining begründet." "The basic personality is
      composed of those elements of personality, which the members of a society share,
      based on communal experiences in early childhood. After that, the emergence of a
      basic personality structure is grounded especially in the socialization practices and
      experiences such as breastfeeding, weaning, hygiene training..." (Renner, "Kultur-
      theoretische und kulturvergleichende Ansätze," 182).
387   Arkoun, *Rethinking Islam*, 54.

118

and agrarian structures in which the ancestral values confirmed and sacralized by Islam were rooted.[388]

Amongst these remarks I spot that Arkoun again contrasts basic schooling with holistic education, an idea with which we are familiar from our investigation into *adab*. Nationalisms and Islamic revivalisms oppress the communication of scientific knowledge and hold back development as did the Catholic Church in the so called 'dark ages'.[389]

Arkoun stresses not only the importance of intellectuals but also that of the *'ulama'* as an informative body for the person and the person's development. They take part in shaping public opinion of Muslim societies as well. But there are shortcomings that need to be overcome: "The traditional ulema's function of critique, employing theological and moral censure, has been completely abandoned. The intellectuals, seduced by the independence of their Western counterparts, choose exile or self-censure [...]."[390] In these ways *'ulama'* and intellectuals become ineffective for building an autonomous civil society.

As we have seen, Arkoun goes even further than calling for critical *'ulama'*. He suggests a metalevel on which all scholars whether religious or not contribute to the knowledge about religion and humankind. He talks about the mechanisms of religious language: the language of the Quranic discourse, the mechanisms of human psychology and the imaginary faculties, the symbolic investment etc. This seems to indicate the belief that human thinking is influenced by many factors. He also says we have to use all tools to analyse these mechanisms in order to reveal them and their power to achieve some kind of liberty. He continually calls for the freedom of thought and research. Education seems a crucial and necessary tool to break the vicious circle of manipulation. In that context, his call for applied Islamology which incorporates his suggestions for reflective research must contribute to this liberation. He also calls for rethinking the emergence of values and it appears as if he aims at a construction of values that suit a global ethos of freedom. Independent disciplines, for example Islamic studies, should contribute to this formulation of values. Arkoun perceives that "it is still difficult to find the sort of intellectual, whether artist or leader, who affirms, protects and defines the destiny of the person as the point and ultimate concern of all philosophy."[391] "The destiny of the person" is the "ultimate concern of all philosophy" and it is the task of the intellectuals to help define and protect the course of the person. The enhancement of human beings cannot be achieved through scientific thought that neglects the dynamics of religions. This dynamic must be integrated "into effort to enhance human beings by means other than the rationalized imaginary, which all too often replaces the mythological imaginary."[392]

---

388   Arkoun, *Rethinking Islam*, 91.

389   "Nationalist ideology and the demand for a return to a mythical version of Islam today exercise the same sort of pressure on scientific rationality as did the legal-theological teaching of the Middle Ages. So-called Islamic thought has never engaged in reflection on the ideological function of religious discourse. As a result, assertions derived from the Qur'an are uniformly taken as truth so long as they are guaranteed by the experts who founded the great schools of interpretation or by the ulema deemed to be authorities by the consensus of believers." (Arkoun, *Rethinking Islam*, 94)

390   Arkoun, *Rethinking Islam*, 92.

391   Arkoun, *Rethinking Islam*, 92.

392   Arkoun, *Rethinking Islam*, 103.

Abu Zayd

1. Reconsidering *'aql* [393]

The philosophical notion of reason underlies numerous of Abu Zayd's reform ideas. One premise claims that the main hindering of re-determining Muslim life today is the gross neglect of rational thinking in both the academia and all other levels of education. I will reflect on how Abu Zayd pictures the benefits of thinking rationally also in religious matters.

Abu Zayd's accounts of reason (*'aql*) can be determined from his book *Politik und Islam* in which he criticizes contemporary religious discourse and its mechanisms of interpretation.[394] Abu Zayd addresses Egyptian discourses which are directed at social and political issues, and in which the partaking groups specifically refer to religion and scripture. The discourse is often held publicly and influences society on many levels. Abu Zayd is very critical of this influence and shows how it prevents the development of an open, democratic society, specifically by ignoring rational approaches to rethinking the role of religion. Often Islam becomes utilized rather than engaged with. The discourse participants are caught up in power struggles and the needs and interests of the populace are neglected. for Abu Zayd it is clear that the people ought to be the primary beneficiary of the discourse and that politicians and clerics shall serve the people.

The populace's neglect is mirrored in the lack of promoting the teaching of autonomous thinking and decision making on all levels of education. According to (refer to Springer article) Abu Zayd, the religious discourse – in contrast to the necessary promotion of critical thinking – even developed mechanisms to exclude people from information, and to limit democratic influence. Even worse, the discourse utilizes pretentious religious argumentation to defame rationality and critical thinking.

One example of how the religious discourse misunderstands human reason is for Abu Zayd the re-labelling of the term *jāhiliyya*. *Jāhiliyya* defines the pre-Islamic period which was in a state of *jahl*, the rule of emotions, as opposed to the rule of reason and self-control (*hilm*).[395] To illustrate the pre-Islamic understanding of *jahl* he cites the Arab poet Zuhair Ibn Abi Salma who describes this principle of *jahl* as follows: "Who does not defend his terrain with his weapon, will be destroyed; who does not oppress people, will be oppressed."[396] Obviously in Salma's presentation *jahl* also entails elements of confrontation and conflict between groups of people, which

---

393   A general account of *'aql* is given by Akhtar: "The word *'aql*, translated as reason or intellect, literally means, in its verbal form, to tie or tether something; perhaps the rational quest needs to be controlled and disciplined. The opposite of *'aql* is not faith but *naql*, meaning imitation, that is, the faithful transmission of a received tradition. The Islamic sciences are divided into *'aqliyy* and *naqliyy*, the rational and the imitative (or transmitted) sciences." Akthar *Quranic Islam and the Secular Mind*, 58.

394   *naqd al-kitāb ad-dīnī* (*Politik und Islam. Kritik des religiösen Diskurses*). Unfortunately there does not exist an English version which might then be titled: *Islam and Politics. Critique of Religious Discourse*.

395   Abu Zayd, *Politik und Islam*, 59.

396   Abu Zayd, *Politik und Islam*, 59. Original: "Wer sein Terrain nicht mit seiner Waffe verteidigt, wird zerstört; wer die Menschen nicht unterdrückt, wird selbst unterdrückt."

are based on the interest of oppression and expansion of the clan. *Jahl* incorporates
factors of injustice. However it illustrates how the term *jahl* was understood to mean
the uncontrolled enforcement of selfish interests. Today the term *jāhiliyya* still incorporates this idea of *jahl* as the state of uncontrolled emotions. But it also refers to the
entire pre-Islamic time. Abu Zayd understands that Islam came as an alternative to
this state of *jahl* (uncontrolled emotions, injustice, instability etc.). Quite the reverse,
the religious discourse today identifies *jāhiliyya* with "violation against God's rule and
the trust in rationality."[397] What is gained from perverting or ignoring the historical
understanding of the term *jāhiliyya*? Abu Zayd finds that those who wittingly ignore
the historical meaning of *jahl* suggest that rationality is something a good Muslim
needs to be suspicious of. A true believer ought to believe in the rule of God, and
this – to the benefit of the clerics – is formulated by a few who claim monopoly over
interpreting religious writings. The marginalization of rationality helps then to secure
power in the hands of a few religious authorities. The submission to the rule of God
is made equal by these authorities to the submission to their interpretations. Here
Abu Zayd's critique goes even further: The identification of human interpretation
with divine rule is in his eyes a sin against both God and human rationality. It is a
transgression against God's oneness (*tawhīd*). Committing any association with God,
by claiming divine authority means to commit *shirk* (idolatry).

In Abu Zayd's argument for a rational approach to the Quran and religion he
shows that even the first Muslims tried to comprehend the compatibility of reason
with revelation. This meant that they even questioned whether Muhammad's sayings were grounded in revelation or personal convictions. If they concluded that
Muhammad uttered his own opinion they took the freedom to either reject or follow
Muhammad's example.[398] Hence critical awareness is not foreign to Islamic tradition
and there are numerous examples of interpreters who applied it to Quran exegesis.
Abu Zayd deduces from Islamic history that *textkritik* is not anti-Islamic, but on the
contrary part of the Islamic heritage.

What follows from this observation is that it must also today be possible to secure
the autonomy of reason. Abu Zayd's reading of Islamic history comes to the conclusion that a reasoned approach is superior to following authoritarian rule by a person,[399]
even if that person is the Prophet. However, for Abu Zayd, it is important to point out
that early Muslims were aware that not all areas of thinking ought to be ruled by the
Quranic text.[400] the Quran does not intend to address every aspect of life. Evidence can
be found within Islamic tradition that independent reasonable thinking was highly
regarded (especially for dealing with ambiguous or contradicting verses in the Quran).
Abu Zayd reflects on the religious discourse when it was still incorporating rationality:

> Der religiöse Diskurs mit seinen vielfältigen Strömungen und Richtungen war im
> Laufe der Kulturgeschichte des Islams immer darauf bedacht, jeglichen Wider-
> spruch zwischen Offenbarung und gesellschaftlicher Realität, der durch die ständige
> Veränderung letzterer und die Unveränderlichkeit der Texte entstand, zu negieren.

---

397   Abu Zayd, *Politik und Islam*, 60.
398   Abu Zayd, *Politik und Islam*, 40.
399   'Reasonable discerning' reads in German: *vernünftige Meinungsbildung*; and in Ara-
      bic: *ray'*.
400   Abu Zayd, *Politik und Islam*, 47.

Fast alle, die in diesen Diskurs eingebundenen sind, waren sich darin einig, dass die Überlieferung durch die Vernunft bestätigt wird, dass aber der umgekehrte Ansatz falsch sei. Die Vernunft ist die Grundlage für den Empfang der Offenbarung. Die Auseinandersetzung drehte sich später um die Frage: Verblaßt die Rolle der Vernunft, wenn sie ihre Rolle bei der Festigung der Überlieferung gespielt hat? Oder bleibt sie beim Verständnis der Texte und ihrer Interpretation wirksam? (...) Der religiöse Diskurs blieb darauf bedacht, die >Übereinstimmung des klar Vernünftigen mit dem richtig Überlieferten< zu betonen (...). Die arabisch-islamische Kultur blieb solange lebendig und aktiv, solange sie ihre Vernunft einsetzte und >Pluralität< und >Meinungsfreiheit< erlaubte. Das dauerte allerdings (...) nicht lange.[401]

As we have discovered in chapter II, Abu Zayd regards rationality as pre-requisite for revelation to take place and to 'make sense'. He believes there are two reasons for this. Firstly, the person who receives revelation needs to understand it. Secondly, the language to which revelations inspired is linked to the understanding of words and their meanings at the time and social setting of the revelation. The communication process, which is how Abu Zayd views the Quranic revelations and their transmission amongst Muslim generations, must be based on the capacity to understand, not merely on the ability to be obedient.[402]

So despite the Quran's divine origin, it is and it must be accessible to human thinking. Proper thinking in Abu Zayd's view even demands the engagement with that which does not meet the eye. He claims that "thinking whose goal is to justify current states of reality cannot be called thinking."[403] Although thinking must analyse reality

---

401 Abu Zayd, *Politik und Islam*, 63: "The religious discourse with its many streams and directions was in the course of the cultural history of Islam always cautious to deny any contradiction between revelation and social reality, which emerged through the constant change of the latter and the immutability of the texts. Almost all, who are involved in this discourse, were to agree that the tradition is confirmed by reason, but that the reverse approach is wrong. Reason is the basis for the reception of revelation. The discussion later turned to the question: Did the role of reason fade, when it had played its role in the consolidation of the tradition? Or does it remain effective in understanding the texts and their interpretation? (...) The religious discourse was careful to emphasize the 'clear line of the reasonable and what has been righteously handed down' (...). The Arab-Islamic culture remained alive and active as long as it operated its reason, and allowed 'plurality' and 'freedom of opinion.' But this did not last long (...)."

402 Abu Zayd, *Politik und Islam*, 66–7. "Wenn, mit anderen Worten, die göttliche Rede, die den Weg Gottes weist, sich bei der Verkündigung der Sprache des Menschen als Mittel bedient – trotz der Allwissenheit, Vollkommenheit und Weisheit Gottes -, so kommuniziert die menschliche Vernunft mit der göttlichen Rede – trotz der Unwissenheit, Mängel, Schwächen und Begierden der Menschen. Der religiöse Diskurs ignoriert diese Wahrheit und öffnet den Weg für eine despotische Herrschaft." "If, in other words, the divine speech, that points out the way of God, uses in its pronouncement the language of the people as a means – despite the omniscience, perfection and wisdom of God, – then the human reason communicates with divine speech – despite the ignorance, deficiencies, weaknesses and desires of the humans. The religious discourse ignores this truth and opens the way for a despotic regime."

403 „Das Denken, das sich mit der Rechfertigung der Wirklichkeit und ihrer Verteidigung begnügt, [kann] nur im übertragenen Sinne, aber nicht wirklich als solches bezeichnet werden." "The thinking, which is satisfied by the justification of reality

in order to address real challenges, it must also go beyond the analysis of profane realities. It must try to discover new horizons. Abu Zayd claims, „Denken ist seinem Wesen nach eine Bewegung zur Entdeckung des Unbekannten, ausgehend von den Grenzen des Bekannten."[404] Abu Zayd supposes that creative thinking can still be respectful to heritage. This is why he re-reads Islamic tradition in a curious manner, looking for notions that can deliver constructive elements for tackling of today's challenges. Subsequently he reflects on ideas from Islamic history while simultaneously considering modern ways of assessing current states of society. Thought which is informed by religious convictions can still be active and divergent but it does not inhabit any sacrality or absoluteness.[405] Religious thinking remains human and fallible and all interpretations of scripture show diversity according to differences in epochs, geography, society, history and race.[406] Hence interpretations are dependent on the numerous influences on the person who is practising exegesis. For Abu Zayd, interpretation must be scientific and remove the mythical elements in order to set free the progressive dynamics of religion. For this endeavour, secularism is the best state system since it allows for this method of religious interpretation.[407] Abu Zayd sees a chance of social justice, economic and political independence to develop in Muslim countries when rationality successfully fights against "mythos and superstition."[408] His plea for a demythologization of dealing with religion is not meant to undermine religion's dynamics, but to set them free.

Just as Abu Zayd secures the distinction between the profane nature of human thought and the sacred origin of the Quran, he also wants to safeguard the distinction between divine and human action. He strictly rejects the idea of divine determinism. A reality that is rendered of only God's will and action will be regarded devoid of human rationality and responsibility. The idea of God as a divine agent in all spheres of life gives power to the *'ulama'* who claim to be the only authorized humans to understand cause and effect in this world, closest to God's will. The explanation of the world might then be formulated in theological terms, disconnected from social reality. Abu Zayd in contrast thinks that since reason is a prerequisite for revelation, human rationality, 'all natural and social laws' need to be taken in consideration.[409] This is the only way God's word can be rendered relevant to today's *umma*. For Abu Zayd, engagements with the Quran via human reason resembles constant conversation with God. As for

---

and its defence, [can] only in the figurative sense, but not really be described as such thinking." (Abu Zayd, *Politik und Islam*, 153)

404   Abu Zayd, *Politik und Islam*, 153. I believe what Abu Zayd calls for is 'divergent thinking.' Thus is essentially opposed to 'convergent thinking', which orientates itself along already known paths: "An aspect of creative thought characterized by the formulation of alternative solutions to problems. The task is to generate answers, whereas in convergent thinking the task is to analyse already formulated solutions." (Corsini, *The Dictionary of Psychology*, 291)

405   Abu Zayd, *Politik und Islam*, 153. „[Das religiöse Denken erwirbt sich] durch seinen Gegenstand, den Glauben, weder Heiligkeit noch Absolutheit."

406   Abu Zayd, *Politik und Islam*, 153–4.

407   Abu Zayd, *Politik und Islam*, 26.

408   Abu Zayd, *Politik und Islam*, 26.

409   Abu Zayd, *Politik und Islam*, 43. („[...] alle natürlichen und gesellschaftlichen Gesetzmäßigkeiten [...].")

Rahman, the reasonably thinking person is not only in the position to interpret the Quran, but also, in Abu Zayd's terms, to 'understand natural and social phenomena.'[410]

2. Reforming Islamic Thought

Abu Zayd's biography *Ein Leben mit dem Islam* gives personal insights into his relationship with Islam and his hopes for a change of thought in Muslim societies.[411] First of all, universal human rights have to be obeyed and religious doctrines must be overthrown if they contradict such rights.[412] The individual person must be nurtured through access to education, the availability of information, free expression, free choice of religion etc. For Abu Zayd, identity cannot only be found through religion. Religion must become a private matter and not entangled with politics or jurisprudence. Although religion is not necessary for establishing these ground rules, for Abu Zayd, Islam can still be the source for meaningful answers to questions in contemporary Muslim societies. In how far one renders Islam to be able to encounter modernity depends also on the expectations of Islam: "It is not Islam that is unable to accept modernization, but the contemporary Muslim. The real obstacle to modernization is Muslim thinking, in particular the way Muslims have been taught to think over a long period of time. They are frightened. They think that modernization will erode their religion and identity, because, in the past, identity has been exclusively linked to religion."[413] Religion can be part of a person's identity, but it is not the sole way of defining who we are nor should one expect religion to fulfil such a role. We see that for Abu Zayd the human identity comes before the religious identity, hence he believes that human rights have priority over religious doctrines. Genuine thinking does not allow for alleged solutions like "amputation of body parts or execution."[414] Such violate universal rights – in this case – that of physical integrity of the human body.

Abu Zayd agrees with his former mentor Hassan Hanafi, whom he later also criticised, that change in religious societies must begin with a transformation of theological thinking.[415] In this endeavour Abu Zayd demands humility and self-effacement from theological exegetes when it comes to questions of interpreting Islamic scriptures and formulating truth claims.[416] In contrast to God, the human mind is fallible, and in this awareness Quranic interpretations must be formulated. They are suggestions and it would be "wrong to claim that any single interpretation describes the text's 'true meaning'. Any ideological approach would be absurd given that the Qur'an derives from oral tradition. The decisive question is, what was the human contribution to the

---

410 Abu Zayd, *Politik und Islam*, 45. („[...] natürliche oder gesellschaftliche Phänomene zu interpretieren und zu verstehen.")

411 I believe numerous concepts and ideas Abu Zayd develops or implements were inspired by his life experiences. This is without doubt also the case with Rahman's and especially Arkoun's thinking. Unfortunately there does not exist an English translation of this biography which might be titled 'A Life with Islam.' However there exists a biographical account of Abu Zayd in a corporation with Esther Nelson: *Voice of an Exile: Reflections on Islam.*

412 Abu Zayd, *Reformation of Islamic Thought*, 95.

413 Abu Zayd, *Reformation of Islamic Thought*, 96–7.

414 Abu Zayd, *Reformation of Islamic Thought*, 95.

415 Abu Zayd, *Ein Leben mit dem Islam*, 97.

416 Abu Zayd, *Ein Leben mit dem Islam*, 118.

124

historical development of the Qur'an? The construction of meaning is always, in the final analysis, a human act."[417]

He argues that the literal reading of the Quran, which has dominated since the 10th or 11[th] century, led to a variety of absolute claims to truth, each of which excluded alternative interpretations. In order to break away from the literal reading of the Quran Abu Zayd considers the metaphorical interpretations developed by mystics and the rational school of Islamic thinking (Mu[c]tazila). Both streams were marginalized by the dominant Ashari ideology, and the Hanbali and Salafi legal schools. It is said that these latter directions of Islamic thought developed through Ibn Taymiyya, into the fundamentalist and politico-religious ideology of Ibn Wahab and Ibn Saud.[418] In contrast, one of the initiators of the Muslim renaissance (*an-nahḍah*) – the Egyptian, Muhammad Abduh – founded a school of Islamic thought which was influenced by theology and law developed by the mystics and the Mu[c]tazila.[419] Without discussing the accuracy of Abu Zayd's account of Abduh's agendas, it is still important to mention that Abu Zayd draws inspiration from Abduh. In addition he draws on Ibn Arabi's philosophy of multiple manifestations of truth,[420] in order to argue for tolerance amongst truth seekers.

> My heart has become able
> To take on all forms.
> It is a pasture for gazelles,
> For monks an abbey.
>
> It is a temple for idols
> And for whoever circumambulates it, the Kaaba.
> It is the tablets of the Torah
> And also the leaves of the Koran.
>
> I believe in the religion
> Of Love
> Whatever direction its caravans may take,
> For love is my religion and my faith.[421]

In Abu Zayd's critique of religious discourse in Egypt he states that proclamations of religious authorities are often in the interest of securing power (their own and those of politicians).Furthermore they lack scientific tools for approaching neither, social reality or the Quran. Hence he is very critical of their teaching and influence. He shows how the interpretation of the Quran was used over many centuries by the *'ulama'* to support political offices. The first obvious case of this link between religion and political authority he detects in the time of the *miḥna* under Khalif Al-Ma[c]mum. The

---

417   Abu Zayd, "A Critical Commentary," 29–30.
418   Abu Zayd, *Ein Leben mit dem Islam*, 104.
419   Abu Zayd, *Ein Leben mit dem Islam*, 105.
420   Abu Zayd, *Ein Leben mit dem Islam*, 129.
421   Abu Zayd, *Ein Leben mit dem Islam*, 129. Ibn Arabi's poem "My heart has become able" is cited in German: "Mein Herz nimmt an jegliche Gestalt, Eine Weide für Gazellen und ein Kloster für Mönche, Ein Tempel für Götzen und eine Kaaba für Pilger, Tafeln der Tora und das Buch des Korans. Ich glaube an die Religion der Liebe. Welchen Weg Gottes Kamel auch nimmt, So ist doch die Liebe meine Religion und mein Glaube." The English translation is by Maurice Gloton.

miḥna centred around the idea that the createdness of the Quran must be a universal doctrine and that those refusing to believe in it ought to be punished.

One of Abu Zayd's major critiques is that Islam is corrupted and alienated through its instrumentalization by state and clerics for the sake of power. He detects five mechanisms of this corruption, employed by all sides of the dominant partners in the religious discourse in Egypt:[422] 1. Assimilation of thinking and belief and the dissolution of distance between subject and object.[423] 2. Interpretation of social and natural phenomena, through their reduction to primary principle or primary cause. 3. Dependency on authority of tradition (*turāth*) and declaring secondary literature to be primary literature, which by the *'ulama'* is regarded as sacred. Often such secondary literature is referred to more frequently than to the Quran. 4. Mental assurance, apodictic peremptoriness, and rejection of intellectual engagement lead to discussions about details and irrelevancies, but never to discourse about basic principles. 5. Neglect and abandonment of the historic dimension.

An escapist attitude to reality adds to these mechanisms by hindering the engagement with the challenges for contemporary Muslim societies. The state claims a paternalistic position towards its people with the help of those who claim monopoly over the interpretation of religion. One example is the prohibition of non-state-conforming literature. This banishing issued by the state is backed by Muslim clerics using 'religious' arguments. In other words, the religious *weltanschauung* promoted by the clerics is systematically politicized and directed to a backward ideology of religion which is oriented along the lines of a constructed original Islam. In addition, this Islam-version relies heavily on the literature produced in many centuries of scriptural tradition.

The paternalistic attitude of the state and clerics towards the people does not promote critical, reflexive thinking or academic sophistication. This makes it easier for the clerics to speak in the name of God in order to declare their interpretations as absolutely authoritative.[424] As a consequence they proclaim that Islam is a fixed ultimate system, which cannot possibly be rethought or modified. Paradoxically the clerics deny that a clergy in Islam exists in the first place, while at the same time these deniers function as clergy. Abu Zayd writes: "At the same time it reveals its ideological nature, [...] because it claims for itself absolute "objectivity" and a complete independence of the natural inclinations and prejudices of the people. [...] any finding, which is not based on the religious discourse and the power of the religious scholars, [is] confiscated."[425]

---

422 Abu Zayd, *Politik und Islam*, 29.

423 This means that belief is confused with thinking, whereas thinking, as a critical and rational ability is distorted.

424 Abu Zayd, *Politik und Islam*, 40.

425 Abu Zayd, *Politik und Islam*, 42–3: Original: "Zugleich offenbart er seine ideologische Natur, [...] da er absolute >Objektivität< und eine vollständige Unabhängigkeit von den natürlichen Vorurteilen und Neigungen der Menschen für sich in Anspruch nimmt. [...] jede Erkenntnis, die sich nicht auf den religiösen Diskurs oder die Macht der Religionsgelehrten stützt, [wird] konfisziert."

Abu Zayd points out that clergy and participants of the religious discourse emphasizes the term 'Rule of God' (*hakimiya*).[426] This concept indicates that all occurrences on earth are directly derived from God's will and action. Hence human reason as a means of orientation in life becomes void. The term 'Rule of God' is a human-made construct that helps to negate responsibility for own actions and therefore does not encourage thinking about ethical obligations and human moral actions. By confiscating human reason and withholding education from the masses, people in power (like politicians and clerics) can manifest their own rule.[427] The clergy oppresses liberal as well as fundamentalist thinking. It is called upon by the government to prevent any substantial trouble caused by a change of religious conscience, which could be brought about by alternative Islamic thinking. The more fundamentalist movements, like the Muslim Brotherhood, are considered a threat to the state and hence the government employs the clerics for countering such developments. The state media supports traditional clerics from the al-Azhar institution by broadcasting conservative, state-conforming teachings. Such instrumentalization of religion can be observed oftentimes in Egypt. The dominant religious discourse in Egypt causes "ideological bewilderment," by not adhering to any scientific standards, while at the same time neglecting human reason and the need for proper education.[428] Some parties within the religious establishment draw only selectively on Islamic heritage in order to find supportive material for their own ideologies. This eclectic approach goes hand in hand with the eclectic acceptance of aspects of modernity. Technological advancements are likely to be accepted because their development could be traced back to innovations by Muslim thinkers and scientists; whilst other developments such as free choice of religion, the idea of universal (non-religious) human rights and civil societies are rejected. That critical thinking is partly a result of developments as embraced and enhanced by metaphysician and logician such as the Muslims polymaths Avicenna or Averroes is thereby ignored. In this way much of the rational Islamic heritage is denied. Abu Zayd warns: „Der zeitgenössische Muslim muß demnach mit seinem Körper in der Gegenwart leben, gestützt auf Europa bei der Verwirklichung seiner materiellen Bedürfnisse. Mit seiner Seele, seiner Vernunft und seinem Gefühl muß er in der Vergangenheit leben und sich nur auf sein religiöses Erbe verlassen." He believes this state of Muslim thought is potentially dangerous since: „Die angenommene Trennung zwischen Islam und Wirklichkeit mutet wie ein unabwendbares Schicksal an. Dies könnte die Unfähigkeit des religiösen Diskurses erklären, umfassende Lösungen für die Probleme der Wirklichkeit vorzuschlagen."[429]

---

426   Abu Zayd, *Politik und Islam*, 30. The term *hakimiyya Allah* was employed by Sayyid Qutb and meant to mark the main difference between the people before and after the *jahiliyya*.

427   Abu Zayd, *Politik und Islam*, 44.

428   Abu Zayd, *Politik und Islam*, 46.

429   Abu Zayd, *Politik und Islam*, 53: "The contemporary Muslim must therefore live with his body in the present, supported by Europe in meeting its material needs. With his soul, his reason and his feelings, he must live in the past and rely only on his religious heritage. [...] The assumed separation between Islam and reality seems like an inevitable fate. This could explain the inability of the religious discourse, to propose comprehensive solutions to the problems of reality."

Alienation of Muslim cultures from their sometimes problematic reality is also caused by a prevalent black-and-white-mentality, which according to Abu Zayd reduces Islam to a box that gives out answers only about what is *allowed* or *forbidden*. A more sophisticated discussion about which constructive answers Islam could give for Muslim societies is lacking. To focus only on what is allowed or forbidden simplifies the complexity of reality and that of Islam and the Quran. In the religious discourse the ethical and spiritual dimensions of the Quran are often lost,[430] and for Abu Zayd the Quran presents above all a spiritual message. The Quran entails only a few juridical instructions and Abu Zayd uses this fact as evidence demonstrating that the Quran is not intended to be primarily a source of law. To recognize the spiritual dimension of the Quran and its interest in addressing each person individually will preclude a discourse of paternalism as present in most political rhetoric. With this Abu Zayd promotes a kind of privatization of religion, but nevertheless hopes that constructive impulses for social developments in Muslims cultures will emerge from within Islam. However, these impulses will be carried out by individuals and people, not by a theocratic state. Abu Zayd recurs to the troubles of rethinking Islam in a statement quoted by Paul Marshall and Nina Shea:

> Muslim religious and political reformers working to lift their societies out of stunting ideological conformity are the first to be silenced. As one such Muslim reformer, the late Egyptian scholar Nasr Hamid Abu-Zayd, pointed out: 'Having been at the receiving end of such allegation – and driven from my home in Egypt to exile in the Netherlands – I can state with conviction that charges of apostasy and blasphemy are key weapons in the fundamentalists' arsenal, strategically employed to prevent reform of Muslim societies and instead confine the world's Muslim population to a bleak, colorless prison of socio-cultural and political conformity.'[431]

3. Rethinking Education

Abu Zayd comments on the impoverished state of education and scholarship, especially as it is found in Egypt. He sees a link between the religious discourse (and its failure to realistically address the urgent problem of education) and the quest for power of its individual participants. The education sector is grossly underdeveloped and abused as battlefield for political struggles. For many centuries the political system in Egypt allowed state affairs (also those carried out on the back of religion) to interfere with public education. According to Abu Zayd this unfortunate condition needs to be remedied (along with a reworking of the religious discourse) and the education system must be reformed. The ultimate aim must be to raise an autonomous critical populace. For Abu Zayd it is clear that only an educated mass can make autonomous decisions and contribute to finding solutions for the crisis of Muslim societies.[432]

---

430   Abu Zayd, *Ein Leben mit dem Islam*, 50.
431   Marshall/Shea, "Afghan Blowback." Marshall and Shea are authors of the forthcoming book *Silenced: How Apostasy and Blasphemy Codes are Choking Freedoms Worldwide.*
432   Abu Zayd, *Ein Leben mit dem Islam*, 49.

Abu Zayd looks back into the history of Egypt to find possible roots for the plight of education. He finds that since 1972 Saudi Arabia and its petrodollar gradually infiltrated Egypt and its learning institutions with Wahabi ideology. For Abu Zayd this stream of 'Petro-Islam' originates in the mentality of a tribal society, which accepts technological innovation but at the same time rejects mental progress. The emergence of an autonomous individual, able to think critically and independent is not favoured by this mentality. A backward-looking version of Islam like this, noticeably led to a radicalization, which was successfully launched in Egypt in 1974. Abu Zayd reckons that this radicalization can also be explained psychologically, it might have been an attempt to compensate for the failure of a Pan-Arabic nationalism.[433] One could interpret Sadat's utilization of Islam as one result of this psychological encountering. Sadat's instrumentalisation of Islam was manifested in 1980 in the announcement of *shari'a* as a "main source for legislation."[434] Since 1981 Egypt was ruled by martial law.[435] This spawned an atmosphere of fear and terror which crept into the universities. Education became more prone to make concessions to Islamist ideas.[436] The overall effect was a darkening of spirits on many levels in education.[437] Consequently, Abu Zayd argues for the independence of educational institutions from political and ideological agendas.[438]

Abu Zayd's *weltanschauung* might be called 'inclusivist' in character. He certainly believes that exclusivism must be overcome.[439] He gives the example of the rich Islamic cultures that evolved since the seventh century by absorbing numerous other societies (Indian, Persian etc.): "This sort of acculturization made Islamic thought very, very rich. So, there is no uniqueness in this culture."[440] If Islam has no thinking essential to it, how can it exclude certain thought, which is labelled un-Islamic? At the same time he finds it very difficult to accept the idea that Europe has an essential culture, because of its many different mentalities and fruitful encounters with other civilisations. This makes it even harder to establish a dichotomous construction of European vs. Islamic culture.

---

433   Abu Zayd, *Ein Leben mit dem Islam*, 161–2.

434   Abu Zayd, *Ein Leben mit dem Islam*, 163.

435   The state of martial law was just lifted in 2011 due to constitutional changes.

436   Abu Zayd, *Ein Leben mit dem Islam*, 164.

437   One climax of this process of radicalization and the blinding of rational thinking was illustrated by the steps taken against Abu Zayd. Even before the charge of apostasy, Abu Zayd's application for full professorship was denied on grounds of one rejection against two supporting votes. The rejection was issued by Prof. Shahin who apparently did not read Abu Zayd's work (neither did the supporting parties). Obviously, the democratic system failed by giving right to a minority vote. This might not be too surprising if one recognizes that Shahin is a conservative member of the academic council with strong links to the 'political elite.' Abu Zayd's case is a 'symptom of an illness' that prevails in academia (even the teaching staff) and politics.

438   One effect of better education Abu Zayd hopes for is that more knowledge will help surmount artificially constructed images of Western or Islamic cultures. Abu Zayd, *Ein Leben mit dem Islam*, 66.

439   Abu Zayd, *Ein Leben mit dem Islam*, 130.

440   Abu Zayd, "Im holländischen Exil," 10.

He supports the introduction of philosophical thinking into general education and promotes engagement with Western philosophy,[441] or for that matter, all sources of knowledge. Abu Zayd's biographical writings show that he is well travelled and received academic training not only in Egypt but also overseas. Hence (and he states this numerous times) he experienced a merging of horizons and dissolving of borders between Western and Arabo-Islamic ideas.[442] We see that Abu Zayd promotes his experience as a valuable biographical lesson, namely the importance of a comprehensive, independent education,[443] and the development of an open mind and engagement with different cultures in order to broaden horizons.

4. Secular Democracy, Pluralism, and Tolerance

Abu Zayd believes that secularism enables humankind to practice the 'true interpretation of religion,' since it allows religion to be free from state influence.[444]

As stated above, in Egypt the link between religion and state seemed to have been promoted by a psychological reaction towards the failure of a united Arab nationalism. In this case relatively late in history *shari'a* and state politics became entangled. However, Abu Zayd perceives the idea of the unity of state and religion to be an artificial product, which originated in political ideologies especially since the 18th century. This unity was a response to the occupation of Egypt by Napoleonic France and numerous European nations of Muslim countries. Some, in facing the gross differences of development between the colonising people and the cultures of the Muslim lands, blamed the backwardness on Islam.[445] For others the problem of development lay within the neglect of Islam in their countries. Both of these opinions reflect an identity crisis and pose questions about the role religion ought to play in state and society, if any. For those who embraced the solution of Islamic states, a recapturing of Islam posed the sole solution. Abu Zayd describes this course of thought with the

---

441   Abu Zayd read works of numerous intellectuals such as Claude Lévi-Strauss, Ferdinand de Saussure, Hans-Georg Gadamer, Friedrich Schleiermacher, Wilhelm Dilthey, Martin Heidegger, Paul Ricœur, and Toshihiko Izutsu.

442   Abu Zayd then also experienced this merging in his encounter with text studies in which he finds various parallels between Islamic thinking, such as by Ibn Arabi, and Western philosophers. Abu Zayd, *Ein Leben mit dem Islam*, 114–6.

443   Abu Zayd, *Ein Leben mit dem Islam*, 200. Abu Zayd writes: "Diese islamische Welt ist ein trauriger Verein." „Das Wesen des Lernens darin besteht, Kopfschmerzen auszuhalten, und nicht, sie zu vermeiden. Alles verursacht Kopfschmerzen, vor allem die Freiheit." "This Islamic world is a sad club." "The essence of learning is to endure headaches, and not to avoid them. Everything causes headaches, especially freedom."

444   The example of the al-Azhar in Cairo shows how religious institutions become an instrument for political agendas. Some teachers are so closely linked to political power that they instrumentalize Islam in various ways to support political schemes. Since al-Azhar's claim monopoly over the interpretation of Islam, Abu Zayd hopes that secularism will enable a multiplicity of interpretations through breaking the established power of such religious institutions. Without the political influence and mutual backups between political and religious programs, religion can find manifold expressions. Abu Zayd hopes for the dissolving of subservience (*Authoritätshörigkeit*) towards self-proclaimed religious elites with strong links to politics. Cf. Abu Zayd, *Ein Leben mit dem Islam*, 40.

445   Abu Zayd, *Ein Leben mit dem Islam*, 57.

motto: 'Islam is the fuel that fires the engine of development.'[446] In contrast Abu Zayd envisages religion as a private matter.[447]

Abu Zayd is sceptical about whether one can refer to the Quran to argue for a democratic state system. The Quranic term *shūrā* is often interpreted by pro-democracy groups to present a prototype of democracy. Contrary to Rahman, Abu Zayd does not find that the Quranic term *shūrā* can be applied today. He believes *shūrā* is a pre-Islamic practice which does not resemble a modern system of democracy.[448] Although he does not find specific support in the Quran for a democratic system, Abu Zayd asserts that there is nothing in Islam that is immanently at odds with democracy. Hence he generally grants Muslim societies the ability to establish democratic society, which means he does not believe that living a Muslim life is inherently incompatible with living in democracies: "it is not Islam that stands against democracy, progress or modernity."[449] The positive side effect Abu Zayd hopes for is that democracy will prevent any sort of fundamentalism:

> I mean, the fact that you believe in any system of thought and you think that this is the absolute, you are in fundamentalism. [Fundamentalists] don't believe in a possibility of other forms, other expressions, other manifestations of truth. Such people, they are not ready to listen, they don't listen. They are by definition, have a mentality that has been formed once and forever. And you can find people like this everywhere. I'm not really interested in those people. I like very much people who are able to communicate because I love this kind of communication. This is what makes me human! Communication.[450]

Abu Zayd generally calls for freedom of speech, thought and expression. At the same time he points out that many regimes hinder the development of freedom in society.[451] If these regimes instrumentalise a religion in support of their agendas, create a deep divide between religious groups. Abu Zayd reflects in his biography that in his youth he did not experience mutual exclusivism between members of different faiths. In contrast, people were much more relaxed about religious ideas and not shy of joking about either Muhammad or God, without causing major conflicts.[452] He hardly witnessed personal identification through religious affiliation and its demonstration through displaying religious symbols like miniature crosses and Qurans in cars in the Egypt of the 50's and 60's.[453] People identified themselves much more as Egyptians. Nationality, not religious affiliation was the first aspect of recognition. Today, despite more publicly demonstrated religious affirmation, Abu Zayd detects a decline in compassion and ethics:

> Religion becomes like a political means. And therefore loses its dynamic spiritual power. Sometimes, I feel the more religion is used as a political vehicle, the more there is no religion any more. For example, you can see now in Egypt people going

---

446   Abu Zayd, *Ein Leben mit dem Islam*, 60.
447   Abu Zayd, *Ein Leben mit dem Islam*, 52.
448   Abu Zayd, *Ein Leben mit dem Islam*, 62.
449   Abu Zayd, *Reformation of Islamic Thought*, 96.
450   Abu Zayd, "Im holländischen Exil."
451   Abu Zayd, *Ein Leben mit dem Islam*, 63–5.
452   Abu Zayd, "Im holländischen Exil."
453   Abu Zayd, "Im holländischen Exil."

into mosques. Mosques are very crowded on Fridays, you have all the slogans, religious slogans all over streets, villages, everything, but in the meantime, you have a society with no ethics. You have a society where the powerful and rich do not give a damn about the weak or the poor. You have a society in Egypt now, where rich people make a show. I mean, they invite poor people to have food, but they don't really help them to find jobs, for example. So, it's a society of charity. There is no real religious society. So, there is a lot of religion in the air, on the public, but there is not this deep feeling of religious ethics. I think, it's not only in religion, it's in politics as well. So, for some reason, this kind of politicization of religion has evacuated religion of its moral ethical spiritual power as it used to be.[454]

Pluralism of opinions combined with freedom of expression is essential for a common civilisation and its 'universal discourse about human rights and democracy.'[455] Intellectuals are crucial actors in this debate.[456] Abu Zayd thinks they do a service for the people, like any street sweeper.[457] It is their duty to inform the populace about the facts of society and constructively communicate their ideas for future projects with the public.[458] The example of the execution of Muhammad Taha on charge of apostasy is a gloomy example of what happens when this principle of pluralism is not established.[459] Abu Zayd demands an open society: "But let's just agree on a way of debating, that is the point. And I think we are approaching this point in Egypt. But the authoritative political power is really fighting its last battle. [...]. I think the civil society will succeed in overthrowing this authoritative power. Hopefully."[460]

Evidently Abu Zayd's life demonstrates what exclusivism of religio-political powers can do.[461] Intriguingly, he recognizes a positive element in his experience, namely that the court system found application rather than immediate execution.[462] Here he sees a sign of progress, although he would not go as far as describing this step as one carried out by a truly civil society. When asked, whether his attitude towards Islam changed while he went through the trial, Abu Zayd answers:

> No, I don't think it did, because I have viewed the whole affair not as really a religious affair, but as a political affair. If you look to the context, this was in the nineties, in the early nineties, 1993 the beginning of the case. If you look at the society where there were at least two powers, secularists so to speak, and Islamists, and they don't have any space to communicate on a democratic way. There are two extremes of

---

454   Abu Zayd, "Im holländischen Exil."

455   Abu Zayd, *Ein Leben mit dem Islam*, 67.

456   Abu Zayd, *Ein Leben mit dem Islam*, 68.

457   Abu Zayd, *Ein Leben mit dem Islam*, 65.

458   "I think we – Muslim scholars – should find a way to communicate with the ordinary people. I'm struggling for that. Because talking to intellectuals like you doesn't take you anywhere. How can you find a way to reach ordinary people without hurting their religious feeling? How can you convince an ordinary Muslim that believing in the human aspect of the Quran does not mean violating it's divinity? It's a hell of a job! So, I started to realize that still we are, to a great extent, an oral culture. Culture of face-to-face communication" (Abu Zayd, "Im holländischen Exil").

459   Abu Zayd, *Ein Leben mit dem Islam*, 109.

460   Abu Zayd, "Im holländischen Exil."

461   Abu Zayd, *Ein Leben mit dem Islam*, 136–8. Re. the principle of *hisba*, ibid, 160.

462   Abu Zayd, "Im holländischen Exil."

which you can speak. We have the government, we have the Islamists and we have the secularist. The government is playing with both.

The government is playing with the Islamists, claiming religion, claiming Islam, and at the meantime claiming a civil society. While we didn't have civil society, we have military society. In this context, people wanted to fight [...].[463]

Comparison

Most strikingly all three thinkers promote an advancement of education as a way to achieve an autonomous civil society that is able to make reflexive decisions. Critical engagement with the own heritage (*turāth*), the reconsideration of marginalized Islamic philosophies and the inclusion of non-Islamic sources must be promoted. They call for the creation of democratic structures, with freedom of thought and expression. In this vein they hope autocratic regimes as well as ideological infiltrations (e.g. extremism) will be challenged. One common hope is that democratic structures will allow for the plurality of world views. Even though all three are primarily dedicated to the discussion of Islam, they hold that religions are only different manifestations of truth and that absolute truth claims and superiority are to be avoided.

Rahman, Arkoun and Abu Zayd assert that true thinking must consider the metaphysical or unseen. They try to break down seemingly artificial borders between religious and scientific thinking. For Rahman Islamic metaphysics must inform all forms of knowledge, in order to develop society towards the Quranic ideal of justice. For Abu Zayd religion is part of society but should be a private matter and not intermingle with politics, at least as long the religious leaders keep on misusing religion. Arkoun likewise calls for the necessity of secularism. Both Arkoun and Abu Zayd find that secularism entails a liberating element for religion. However, because Rahman believes that the Quranic term *shūrā* can be developed into a modern democratic principle, he strongly promotes the establishment of a genuinely Islamic state. In contrast, Abu Zayd denies that the Quranic term *shūrā* is applicable to contemporary society.

Their shared claim, that it is valuable to broaden horizons and engage with non-Islamic philosophies and other sources of knowledge, seems to be partially inspired by their biographies. All three received education in their home countries and abroad, learned different languages and travelled widely. Such experiences seem to be common factors leading to more sensitivity and respect for different world views. In addition Rahman and Abu Zayd experienced first-hand the effects of exclusivist and extremist ideologies that refuse rational conversation about what is at stake in Muslim societies. Both argued against the internal power struggles of religious and political elites, in order to instead concentrate on analyzing the prerequisites which are necessary for an improvement of the human condition. Both were forced to leave their home-countries. Also Arkoun was accused of heresy.[464] But despite these perturbations, all three intellectuals continually engaged deeply in the discussion about ethics and values that could promote a contemporary humanism.

---

463   Abu Zayd, "Im holländischen Exil."

464   Today's Muslim intellectuals with teaching positions at state universities continue to face opposition and accusations. Cf. Völker, Katharina (2013), "A Danger to Free Research and Teaching in German Universities? The Case of Muhammad Sven Kalisch," 175–85. And, ibid. (2014), "Parameters of Teaching Islam *Freely*," 209–224.

133

Chapter V – Exegesis and Hermeneutics

Rahman

When we look at Rahman's ethical views and proposals for reform as set out in previous chapters, these appear at first sight to be derived from his Quran exegesis. Yet several ideas appear to originate in sources other than the Quran. For instance his demand for a charismatic leadership in the initial stage of setting up Islamic states seems to be inspired by Islamic historiography, in which Muhammad appears as a key figure. In Muhammad's quest for unifying the first *umma*, he had to establish socio-political order to implement the guidance and instruction of the revelations. That a state-leader must today be elected by the *umma*, might be an idea deduced from Rahman's understanding of the Quranic term *shūrā*. According to Rahman, *shūrā* implies consultation between all parts of society. However, that Rahman regards the *umma* as a mass movement seems also to come from Islamic historiography in which the first Muslim community is described as exemplifying a model for a successful and united group. From within the Quran there is not sufficient information on the first *umma*, which suggests that Rahman relies in his interpretation practice on secondary material, such as the life of Muhammad and information about the first Islamic society. For example, his insistence on a strong military looks as if it is traced from sociological or historical requirements for the establishment of Muslim nations. The same is true for his wish for an initial one-party-system that can only be replaced when the populace is sufficiently familiar with democratic structures. So it cannot be said that Rahman's ideas are drawn solely from his reading of the Quran. Nonetheless, the Quran is clearly a key text in Rahman's thought.

In the following investigation I will enquire into Rahman's proposals for Quranic interpretation, before continuing with giving concrete interpretation examples. The following section displays Rahman's demand for categorizing verses, rethinking traditional methods (*asbāb al-nuzūl/naskh*), reading in the spirit of the Quran, and the application of the *double movement*.

1. Methods and Terminology

1.1 Categorizing Verses

When discussing Quranic verses, Rahman distinguishes between the *ideal* and the *contingent*. It is important to understand that he discerns two characters, not two different kinds of verses. This means that each verse potentially entails both natures: the *ideal* and the *contingent*. The ideal has to do with the goal of establishing a just society. However, the fulfillment of this ideal is not bound to the time of revelation. Here Rahman differs significantly from revivalists, who think the ideal was already achieved at the time of Muhammad. For Rahman the ideal is what the believing community must strive for and this incorporates development and change, not withdrawal into an imaginary 'lost paradise.' The *contingent* in verses on the other hand is what was revealed for a certain temporal purpose at the time of revelation.[465] Identifying the

---

465 Saeed, "Fazlur Rahman," 62: "His emphasis on the context of the revelation has had far reaching influence on the debate among Muslims of questions such as human

contingent in a verse does not mean that this verse does not carry a lesson for today. This is because even in its temporal nature it was meant to persuade the audience to certain beliefs and actions which should instruct the newly established community to develop socially and religiously. Rahman asserts: "If we look at the Qur'ān, it does not in fact give many general principles: for the most part it gives solutions to and rulings upon specific and concrete historical issues [...]."[466] Hence, the verses should be read in their socio-historical contexts. Overall Rahman prefers a logical arrangement of verses that considers the inner relation of the texts,[467] reflection and study on the chronology of verses,[468] and – most essentially – their socio-historical background.[469]

1.2 Rethinking Traditional Methods

According to Rahman Islamic tradition has often overlooked the general spirit of the Quran and has relied much upon the use of secondary literature such as *hadith, sīra* and *sunna*. At times those secondary sources are treated as equal in authority to the Quran. In addition, Islamic law fabricated rules, which were often not based on Quranic content or lacked consideration of the Quran's general character. Since Rahman sets out to rediscover the spirit of the Quran he pleads for a rethinking of traditional exegesis. This is not to say, as we have already seen, that Rahman does not utilize secondary literature. His emphasis on knowing the circumstances of revelations makes himself draw on supporting, non-Quranic documents. This is most noticeable in his depiction of Muhammad's mind at certain stages in the revelation process. Nevertheless, in his work *Major Themes of the Quran*, which I regard as the most comprehensive source for his exegesis, is demonstrated that he genuinely tries to interpret the Quran by the Quran.[470] I will now explain how Rahman hopes to rethink traditional methods such as the use of *asbāb an-nuzūl* literature and the practice of abrogation (*naskh*).

---

rights, women's rights and social justice. Rahman's approach has been utilized by an increasing number of Muslims to relate the Qur'an to contemporary needs; it will likely continue to be influential among the younger generation of Muslim intellectuals."

466 Rahman, *Islam and Modernity*, 20.

467 Rahman, *Major Themes of the Quran*. Rahman holds it impossible to arrange verses passage by passage. Hoffman explains in her article "Qur'anic Interpretation and Modesty Norms for Women,": "The approach taken by traditional Qur'ānic exegesis is to analyze Qur'ānic verses phrase by phrase or word by word; to ascertain the meaning of individual words by their root meanings and usage in Arabic poetry from the time of the Prophet; and to use Hadith to provide interpretations of the legal import of verses and the historical circumstances (*asbāb al-nuzūl*) in which a verse was revealed." (90)

468 Rahman notes: "With regard to the chronological studies of the Qur'ān, the monumental work of Nöldeke-Schwally, Geschichte des Qorans, still sets the standard and cries out for an English translation." (Rahman, *Major Themes of the Quran*, vii.)

469 Rahman proposes that a grasp of the background of the Qur'ānic passages and of the chronological order (to the extent possible) is crucial for a correct understanding of the purposes of the Quran. Cf. Rahman, *Major Themes of the Quran*, xvii.

470 Such interpretation in essence is called *tafsīr al-Qur'ān bi'l-Qur'ān*, a practice often applied by Islamic modernists such as the reformist Muhammad Abduh or the Quranites (*Ahl al-Qur'ān*) to which belonged for instance Rahman's contemporary Ghulam Ahmed Pervez. However, we will see that since Rahman relies also on secondary material, it cannot be claimed he belonged to the Quranites, who proclaim the Quran as self-sufficient in explaining itself.

Rahman's insistence on using *asbāb an-nuzūl* literature (which is comprised of information derived from the *hadith, sunna* and *sīra*) proves his dependency on source second to the Quran. He sees a great value in consulting such literature for deriving clues on the circumstances of the revelations. Still, Rahman is also critical about the use of this material, especially the way in which it was utilized by classical exegesis (*tafsīr*) and jurisprudence (*fiqh*). He finds that Islamic scholarship failed to use *asbāb an-nuzūl* material in combination with further knowledge about the socio-historical context in which the revelations took place.

> It is strange however, that no systematic attempt has ever been made to understand the Qur'ān in the order in which it was revealed, that is, by setting the specific cases of the *shu'un al-nuzūl*, or "occasions of revelation", in some order in the general background that is no other than the activity of the Prophet (the Sunna in the proper sense) and its social environment. If this method is pursued, most arbitrary and fanciful interpretations will at once be ruled out, since a definite enough anchoring point will be available.[471]

I understand here that Rahman wants to push the idea behind the material on the occasions of revelations further, towards an even more critical but re-constructive encounter with the Quran's social environment. In the context of religious law making considering all available material on the occasions of revelations and their socio-historical circumstance serves the discovery of the *ratio legis* behind Quranic verses.

In contrast to this suggestion, Angelika Neuwirth in her work *Der Koran als Text der Spätantike* (2010) suggests that Rahman does not go beyond the traditional use of the notion of *asbāb an-nuzūl*. To understand Neuwirth's critical analysis it helps to read her proposal for analysing the Quran in the entirety of its contexts, namely as a *fait accompli*. Neuwirth comments (also on Rahman):

> Die doppelte Entwicklung von Text und Gemeinde wird nur aus einer chronologischen orientierten Lektüre des Textes ersichtlich, die dem Prozess der Entwicklung verschiedener von Verkünder und Gemeinde verhandelter Leitideen nachgeht und versucht, deren zeitliche Abfolge plausibel zu erklären. Es ist dieser Verhandlungsprozess, der bisher selbst bei denjenigen muslimischen Forschern außerhalb des Horizonts bleibt, die wie Fazlur Rahman und die (post)modernen türkischen Exegeten die Notwendigkeit einer historischen, d.h. an den überlieferten >Offenbarungsanlässen<, den *asbāb al-nuzūl*, orientierten Lektüre postulieren.[472]

It might well be that Neuwirth is accurate in saying the treatment of the *asbāb an-nuzūl* as put forward by Rahman does not yet consider all knowledge about the contexts in which the revelations occurred. However, we can also say from his demand for the

---

471   Rahman, *Islam and Modernity*, 143.

472   Neuwirth, *Der Koran als Text der Spätantike*, 28: "The dual development of text and community becomes apparent only from a chronological oriented reading of the text, which [such reading] investigates the process of development of various leading ideas, which are negotiated by Prophet and community, and [such reading] tries to plausibly explain their chronological succession. It is this negotiation process, which so far remains beyond the horizon, even within those Muslim scholars, like Fazlur Rahman and the (post)modern Turkish exegetes, who postulate the need for a historical reading, which means a reading that is oriented towards the handed down 'occasions of revelation,' the *asbāb al-nuzūl*."

constant study of sociology and history, that he must have been open to considering further-leading sources. His demand for gaining a coherent knowledge in religious and worldly affairs, as set out in his reform and education proposals leads towards this consequence. Neuwirth later points out that Rahman as well as Abu Zayd do consider the double development of text and community: "Der Koran ist als ein spätantiker Text anzuerkennen, der gemeinsam mit einer sich sukzessiv herausbildenden Gemeinde spätantik akkulturierter Hörer entstand. Eine solche kontextuelle Lektüre steht mit derjenigen einzelner islamischer Gelehrter wie Amin al-Khuli, Fazlur Rahman, Nasr Hamid Abu Zaid (1943–2010), Mehmet Paçaci oder Ömer Özsoy in Einklang."[473] In the list of thinkers just mentioned I would also include Muhammad Arkoun, who proposes the consideration of all material that could shed light on the time of the Quranic discourses. Furthermore, I am in agreement with a further analysis of Neuwirth. She mentions Rahman's focus on the *sīra* literature, which as I said above, is used to reconstruct the biographical and psychological state of the Prophet during the time of revelation.[474] Neuwirth stresses that "this concentration is problematic, since the Quranic text draws a much more complex scenario."[475] Rahman's interpretation shows that he regards the mental state of the Prophet as an important factor in understanding the Quran, although he does neither use many sources of knowledge from outside the traditional Islamic realm, nor does he claim his sources would be all-comprehensive on this matter.

Next to *asbāb an-nuzūl* Rahman considers *naskh* (abrogation) as one exegetical notion that shows the development of the Quran in connection with historical and sociological events during Muhammad's life. The divine act of abrogation, which is even mentioned in the Quran, can be understood as supporting the thought of an evolution of Quranic themes and verses. To accept this idea would mean to understand that the Quran was subject to changes and these changes are not only recognized by the Quranic text but also prove the successive progression of the revelations. Rahman maintains that an evolution of themes does not disagree with the overall cohesiveness of the Quran. He asserts that comprehending the Quran in its spirit will illustrate and safeguard its overall and internal consistency. With this he challenges those Islamic thinkers who assert that contradictions of Quranic verses can be resolved by following the chronology of revelations. Such results in the detection of abrogated verses which were followed by others entailing instructions that differed from those previously entailed.

In the following passages I attempt to understand how Rahman treated the principle of *naskh*. The notion of divinely sanctioned abrogation is proclaimed by the Quran itself, which states that some verses are "cast into oblivion" (2:106). As mentioned, Islamic scholarship developed different understandings of this notion. Amongst some, it was understood as a correction of what had been sent before. The new instructions'

---

473 Neuwirth, *Der Koran als Text der Spätantike*, 73: "The Quran has to be acknowledged as a text from late antiquity, which was created jointly with a gradually emerging community, of listeners, acculturated to the world of late antiquity. Such a contextual reading harmonizes with that of particular Islamic scholars such as Amin al-Khuli, Fazlur Rahman, Nasr Hamid Abu Zayd (1943–2010), Mehmet Pacaci or Ömer Özsoy."
474 Cf. Rahman's trust in Muhammad biographies is for example expressed in *Major Themes*, 61+96 (Rahman refers to Ibn Isḥāq's Muhammad biography).
475 Neuwirth, *Der Koran als Text der Spätantike*, 336. "Diese Fokussierung ist jedoch problemtaisch, denn der koranische Text zeichnet ein viel komplexeres Szenario."

corrective character was associated with bringing improvement to the life-situation of the first *umma*. This account also held that the abrogated content of previous verses must then be either discarded or even actively opposed. One group that stressed the Quranic principle of *naskh* was the Mu'tazila. It found that abrogation as authorized by the Quran supported their doctrine of the createdness of the Quran. We know from our investigation into the revelation process (chapter III Rahman) that Rahman also argues for the created nature of the Quran, but at the same time maintains its *qadīm* (eternal) nature. That's why we are obliged to enquire how he thinks of *naskh*. To envisage the Quran as eternal is a traditional view supported by a literal understanding of the *tablet* (cf. chapter III). When Rahman asserts that the Quran's ethico-legal content is eternal and coherent, his view is close but not identical with the more conservative one, which holds that every word of the Quran was already inscribed in the *mother of the book* (eternal and with God). We are by now acquainted with Rahman's refusal of a literal understanding of the tablet and what comes along with it, namely his negation of the proposition that the Quran endorses determinism. What is more, he believes in the divine reaction to historical circumstances and therefore holds the Quran to be created. We know that the intimate relation between Muhammad's mind and the process of revelation is for Rahman an utmost affirmation of the interconnectivity of the Quran with its historical context. Hence each verse potentially carries traces of this interconnectivity, that is to say the reactions of the listeners, the mental shape of Muhammad, and the social situation. For Rahman it is clear that each verse has its merits and bears a lesson for today's readers. Since he does not read verses literally, but seeks for their underlying agenda,[476] Rahman does not confirm to the actual practice of discarding verses due to abrogation.[477] When he mentions *naskh*, it is not as a doctrine of exegesis but as a proof for the chronological and historical development of the text.[478] He approves of the idea that the so called 'satanic verses' were abrogated by God,[479] but holds that these verses were not Quranic, and hence did not originate in the divine source in the first place.

However, Rahman asserts that in the course of revelations some verses' contents were at their time of sending more applicable and fitting then other verses of preceding revelations. This was of course due to changed situations and circumstances. Then, *naskh* as mentioned and practised by the Quran is a contingent measure which must be understood as a way of pre-eminent appropriating the divine message and catering for the dynamics it sought to release. This stance allows Rahman to continue his search for the Quranic hints into the direction of the ideal, now also in potentially abrogated verses. We are reminded here that Rahman believes the Quran to be mostly explicit about how to weigh contradicting verses and that the overall message is coherent. Rahman's restriction of *naskh* becomes apparent when he refuses the interpretation which holds that the *sword verse* would abrogate all previous revealed verses calling for a more liberal treatment of unbelievers. In other words, he does not allow *naskh* to be used against his understanding of the Quranic élan, which attempts to bring about equality and justice amongst humankind.

---

476   This is coherent with the totality of the Quran.
477   Rahman, *Major Themes*, 62.
478   Rahman, *Major Themes*, 7.
479   Rahman, *Major Themes*, 62.

1.3 Double Movement

Rahman's double movement requires explanation in all discussions of his thinking, since it is essential to his overall method. It is sufficiently explained in numerous works,[480] so I shall display it only briefly. The Quran is for Rahman of functional character. Not as a theological speculation but as practical guidance (*hudā*) it is given by God in all mercy in order to bring humankind to the straight path which leads to salvation. The Quran was revealed piecemeal into certain situations through the Prophet Muhammad. As we have found out in chapter II the Quran is hence involved in many situational matters. At the same time each contingent message entails a rationale that reflects the spirit of the Quran as intended by God. To understand the Quran today means to comprehend it in its contingency, then to filter out the essential message or dynamic. After having thoroughly studied the current situation's social requirements, this dynamic or basic idea needs to be implemented into today's contingent circumstances, by contemporary means. Such an assessment of the Quran's spirit must be an ongoing process in order to enable the Quran to remain an ever vital guidance to humankind.

2. Exegesis and Hermeneutics

When secondary works about Rahman refer to his interpretations, most common illustrations are his stances on the status of women,[481] banking interest,[482] and *shūrā* (principle of democracy). These examples are often mentioned in the context of discussing Rahman's attitude towards Islam as development-advisor in Pakistan, where his ideas were strongly rejected in the 1960s. I now choose examples that are not frequently discussed in detail but which seem to be crucial in understanding Rahman's Quran reading as well as his hopes for reform. The two themes I shall discuss are the ideas of determinism and equality.

2.1 Determinism

Many of Rahman's reform ideas rely upon the notion of free will, free thinking, and free decision making. On those rests the ability to become a responsible citizen who is ably to chose, therefore vote for her or his own leader, religion and social laws. By insisting that "the Qur'ān states repeatedly that every man and woman individually and every people collectively are alone responsible for what they do–a doctrine that underlies the Qur'ānic rejection of redemption,"[483] Rahman points out that the Quran not only refuses determinism but also the concept of original sin.[484] However, there are numerous verses in the Quran that can be understood as supporting determinism.[485] Certainly, within the history of Islamic thought this puzzle kept many theologians

---

480 As for example by Tamara Sonn (1991), Yusuf Rahman (2001), Jon Armajani (2004), Kenneth Cragg (1985), Donald Berry (2003), Fredrick Denny (1989), and Abdullah Saeed (2004).

481 cf. Y. Rahman (2001), and Jon Armajani (2004).

482 cf. Berry, *Islam and Modernity.*

483 Rahman, *Major Themes of the Quran*, 13.

484 Rahman refers in *Major Themes of the Quran*, 13 to Q 2:37, and 29:12.

485 Rahman mentions numerous verses. 2:7, 142, 213, 272; 14:4; 16:93; 24:35; 28:56; 30:29; 35:8. (*Major Themes of the Quran*, 10)

140

and philosophers occupied. As we saw in chapter II, Rahman states that although humans have to serve God, hence practice *'ibādah*, they must choose to serve by free will. The need for *'ibādah* arises from the goal of gaining salvation, which can only be achieved by believing "in God and the Last Day and do[ing] good deeds."[486] People are free in their choice of obedience or disobedience, namely the decision to serve either God or one's self. The failure to serve is disobedience (*kufr*).[487] We see here that Rahman's understanding of the term *kufr* goes much further than the often claimed identification of the term with non-Muslims. It is much more that the belief in one's utter independence of God entails the idea of human omnipotence which is in Rahman's view *shirk*.[488] On the other hand, the thought of being utterly dependent and unfree suggests the human individual is not responsible for actions and thought.

These explanations lead to asking the question: How do people find faith that incorporates the three requirements: the belief in God, the Last Day and the practice of good deeds? We know already one answer given by Rahman, namely his assertion that the Quran's ultimate purpose is to lead to faith, which includes a genuine notion of morals and rightful behaviour. We remember the role of the Quran is that of guidance towards the creation of earthly justice, which ought to strive to resemble God's righteousness. To believe that the Quran teaches determinism means "not only to deny almost the entire content of the Qur'ān, but to undercut its very basis: the Qur'ān by its own claim is an invitation to man to come to the right path [...]."[489] The Quran in Rahman's view consequently attempts to persuade and not to dictate. Acceptance or refusal of this invitation equals an individual decision.

To reflect on the Quranic verses that seem to teach determinism, Rahman comments on the perception of this concept in pre-Islamic times. The Quran describes God's power as the 'measuring out' (*qadar*). In pre-Islamic time the term *aqdār* (plural of *qadar*) denoted general fate such as birth and death over which humankind had no control. Quite in contrast to this pre-Islamic account of determinism, in the Quran the term came to mean that God "'measures out' everything, bestowing upon everything the range of its potentialities, its laws of behavior, in sum, its character."[490] Another connotation of *qadar* (to measure out) is *amr*, the divine command. Rahman points out, that nature is forced to follow this *amr*, whereas humankind has the choice. This is also how the relationship between God and humankind receives a moral component.[491] One more connotation of God's power is (as we have seen before) not only the term *amr* (command) but also *hudān* (guidance). Through the power of God, described as *qadar*, *hudān* and *amr*, the entire creation receives potentialities and limits: "When God creates anything, He places within it its powers or laws of behavior, called in the Qur'ān 'guidance,' 'command,' or 'measure' whereby it fits into the rest of the universe [...]."[492] The concept of *qadar* does therefore not support 'a theory of predetermination, although it does mean a kind of 'holistic determinism.' This is clear from the references

---

486 Rahman, *Major Themes of the Quran*, 115. He interprets verses 2:62 and 5:69.
487 Berry, *Islam and Modernity*, 68. Cf. *Major Themes of the Quran*, 14.
488 Rahman, *Major Themes of the Quran*, 46.
489 Rahman, *Major Themes of the Quran*, 20. see also Rahman, *Islam and Modernity*, 2/155.
490 Rahman, *Major Themes of the Quran*, 8.
491 Rahman, *Major Themes*, 9.
492 Rahman, *Major Themes*, 46.

where 'measured' does not mean 'predetermined' but 'finite' or 'limited.'[493] In that sense it is reminiscent to the pre-Islamic notion of *qadar* meaning those unavoidable facts of life like birth and death that define the frame by which human existence is ultimately circumscribed.

We still need to examine how Rahman hopes to reconcile his idea of free will with passages in the Quran that potentially contain support for determinism. Although Rahman recognizes these passages in the Quran, he is quick to state that "far more often it says that 'God does not lead aright the unjust ones.' [...] This means that man does something to deserve guidance or misguidance."[494] So it seems Rahman grants certain statements in the Quran more importance than others, based on number of appearance Furthermore, Rahman provides a psychological rationalization of those verses that suggest God seals people's hearts.[495] Rahman replaces what is described by the Quran as 'the act of God sealing hearts' with a certain 'state of the human spirit'. This unfortunate state is caused by freely chosen ungodly deeds, which lead to cloudiness of the mind and soul. Although Rahman tries to interpret the alleged verses metaphorically (by replacing God as an actor with a freely human-made decision to choose ungodly deeds) he also refers to the other set of verses which mention that God seals hearts 'not without reason.' Here Rahman's interpretation is clear: the blinding is caused through the earthly, punitive action of God. This interpretation avoids the metaphorical reading. From this we see that Rahman reads metaphorically those verses that do not support his notion of free will and those literally that do support his concept.

2.2 Equality

Rahman asserts in all his reform ideas that the rationale of the Quran is to bring instructions and guidance to humankind in order to implement justice on earth, which ought to reflect the divine principle of justice. We have noticed so far that he speaks from within a Muslim's perspective and hence almost exclusively addresses Muslims with his proposals. This becomes apparent in his demand that establishing an Islamic state would be paramount in order to create a people and community that approximates God's ideal for a human society.

However, this centrality of the Quran and Rahman's proclamation of the necessity of an Islamic state might fuel some conflicts with world views that do not accept Islam as a way to salvation. And since Rahman proclaims that equality amongst humankind is an outcome of the successfully enacted principle of justice, he must have addressed this question. So what does Rahman say about these people outside the realm of Islam and their chances for salvation?

We know by now that Rahman sees the aim of revelation as a godly life that seeks to establish justice amongst humankind. In his thinking, living a godly life means that one trusts in God's guidance. Rahman also values highly the doing of good deeds, as a form of *'ibādah*, but nowhere asserts that simply doing good deeds earns salvation. Ungodly behaviour, Rahman declares, follows when "people belittle or ignore or even rebel against God, because they view the processes of nature as having self-sufficient causes, normally regarded by them as ultimate. They do not realize that the universe

---

493   Rahman, *Major Themes*, 46.
494   Rahman, *Major Themes*, 10.
495   Rahman, *Major Themes*, 13–4.

is a sign pointing to something 'beyond' itself, something without which the universe, with all its natural causes, would be and could be nothing."[496] The entire nature and universe must be recognized as a divine miracle, hence people ought to be persuaded to believe in a divine being as the source of everything.[497] Rahman suggests that natural laws and mechanisms equal the disobedience (*kufr*) towards God. In other words a person who does not recognize God (the alleged author behind nature) will live an ungodly life. This still does not answer the question, why not all people recognize God behind nature and all existence. Rahman admits that "[...] although a 'sign' in the religious sense points beyond itself to its Author, and the transition is in this sense rational or at least reasonable, it is nevertheless not equivalent to rational proof. In order to determine the meaning of a sign, one must have, in addition to reason, a certain disposition, i.e., the capacity for faith." One hence needs a "mental-cum-spiritual attitude so that one may 'really hear, really see, and really understand'."[498] In that case we are inclined to ask how or why anyone might lose this capacity of faith. But Rahman does not answer this. Instead he goes on explaining with reference to multiple verses the different types of persuasive elements within the Quranic signs.[499] For now I find that for Rahman the conclusion is clear: the Quran itself, each of its verses, plus the entire nature and universe are cogent proofs of God's existence. This would also mean that all people, even if they have no access to the Quran or have never heard of the notion of God, let alone the monotheistic image of God, should be convinced by the powerful sign of nature that there is a creator, who made everything. Then faith in this creator and subsequently the belief in the Last Day will follow, if a person is rightly disposed. However, in the end Rahman nowhere explains satisfyingly why some people have the capacity of developing faith and others do not.

What about other religions? Rahman mentions that all revelations to people came from the same divine *amr*. Since within Rahman's thinking this *amr* emanated from a monotheistic God and utilizes Prophets to spread its message, we can assume that at least those religions that recognize a monotheistic God and believe in revelations and Prophets, had at one stage access to the guidance that leads towards salvation. The Quran seems to suggest that "for every people a guide has been provided" (13:7).[500] But Rahman remains thinking in categories of a monotheistic God and Prophets, just as the Quran: "True, different Prophets have come to different peoples and nations at different times, but their messages are universal and identical. All these messages emanate from a single source: "the Mother of the Book" [43:4; 13:39] and "the Hidden Book" (56:78). Since these messages are universal and identical, it is incumbent on all people to believe in all divine messages."[501] So it is not clear whether Rahman reads the Quran to be saying that all people (including the Pantheists, Pagans, and Buddhists etc.) have received messages. Apparently they do not believe in a monotheistic God, and not necessarily in Prophets for that matter. What went wrong? According to Rahman the Quran admits the split of

---

496 Rahman, *Major Themes*, 47.
497 Rahman, *Major Themes*, 48.
498 Rahman, *Major Themes*, 48. One could ask further: Did all people have this capacity at one time and then for some reason lost it? However, Rahman does not dwell on this, in my eyes quite important issue.
499 Rahman, *Major Themes*, 50–3
500 Rahman, *Major Themes*, 113.
501 Rahman, *Major Themes*, 113.

humankind into different religions is a "divine mystery, for if God so willed, He could surely bring them to one path."[502] Surely, God would then take away the free will and choice of people to choose whether to follow the divine guidance or not.

But here also a different problem arises, for the Quran seems to indicate a plurality of religions, not only a difference between godly and ungodly existence. The plurality of religions raises the problem of authority, namely that one religion claims to be the only right one. Rahman points out that the Quran (sura 2) reacted against exclusivist claims: "The Qur'ān's reply to these exclusivist claims and claims of proprietorship over God's guidance, then, is absolutely unequivocal: Guidance is not the function of communities but of God and good people, and *no* community may lay claims to be uniquely guided and elected. The whole tenor of the Qur'ānic argument is against election."[503] Hence Rahman concludes that it is not up to humans to make exclusive claims, since God chooses the way of guidance. And if God apparently sent guidance to all people, it is not up to humans to judge which religion God favours. However, Rahman dedicated his entire life to the study of Islam, and thought of Islam as offering the criteria for an ideal human society. But he was too dedicated to the humbling concept of *taqwā*, which does not allow speaking in absolute certainties, and hence he nowhere diminished the status of other religions.

Arkoun

In this section on Arkoun's treatment of the Quran I attempt to formulate some of the interpretative principles that can be found in his writings. Some of his views on the Quran and more specifically on the original discourses and revelation might take more concrete shape. Arkoun frequently focuses on specific verses, in order to argue for some of his underlying philosophical stances such as humanism and the emergence of a responsible person. Hence I try to follow his argument and want to show in which way he refers to the Quran in order to support several of his reform ideas. My examples cover the themes of understanding *imān* and *islām*, violence and the emergence of the responsible person.

1. Methods and Terminology

We have already discovered that Arkoun's exegesis aims at reconstructing the first audience's comprehension of the discourse (discourse analysis). While saying this, I have to repeat that Arkoun does not claim to deliver a Quranic exegesis. Of course he engages with the Quran and speaks about the meanings that emerged in the interpreting corpora and he also assesses some of them (as becomes clear from his proposed deconstruction), but he nowhere suggests that he is offering a comprehensive interpretation. Arkoun's aim is first of all the deconstruction of conceptions and representations, which were generated about the Quranic content in accordance to mythological consciousness, *imaginaire, episteme,* and *will to power.*

One, but not the only, aim of Arkoun's deconstruction of Quranic interpretations is to establish a foundation for a reconstruction of Islamic thought. Let us recall the numerous consequences which derive from Arkoun's deconstruction. This includes

---

502   Rahman, *Major Themes*, 113.
503   Rahman, *Major Themes*, 114.

144

the liberation of the Quranic text from obsolete layers of thought; new perspectives on the Quran, closer to the original understanding and purpose of the revelation; higher but not total objectivity; and new meanings based on knowledge derived from diverse disciplines.[504] For the concrete act of exegesis this means that the reading of the Quran is not determined by former interpretations, and all knowledge gained from various disciplines about the time of the Quranic discourse needs to be implemented (discourse analysis). Arkoun is aware of course that also the contemporary reader will bring her or his own pre-concepts and ways of speaking about reality into the process of understanding the Quran. This is precisely why one needs to be aware of discourse mechanisms; those of the reader's contemporary discourse and those of past discourses that are entailed in secondary literature, and those which were prevalent at the time in which original material appeared. In all this, claims to absolute truth and knowledge become impossible.

Since suggestions for how one might interpret the text are very rare and un-systematically distributed within Arkoun's many works, it is not possible to categorize concrete methods, as it is possible for the exegesis carried out by Rahman and Abu Zayd. This of course comes down to the fact that these two are actually proposing tangible interpretations, which Arkoun does not. However, I hope his 'exegesis' will crystallize in the examples subsequently given. For a start, let us recall that Arkoun proposes that his text treatment will transform not only text understanding but also the awareness of the nature of the text (cf. chapter II. 3+4).

> By invoking the existence of a Qur'anic discourse that is cognitively open, I am not falling back into the dogmatic closure I have been warning about. I envisage the Qur'an as a linguistic space where several types of discourse (Prophetic, legislative, narrative, sapiential) work simultaneously and intersect each other. Purely linguistic and semiotic analysis serves to distinguish the existence of a central mythical structure calling upon symbol and metaphor to confer potential meanings on all Qur'anic enunciations, which are constantly made actual in recurrent existential situations.
>
> The contrast between closed and open is not speculative or an act of faith. It can be verified linguistically and historically by revealing the constant interaction of language, history, and thought – three realms for the production of meaning. The reading of the Qur'an requires us to join the three realms, which are customarily explored separately by specialists: linguists, historians, and philosophers.[505]

It will be interesting to see in how far his approach helps to develop an understanding of the Quran that does justice to the available knowledge about the original circumstances of the emergence of its discourses.

1.1 Analysing the Semiological Environment

Arkoun refers to the semiological environment of the Quranic reality (QR) in his attempt to understand how the first audience might have understood the messages uttered by Muhammad. This brings to mind the question of how Arkoun treats the chronology of the Quran, about which different accounts exist. He expresses clear scepticism towards attempts at a chronology, which are for him products of

---

504 Disciplines such as sociology, history, archaeology, and linguistics.
505 Arkoun, *Rethinking Islam*, 94.

speculation.[506] He insists that the researcher has to reflect on the interests and persuasions of those who compiled the texts into their final form: "Certainly, those who gave to the *Mushaf* the form handed down to us had their own motivations and purposes that we can only guess."[507] The 'surest way' of exegesis he asserts is to read the Quran by the Quran,[508] although Arkoun often mentions the chronology of verses and relates the interpretation of some verses to the overall dynamic of the Quran. Nevertheless, he does so with caution, since

> in the absence of complete accord about the chronological classifications proposed for the sūras and *a fortiori* for the verses, one may not employ this perspective except for the rare cases where there are relatively reliable and coherent indices upon which to base such judgements. One knows how the collective concurrent memories were construed during the first Islamic centuries and how this mythological and ideological appropriation informed what was to become the paradigm of the earthly history and the salvation history of the Muslim community.[509]

Furthermore, in all attempts of dealing with the Quran, simplification and reduction of meanings should be avoided.[510] Studying the Quran's semiological environment implies investigation of grammatical, rhetorical, and semantic aspects; the identification of addressee, addresser, protagonist, subject, and object. This requires linguistics and the study of linguistics. Arkoun believes that "the semiotic structure [...] underlies all Qur'anic statements"[511] and hence must be subject to semiological analysis, which "is an excellent, performing tool applicable to all the linguistic levels where meaning is generated."[512] Arkoun believes that the language mechanisms (linguistic, semiotic, rhetoric, stylistic) within the Quran have the power to generate meanings which change history. How these mechanisms operate must be scrutinized through discourse analysis.[513]

Thus reconstructing the Quran's semiological environment requires more than considering *asbāb an-nuzūl* material. The semiological environment is highly complex: it involves places and people present at the time of the verses' reception, the state of affairs to which revelation reacted, and the dynamics brought about through prophecy.[514] That is why exegesis ought to take place via systematic reference to Quran verses, opposed to selective selection. By 'systematic,' Arkoun means a kind of thematic orientation, which entails more than the topical categorizations. As we will see shortly, the themes Arkoun follows up represent the dynamics of the Quran which manifest themselves until today within social spheres of human action and belief. Furthermore exegesis incorporates the analysis of its metaphorical organization and inter-textuality.[515]

---

506 Arkoun, *Reform or Subvert*, 124. *Islam: To Reform or to Subvert?* was originally published as *Unthought in contemporary Islamic thought*. London: Saqi Books, 2002.
507 Arkoun, "Revelation Revisited," 13.
508 Arkoun, *Reform or Subvert*, 124.
509 Arkoun, "Islam," EQ.
510 Arkoun, *Reform or Subvert*, 85.
511 Arkoun, *Reform or Subvert*, 127.
512 Arkoun, "Revelation Revisited," 14f.
513 Arkoun, "Islam," EQ.
514 Arkoun, "Revelation Revisited," 12.
515 Arkoun, "Revelation Revisited," 13.

Whether it be the Bible, the Gospels or the Qur'an, when reading a verse or a longer textual unit three levels of contextualisation must be kept in mind: 1) the *discourse situation* of the first oral enunciation; 2) the immediate textual context where the verse or fragment has been inserted; 3) the context incorporating the Closed Official Corpus (the whole of the tales, the fragments, the large units collected and divided up in the volume called Bible, Gospel or Qur'an).[516]

Here Arkoun again calls for the priority of the intellectual approach as opposed to that which seeks religious affirmations. In all this, however the reader – as we have said above – must also develop a respectful attitude towards the history of the text and the historical gaps between the readers' time of existence and the period of the Quranic reality.

2. Exegesis and Hermeneutics

Arkoun does analyse three sections of the Quran in more detail: The allegedly first revealed sura 96, and the last two, 49 and 9. In his essay 'Revelation Revisted' he states: "For the specific purpose of this chapter, I shall examine two different *sûra*: the *The Blood Clot* (*al-ʿalaq*) numbered 96 in the *Mushaf*, and the 9th one presented with two titles: *Repentance* or *Immunity*." For the sake of consistency with the discussion of Rahman and Abu Zayd I follow the themes on which Arkoun's reflection deliver most insights. Having regard to Arkoun's reform ideas, I choose specifically these subjects: *islām/imān*, violence/*jihad*, and the emergence of the responsible person.

2.1 *islām/imān*

In Arkoun's enquiry into the Quran's use of the terms *islām* and *imān*, he analyses sura 49 and mentions the importance of sura 9. Sura 49 is placed before sura 9. It was probably revealed after around 20 years of Quranic preaching.[517] However, Arkoun is sceptical about relying on the (numerous) chronological orders of verses which were established within Islamic and Oriental scholarship, even though in some cases the chronological order of verses is useful in the quest.

However, Arkoun does not believe it is enough to follow up all verses in which the literary term appears in one or another form. He is not persuaded by the purely lexical analysis of terms. In addition he asserts that the search for the meaning of *islām* by Muslim historians is already not 'innocent.' This is because they already assume that Muhammad is the Prophet through whom the revelations came from a monotheistic God, and that these revelations are the words of God which have manifested in the written Quran. Arkoun seems to consider this acceptable: he is writing in the first place about Muslim historians. At the very least, a researcher in this field ought to be one for whom God has not "become a useless hypothesis" and who does not believe in a modernity that "insists that humans take responsibility for their destiny and substitutes an image of progress by science for the image of eternal salvation guaranteed by a loving and compassionate God."[518] So even of the non-Muslim historian Arkoun

---

516 Arkoun, "The reflexive History of Thought Seen as Problematisation of Truth," 13.
517 Arkoun, *Reform or Subvert*, 128.
518 Arkoun, "Islam," EQ.

expects openness towards the possibility of the actuality of revelation and religious truths (cf. chapter IV, Arkoun, 2.).

Again, Arkoun points out the risk of approaching Quranic terms with a method that does nothing more than investigate "etymologies of a semantically rich vocabulary." Such study he considers functional to a certain degree but "the danger of such research lies in the tendency to rest content with partial or fossilized meanings that are only poorly related to the living continuation of a no-longer extant language and society."[519] If the aim is to discern the text's meaning that is relevant for today's horizons of comprehension the engagement with the Quran must go further. Arkoun reflects on Bravmann's study of the terms *islām* and *imān* and of their development in meaning in the course of the evolution of the Quran: "islām has meant confronting death, sacrificing one's life for a higher goal and thus, by extension, defending one's honor (q.v.), and giving oneself unconditionally to God [...as well as] dying for the honor of the clan [...]." Arkoun recognizes these meanings in his article 'The Notion of Revelation.'[520] But he advances their interpretation by looking at how the Quranic text uses these terms and invests them with certain psychological qualities. However, he does not give a clear account of how to understand these terms today or what they should mean today. His overall project is more concerned about how scholarship did and ought to deal with the terms.

Arkoun notes that, in the absence of a yet established Muslim community, the term 'Muslim' not only meant a member of Islam but much more classifies "internal submission of faith which is contracted in the alliance *(mīthāq)* with God" and "an internalized religious attitude that is well symbolized by the conduct of the qur'ānic Abraham." Here we could glimpse a possible meaning of the term which Arkoun would prefer to be read from the Quran today. Outside the context of battle and fight for emancipation of the emerging religious community, this reading brings forth a more general understanding. Arkoun does not express a clear preference for this account, but he insists that discerning *islām* and *imān* today only as understood by the first audience will be an insufficient approach. It will not achieve the 'deployment of the optimal human condition,'[521] which he sees as a possible Quranic ideal. For this, an understanding of *islām* as the inner disposition of one's soul towards God and the covenant *(mīthāq)* between the Divine and humankind is preferable.

In understanding the term *imān* (belief) then Arkoun attempts to follow "the developments within the qur'ānic discourse of the social and linguistic construction of the categories of 'believers' and 'nonbelievers,' as these relate to what would be called 'Islam' [...]."[522] First Arkoun notices that sura 49 addresses repeatedly "the category of *mū'minūn*, translated as believers." He continues to analyze how the sura understands *imān*, the root for *mū'minūn*. Here he refers to Blachere's analysis of the term *imān* in this sura, listing diverse features of *imān* (and *islām*) and concludes that the sura contains numerous "imperatives of social ethics and personal control [to which] are added definitions of greater religious and political significance." *Imān* constitutes not only a "new ethico-political code of social bond," but also delivers material for the development of "a spiritual theology of the human person and even of a philosophical

---

519   Arkoun, "Islam," EQ.
520   "The Notion of Revelation" is based on the unpublished paper "Revelation Revisited."
521   Arkoun, *Reform or Subvert*, 318.
522   Arkoun, "Islam," EQ.

148

subject [...]."[523] How the sura constitutes all this Arkoun does not spell out in detail. However I understand from his writings that the term *imān* can have various meanings. And given the centrality of this term for Islamic identity, Arkoun wants to show how the Quran's ambiguities cater for the formulation of different meanings, which nonetheless can be of existential significance. He even concludes that the sura delivers substance for the development of a new human ethos.

2.2 Violence/jihad

Arkoun detects the roots of what he calls an anthropological triangle of *violence-sacred-truth* in the Quranic passages that were revealed during the 'Medinan experience,' hence in the course of the emancipation of the young religious community. Those verses merged profane actions and ideas with a rich religious symbolic capital. Arkoun asks: "How does the concept of violence emerge from the Qur'ānic corpus?" A look at the words used to denote forms of violence or aggression in various contexts reveals that the Quran mostly connotes violence as an action against oppression. As a remark, in this context various forms of the root *z-l-m* (injustice) are found 319 times.[524] For this reason, Arkoun concludes "the strategy of Qur'ānic discourse [...] is concerned with stigmatizing, rejecting and condemning unjust conduct, by referring to it insistently." In addition, "the Qur'ān is never interested in violence in itself, whereas today, a focus on violence has become a major anthropological theme."[525] The Quran does not portray violent behaviour as having value in itself. Violence is generally mentioned in contexts which picture transgression against the truth or the believers who in consequence have to defend their Islam. Sura 9 includes the so called *sword verse* (9:5) which Arkoun cites in full. We will later reflect also on comments about Arkoun's reading of this verse, as put forward by Robert Gleave.[526] For now we accept that the interpretation of the *sword verse* is crucial for setting ethical ground rules on relations between Muslims and non-Muslims. It is also of particular importance since some exegetes interpret it as abrogating much more numerous verses that call for tolerance towards non-Muslims. I mention this fact here since it is a crucial issue in discussing the topic of violence as interpreted from within the Quran. Arkoun asserts that "the designations of the forms and shapes of "violence" are never named as such but always aiming at an attitude, or at intolerable conduct that rejects values, knowledge, and the "limits" (*ḥudūd*) fixed by God and his envoy."[527] The Quran identifies violence with defence and not with the mere gaining of power. It invests the meaning of violence with the significance of fighting for the right cause. At the same time violence is not only legitimized but undergoes humanization. This is because the violent act is carried out by the individual who is indebted to the covenant: "On this essential point, the Qur'ān continues, in its

---

523   Arkoun, *Reform or Subvert*, 128–30.
524   Cf. Abu Zayd's mentioning of *ẓulm al-nafs* (injustice by the soul).
525   Arkoun, "Violence," EQ.
526   Arkoun, "Revelation Revisited," 23. The Arabic Studies scholar Robert Gleave brings to attention Arkoun's interpretation of the sword verse in a short, but not insignificant article. Gleave, "Arkoun and the 'Sword Verse,'" LIVIT Blog (A three year project called: Legitimate and Illegitimate Violence in Islamic Thought, 2010–2013).
527   Arkoun, "Violence," EQ.

own style and in a different context, the work of the Bible and the Gospels, which convert archaic usages of 'violence' in tribal societies into a 'violence' contained in a new symbolism." The Quran therefore transcends the previous meanings into concepts that support the Islamic cause. In this socio-anthropological investigation into the Quranic understanding of violence, Arkoun does not offer an exegesis for today's believers.

Arkoun's investigation of sura 9 regarding the 'new code' or 'social contract' may shed more light on how he views the function of Quranic display of violence. Arkoun does not examine each verse of the sura, but begins with a thorough categorization of its vocabulary and word groups. Here an example: the sura speaks of the

> [...] holy mosque and the houses of ungodly worship; the calendar inaugurated by God ('from the day He created heaven and earth') and the pagan calendar marking impious acts; alms given out of a desire for proximity to God (*sadaqa, qurubât*) and the tributes (*maghram, jizya*) exacted in a spirit of humiliation; treaties in emulation of the holy Alliance and truces violated out of self-aggrandising motivations.[528]

The sura works with categories such as concrete groups and places that receive identification by contrasting these with one another. Identification comes down to either the membership in the right or the wrong group, expressed by correct or erroneous deeds, as defined by the new message, with its "effective functions of the discourse as a ***new starting cultural code*** (nouveau départ de code) in the Arabic language, taking over a singular history of a particular social group (i.e., the Arabs in the Hijaz)."[529]

A first glance at the word groups helps to realize the language's play with polarities, in order to display demarcations between the followers of the Islamic faith and other groups. For Arkoun these polarities are a result of a time of conflict between the emerging group and the established others. The scene sets a struggle for emancipation of the new community from the former shackles. However, this concrete historical setting is used by the text as a background on which it establishes the notion of the righteous *umma* with universal character. We also remember that Arkoun understands revelations as beneficial for societies since they establish 'vistas of liberation,' by which he probably means in the historical context of the Quran the liberation of humankind from tribal and *jāhili* culture. "From this perspective, the Revelation of Islam is only one attempt, among many others, to emancipate human beings from the natural limitations of their biological, historical, and linguistic conditions."[530] Later Islamic discourse tended to generalize the contingent polarities.[531] Arkoun's deconstruction of such generalizations and his proposed restoration of the conditions in which this particular text emerged, tries to avoid consequences that could arise from oversimplifications. For example, the disparagement of non-Muslims will create insurmountable obstacles for the striving towards a peaceful human condition in today's globalized world. We remember that

---

528   Arkoun, "Revelation Revisited," 29.

529   Arkoun, "Notion of Revelation," 72–3.

530   Arkoun, *Rethinking Islam Today*, 210.

531   In example, as Camilla Adang shows, the 'impurity of unbelievers' as stated in verse 28 "came to be interpreted in the Mālikī and Ja'farī schools of law as prohibiting all non-Muslims from entering Muslim places of worship and led to discussions about the nature of the unbeliever's impurity [...]." (Adang, "Belief and Unbelief," EQ)

150

Arkoun was a vigorous supporter of a global ethics that is committed to a culture of non-violence, solidarity, just economic and social order, tolerance, truthfulness, and respect for life. It is clear that Arkoun does not insist that all these incentives could be read from the Quran. But at the same time his critical assessment of the text helps to point to both the historical and contingent dimension of the Quranic verses, and to an explanation of behavioural dynamics that are still prevalent in Muslim societies and originate from the Quran's symbolic reinvestments.

We might dwell further on these reinvestments in order to really understand how Arkoun wants to demonstrate the force that it entailed in the Quranic text. Generalizations such as those applied to the meaning of sura 9 find support in a special linguistic feature of the Quran. This is the symbolic identification of profane and merely socially functional actions with deeds that are willed and demanded by God. Sura 9 "blends worldly and political ends with religious purposes."[532] Examples are prayer, warfare and alms-giving as signs that one is a follower of Allah. One can understand the demand for these deeds as an expression of the need to demonstrate membership of the newly established social group. But the sura also indicates that these actions are a condition for gaining salvation. Giving alms, for example, fulfils both a social and spiritual function. In the course of Quran exegeses throughout the history of Islamic cultures the profane actions become even more 'ontologised' until they come to be actual premises for salvation. Eschatology then argues for the salvific character of socially profane actions and further ontologises and sacralises them as a means for salvation. Generalization of contingent meanings leads to universal and absolute claims.

> It is this constant traffic from an actual social-historical process to paradigmatic utterances of **existential** import (presenting ideal objectives for human existence) that invests the Qur'anic discourse with an inexhaustible fund of energy in socio-historical situations resembling its own. It is here that the **revelatory power** of the Prophetic discourse is to be found. This revelatory function, detectable in the linguistic mechanisms of discourse, served as a concrete basis for the theological construct of revelation.[533]

Arkoun argues that what he detects as revelatory power is what the *iʿjāz*-literature tried to describe as the wonderful powers of the Quranic language. As one example of the symbolic identification of profane, merely socially functional actions with godly intent, Arkoun reads verse 60, which goes: "'Alms are only for the poor and needy, and those who work for them, and those whose heart are to be reconciled (to be converted to Islam), and those in captivity, and those in debt, and those who are on Allah's path, and for the wayfarer. This is an ordinance from Allah, for Allah is Knower, Wise'." Arkoun writes:

> It is in fact all the more in so far as the beneficiaries listed in verse 60 are a product of conditions of war and recruitment imposed on the believers. Objectively, then, what was happening was a confrontation between two systems of solidarity underlying two competing regimes of truth and political ruling. Despite its contingent and

---

532   Arkoun, "Revelation Revisited," 29.
533   Arkoun, "Revelation Revisited," 30.

profane origins, the system that was to become 'Islamic' would retain, thanks to the Qur'ân and its amplification through exegesis, a sacred and sacralising value.[534]

It is significant that verse 5 uses terms to indicate a context of conflict and war (*arrest, besiege, lie in ambush*, see verse 5) and other verses within sura 9 can be read in this same context. Arkoun's reading shows that he approaches the text as one that was produced in such situation of conflict.

The *sura's* title *repentance* (*tawba*) also represents one theme of the text. From Arkoun's reading we can infer that joining warfare (*jihad*) was a powerful sign of following the newly emerged *transforming hero* (Prophet Muhammad). But this is not the first sign of membership of the *umma*. According to sura 9 we see this by looking at the conditional nature of verse 5, which indicates that idolaters ought not to be killed *if* they performed *salat* and *zakat*: "If they repent (*tâbû*) and take to prayer and render the alms, allow them to go their way. For God is forgiving and merciful."[535] If we also consider the prior sentence which reads "arrest them, besiege them and lie in ambush for them everywhere," we can infer that the idolaters were given the chance to repent before their slaying was considered. Repentance is usually translated as "returning to God," but within the context of sura 9 it receives a much more practical meaning, namely the submission under the new laws (praying and alms giving).[536]

Like Abu Zayd, who criticises how traditional Islamic discourses deny the historical dimension of the Quran, Arkoun discerns the practice of traditional Quranic interpretation which uses "discursive techniques of integration, or better, cancellation of concrete and profane historicity in order to vest it in the framework of History of Salvation. These techniques, well analysed by P. Ricœur in *Temps et re'cit*, are in operation in the founding narratives using literary devices for the accounts of transfiguration, appropriation, insertion of the profane in the sacred."[537]

Arkoun points out that the new group renamed the act of giving alms or tax for the poor: from *maghram* it became *sadaqa* or *zakat*. For Arkoun is clear the new terms "took on a religious significance while still fulfilling the same socio-political function. This meant breaking with traditional loyalties, leaving fathers, wives, children and goods behind in order to join a new group.[538] Probably, the ultimate *tawba* was still for former opponents to become jihadists. Here repentance receives again a slightly different meaning. Arkoun claims that *tawba* enabled the new group member to become a fighter for the novel faith. From Arkoun's reading I understand him to be saying, although he is not explicit on this point, that killing the unbeliever is not an ideal, universal obligation but was asked of former opponents to prove their loyalty to the new messenger. It was only one sign of loyalty and only to be performed in this social setting of the crucial first inauguration of Islamic community. In addition even in this tense situation, the unbeliever ought not to be killed, if they performed other signs in order to repent. Again the common practice of *jihad* was transformed by later commentators into a divine struggle in the name of the Divine: *Jihad* "was presented as a struggle on behalf of God, in practice the jihad

---

534 Arkoun, "Revelation Revisited," 34.
535 Q. 9:5.
536 Arkoun, *Reform or Subvert*, 130–1.
537 Arkoun, *Reform or Subvert*, 123.
538 Arkoun, "Revelation Revisited," 30.

152

was fought by means of tactics (of siege, ambush, murder, capture and looting) and for the sake of objectives (conquest, expansion and consolidation of the state) which were commonplace in confrontations between social groups of all various sizes."[539] Later the sura displays which rewards the believers receive, if they perform certain deeds and take on internal attitude of obedience. Again the text invests religious capital into profane actions.

I find that my understanding of Arkoun's stance is supported by Gleave's look at Arkoun's sword-verse interpretation. Gleave writes:

> Violence becomes sacralised in the defence of truth. Q9.5 is understood as a "micro narrative" within a "macro framework" of the Quranic discourse on salvation history, in which God sends a Prophet whose message is rejected by all but a few; the majority suffer defeat and the few become justified in the eventual victory. [...] his exploration of Q9.5 does provide us with an alternative approach to the supposed scriptural justification of violence.

Gleave suggests here that Arkoun does not promote a purely contextual reading of the verse, in order to dismiss its significance for today. But even if Arkoun's reading explains how the mechanisms of symbolic investment and generalization are rooted in the text, this does not really guide towards an alternative understanding of the text's meaning. I appreciate Arkoun's demand for understanding the mechanisms, but the questions remain: Shall we approve of these mechanisms? What does the text tell us with sura 9 today? These implications Arkoun leaves to those who want to go on with the reconstruction of the conditions of the Quranic discourse.

2.3 Emergence of the Responsible Person

The birth moment of the Muslim personality is charged with rich symbolic investments of formerly profane actions. Violence is one of these notions that the Quran turns into a sacred action, when carried out for the defence of *al-ḥaqq*. We have already seen in chapter IV that Arkoun pays much attention to sura 49 and 9 when it comes to talking about the emergence of the person, even though, as mentioned above, it is not clear how he hopes to establish his ideas from the Quranic material. One reason for Arkoun to have chosen to dedicate a great deal of attention to sura 9 could be that it includes themes particularly important for formulating Islamic beliefs: the pact between Muhammad and others (9:1), the covenant between God and God's people (112) [1], believers/unbelievers (9: 20, 23–4, 29, 30, 54, 71, 75, 80, 84) [2], oaths between believers and opponents [3], victory and triumph (9:14, 72, 89, 100, 111), gaining paradise (9:72), dooming in hell (9:35), belief/unbelief in afterlife (9:85), fight against unbelievers/warfare (9:5, 16, 20, 24, 41, 44, 73, 81, 86, 88, 90–94), *al-ḥaqq* (9:29), ethics (9:100), *hajj* (9:3). The sura states what the person has to do in order to gain

---

539   Arkoun, "Revelation Revisited," 30.

salvation.[540] It becomes clearer now that Arkoun in concerned with the sociological and anthropological reading of the Quran:[541]

> The discourse of transcendence and of absoluteness opens an infinite space for the promotion of the individual beyond the constraints of fathers and brothers, clans and tribes, riches and tributes; the individual becomes an autonomous and free person, enjoying a liberty guaranteed by obedience and love lived within the alliance. The consciousness of the person thus liberated does not even require the mediation of another human consciousness, as it does in Christianity, which depends on the mediation of Jesus; the ontological access of a Muslim is direct, total, and irreversible. [...] Qur'anic discourse has broadly demonstrated its efficacy as a space for the emergence, training, and deployment of the free person, who enjoys guarantees of life, property, family, and private domicile not as "citizen" of a civil society managed by elected representatives or by universal suffrage (sovereign of the nation founded in 1789 by the French Revolution) but as God's partner in an eternal compact.[542]

Arkoun also explores the dialogical nature of the Quran. Arkoun identifies a general technique of the Quranic discourse which is mostly comprised of: "'**We**' of the addresser (called God in the discourse of faith), the '**thou**' (Muhammad), the '**you**' comprising the believers, '**he**' and '*they*' (man and the people still outside the new emerging space of communication). This configuration of pronouns establishes the basic, constant space of communication and meaning in the entire discourse of the Qur'an." Throughout the Quranic discourse there is a tension amongst these protagonists (addressee and addresser, subject and object): "[...] through which there emerges a consciousness of **culpability**. Through it, man thereby comes to be transformed into a conscious, reflective subject in the sphere of ethics and law. He becomes responsible for every thought, action and initiative in his life."[543]

> From this third perspective, it suffices to establish that what can be called the qur'ānic stage, the instantiation of a new religion, is a complex historical process engaging simultaneously social, political, cultural, and normative factors. These are entangled with ritual, customs, ethics, familial structures (see family; tribes and clans; kinship), competing structures of the imagination and the collective interactive memory of such entities as Jews, Christians, Sabians (q.v.), polytheists (frequently termed "pagans"), and all cultural groups of the ancient Near East. All these modes and manifestations of the historical existence of such social groups in Arabia are not only present in the qur'ānic discourse but transformed. They have been sublimated, uprooted from their local conditions to constitute an "existential paradigm" of the

---

540 In sociological terms we can say that Arkoun speaks of the 'myth of probation; (*Bewährungsmythos*) and the origin of the basic Muslim personality (this last expression is used by Arkoun numerous times). The sociologist Ulrich Oevermann uses the term *Bewährungsmythos*, to describe the myth of religion that claims the necessities for gaining salvation.

541 Schönberger, p.11 comments on Arkoun, *The Unthought in Contemporary Islamic Thought*, 50. "Although the Qu'rān is the basis of the imaginaire, it is not a static concept; it is rather a dynamical one that is interdependent with the ethic of Islam. In doing so, Arkoun's anthropological orientation is to unearth the 'myth of origins' and the 'regimes of truth.'"

542 Arkoun, *Rethinking Islam*, 57.

543 Arkoun, "Revelation Revisited," 12–3.

154

human condition. Divested of its particularity, this qur'ānic paradigm is capable of producing and informing individual and collective existence within the most diverse cultural and historical contexts.[544]

Furthermore he suggests a semiotic analysis as displayed in a diagram in the article "*Notions of Revelations.*"

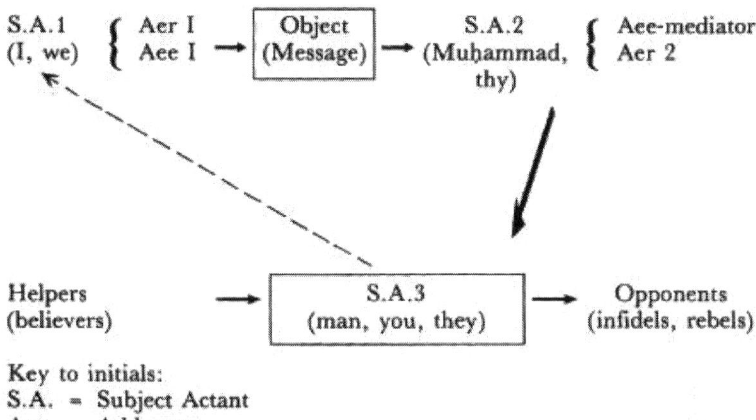

Sura 9 delivers all material for this "dramatic structure" of the Quranic discourse. Reading it according to the diagram restores its possible meaning to the first audience in its historical context. As said before, the sura needs to be read in the light of the different protagonists, whose interaction establishes profound tension within a "historical paradigmatic drama."[545] In the context of reading sura 49 and 9 Arkoun writes:

> The groups of protagonists are transformed into protagonists of a **spiritual drama** [sic]. The political and social situations and what is actually at stake are sublimated into paradigms of conduct and recurrent choices inexorably involving the ultimate destiny of every soul (person) confronted at the same time with temptations, constraints and solidarities of the immediate life (*al-dunyā*, or 'society' as we could call it today) [...].[546]

The Quran involves the addressees into a dialogue that leaves them transformed. The drama displays the individual's struggle for salvation against the odds of its own social, political and historical reality.[547]

---

544   Arkoun, "Islam," EQ.
545   Arkoun, *Reform or Subvert*, 126.
546   Arkoun, *Reform or Subvert*, 127f.
547   Regarding the emerging of the consciousness of the self see Arkoun, *Reform or Subvert*, 279–80 (re. verse 9:5).

Abu Zayd

After some reflections on Abu Zayd's literary study of the Quran, I will focus on the question of whether he considers the aim of interpretation to be the discovery of the author's intention. I will then look more generally at his interpretative principles, examining the similarities between Abu Zayd's hermeneutic and that of Hans-Georg Gadamer. Finally, I will discuss some examples of Abu Zayd's Quranic interpretation.[548]

1. Methods and Terminology

As we know, the need for exegesis arises amongst others from the fact that the Quran entails not only clear but also ambiguous or contradictory verses. Notwithstanding this difficulty, Abu Zayd attempts to contribute to the development of an interpretation that does justice to what he sees as the human nature of the Quran. One aim of a literary reading is to determine the meaning of verses in the understanding of the first audience.[549] Even if Abu Zayd takes on this task, he does not hold this primary understanding as authoritative for Muslims today. However he values highly the attempt to reconstruct this first understanding. Furthermore Abu Zayd in later stages of his career approached the Quran not only as a literary text but as a product of discourses as well as the initiator of discourse. The communicative character of the text necessitates what Abu Zayd calls a humanistic interpretation of the Quran.

We are tempted to ask at this stage what it is that an interpreter will seek to understand from the Quran. Is it a specific intention put forward by the author, in this instance God? In any case, to view the Quran as a human product (cf. Chapter II 3.2)

---

548   Some remarks on relevant literature: Abu Zayd's hermeneutic is in most detail analysed in two unpublished PhD theses, namely by Yusuf Rahman (*The hermeneutical theory of Naṣr Ḥāmid Abū Zayd*, 2001), and Peter Matthews Wright (*Modern Qur'anic Hermeneutics*, 2008). Y. Rahman analyses Abu Zayd's hermeneutic with reference to numerous of Abu Zayd's Arabic works, and hence provides helpful access to Abu Zayd's Arabic terminology. Wright scrutinizes parallels in Abu Zayd's thought to literary romanticism which reveals further facets of the work of Abu Zayd as it emerged in a particular intellectual environment. In the course of finding support in Abu Zayd's hermeneutics for his reform hopes I briefly reflect on some key ideas extracted from Y. Rahman's and Wright's theses which seem germane. However, I chiefly consult Abu Zayd's original works.

549   We will see later that Y. Rahman identifies al-Khuli's understanding of the first audience as *canonical meaning*. The idea of discerning the first audience's understanding is inspired by Abu Zayd's "real intellectual influence," the Egyptian scholar Amin al-Khuli (1895–1966), one of the forefathers of applying literary reading in Quran exegesis. Sukidi writes and cites Abu Zayd: "'My real intellectual influence,' Abū Zayd himself acknowledges, 'is Sheikh Amīn al-Khūlī.' If al-Khūlī has approached the Qur'ān as a literary text (*naṣṣ adabī*), Abū Zayd approaches it as a linguistic text (*naṣṣ lughawī*)" (Sukidi, "Naṣr Ḥāmid Abū Zayd," 208). Khuli's approach is discerned by Y. Rahman (2001: 48–58), Wright (2008: 75–7/81–3), Wielandt (1996), Abu Zayd (2006: 55–6), Hildebrandt (2007: 363–9). For Khuli's 'art of discourse' (*fann al-qawl*) arises the problem that the author of the Quran cannot be identified as it is often possible for other literature. Hence biographical, geographical, historical data on the author is lacking. If one considers God as the Quran's author, there is no primary information on God than from the Quran itself.

means for Abu Zayd to weaken the certainty of grasping the divine intention. This kind of scepticism becomes apparent in Abu Zayd's belief in the created nature of the Quran and the numerous human influences on the text. However, pointing out the human aspects of the text should, according to Abu Zayd, not rule out the possibility of 'getting it right'. What drives a believer to engage with the Quranic text is this urge to enter a process of understanding the text and the hope with that to recognize God's will. For this reason the notion of the accessibility of the text ought never to be violated. Abu Zayd criticises the religious authorities for emphasizing the inscrutability of the text.[550] This notion enables the monopolization of their 'official' interpretations. By way of contrast, knowledge about the created nature of the Quran makes the text more accessible for human reason in general.

For his agenda and speaking from within the academic realm Abu Zayd holds the literary study of the Quran as the most adequate approach. This idea seems to be inspired by al-Khuli who asserts that "the Arabs accepted Islam on the basis of evaluating the Quran as a literary text. This means that the literary method should supersede any other approach [...]."[551] Al-Khuli and Abu Zayd must have in mind here the success story of the spread of Islam supported by the distribution of the written Quran (*mushaf*) as medium of authority. Even though the Quran is a religious text, a literary reading which analyses themes, "stylistic and rhetorical qualities," historical context, chronological evolution, and psychological and sociological effects of the text,[552] can be applied without necessarily seeking theological knowledge.[553]

---

550 Abu Zayd, *Politik und Islam*, 87.

551 Abu Zayd refers to al-Khûlî, A. (1961) *Manâhij 'Tajdîd fi 'l-Nahw wa 'l-Balâghah wa 'l-Tafsîr wa 'l-Adab* (Method of Renewal in Grammar, Rhetoric, Interpretation of the Qur'ân and Literature), Cairo: 97–8; 124–5 (cf. Abu Zayd, *Reformation of Islamic Thought*, 55). Abu Zayd writes that Khuli "states very clearly that the literary approach to the Quran is the only possible way of saving Muslim intellectuals from schizophrenia. Muslims can truly believe in Islam and the holy Quran without necessarily believing that the stories mentioned in the Quran are historically authentic [...]." Abu Zayd refers to Khuli's foreword to Khalafallah's "second edition of *al-Fann al-Qasasi* (Cairo 1957)" (Abu Zayd, ibid, 57–8).

552 Wielandt, "Wurzeln der Schwierigkeit innerislamischen Gesprächs," 258. An example of studying the Quran according to its stylistic and rhetorical qualities can be found in some *i'jāz*-theories. One of the traditional arguments for the Quran's *i'jāz* (inimitability) was based on its supreme grammar (*balagha*). Khuli promoted that the study of *balagha* ought to be carried out by applying modern methods of grammatology. Abu Zayd points out how Khuli hoped subsequently to this modern approach that psychological implications of Quranic grammar will be discerned (cf. Abu Zayd, *Reformation of Islamic Thought*, 55: "The study of balaghah should then focus on the study of the literary style and its emotional impact on the recipient/ reader [...]."

553 Abu Zayd, *Reformation of Islamic Thought*, 55. As well, Abu Zayd refers to Khuli's student Khalafallah (1916–1998), who enhanced the literary study of the Quran. Khalafallah's approach is discerned by Hildebrandt (2007: 369–373), Abu Zayd (2006: 56–7), and most detailed in Y. Rahman (2001: 58–75). As mentioned above Khuli's reading of the Quran was not met with much sympathy. When Khalafallah, a student under his supervision, submitted a thesis in which he applied and developed Khuli's ideas, a "group of the Azharite 'ulama,' called *Jabhat 'Ulama' al-Azhar*" declared Khuli and Khalafallah infidels and demanded the Egyptian government to withdraw

It is important to note that Abu Zayd adds a further dimension to the elucidation of the Quran, now not only treating it as text but also as discourse.[554] In a way that resembles Arkoun's discussion. Abu Zayd holds that the Quran is partially a product of discourses.[555] Even further he declares that the Quran can be treated as a discourse today, so that one can step into communication with the text. Hence, he asks who is speaking in the Quran, and who is addressed in which context, and for which purpose? The most adequate method is the literary reading which must aim at understanding the use of language, metaphors, and symbolic expressions of the specific time of the emergence of the discourses.[556] Abu Zayd further considers "the mode of discourse under investigation, whether argumentative, persuasive, polemic, proscriptive, prescriptive, descriptive, inclusive or exclusive etc." He does not "deal with the sūra (chapter) or with the ʿāya (verse) as independent units; the unit is the identified discourse [...]."[557] He identifies also thematic frames in which the Quran expresses itself, such as cosmology, Divine-human relationship, ethical and moral dimension, society, and punishment. This does not mean that he favours interpretation along thematic themes. But he hopes to reconnect the different levels of Quranic expression, which were fragmented by diverse Islamic sciences.[558]

We will now explore the more concrete forms of interpretation and the terminologies proposed by Abu Zayd. Let me start by citing a core statement on his exegesis: "Erst ein Verstehen auf der Basis umfassenden historischen und philologischen Wissens setzt uns in den Stand, den koranischen Text richtig zu interpretieren, somit den überhistorischen Kern einer Botschaft zu erfassen und dann zu entscheiden, was er für uns Gläubige heute bedeutet."[559] In the following pages, six interpretative techniques

---

both from the academy (Y. Rahman, *The hermeneutical theory of Naṣr Ḥāmid Abū Zayd*, 61). Abu Zayd states that Khalafallah was subsequently "transferred to another job outside teaching" and Khuli "continued as a university professor but was confined to teaching Arabic grammar, rhetoric and literature. A few years later, in 1954, al-Khuli would be among a group of about 40 university professors who were transferred to jobs outside teaching. Ironically enough, this decision was made by the new military regime of the Free Officers Movement (*Harakat Dubbat al-Ahrar*), supposedly to cleanse the university of corruption." (Abu Zayd, *Reformation of Islamic Thought*, 58)

Abu Zayd and Y. Rahman both refer to Khalafallah's *al-Fann al-Qasasi*.

554 Abu Zayd writes: "Realizing the fact that the Qur'ān was originally a series of discourses, each of which has certain historical context and certain degree of independence, I suggested a redefinition of the Qur'ān as discourse(s)." (Abu Zayd, "Research Profile")

555 This assumption of course opens the door for considering numerous research disciplines to be applied to the text.

556 Generally, Abu Zayd supports Arkoun's understanding of the Quran as a text with history. The Quran was collected into a *muṣḥaf* which in addition lacks chronology of narratives. However, Abu Zayd does not, like Arkoun, speak of a selection of verses but of 'collection' (*Sammlung*) and 'arrangement' (*Arrangieren*) (Abu Zayd, *Mohammed und die Zeichen Gottes*, 77). The written text has a human history in addition to being difficult to follow in its narratives.

557 Abu Zayd, "Research Profile."

558 Abu Zayd, "Research Profile." He specifically refers to "fiqh, theology, philosophy and mysticism."

559 Abu Zayd, *Mohammed und die Zeichen Gottes*, 9.

will be explored: The rational approach, categorizing Quranic verses, determining *Meaning* and *significance*, practice of *ta'wīl* and reassessment of *turāth*, the reading in the light of the spirit (*maqsad*) and two dimensions of the Quran.

1.1 The Rational Approach

I have already spoken about Abu Zayd's call for a reintroduction of critical rational thinking, in our investigation into his reform ideas. Of course, rationality also plays a crucial role in exegesis. For Quranic interpretation this means that individual, critical thinking is favoured over blind adherence to traditional accounts,[560] a literal reading, or mystical insight.[561] The necessity of rational reflection becomes especially apparent in the course of discerning the meaning of ambiguous verses, but is generally required for any act of realistic understanding and its adequate appropriation. Reason is a "dynamic, social and historical force,"[562] which in Abu Zayd's view is able to change reality and hence influences history just as Muhammad applied his rationality to the revelations and applied his interpretation to his social environment.

However, a rational approach to the Quran will not lead to absolute knowledge and truth claims.[563] The scholar of Abu Zayd's work Navid Kermani writes: "In Abu Zayd's view, an individual's interpretation is never absolute *(jahm mutlaq)*. It is always relative *(jahm nisbi)*, since the 'information' in the divine 'message' varies according to whoever 'receives' it."[564] The information gained will be influenced by the knowledge and experience the individual brings into the understanding process.[565]

1.2 Categorizing Quranic Verses

Although the Quran describes itself as containing both clear and ambiguous verses,[566] it also "maintains that, as a text authored by God, it has no contradictions.[567] Yet the phenomenon of contradiction does exist [...]."[568] Islamic tradition distinguishes clear (*muhkam*) from ambiguous (*mutashabih*) verses,[569] and also developed subcategories.[570] For Abu Zayd these still seem to be a simplification that does not do justice to the Quran's complexity and hence he calls for further demarcation that helps to

---

560   To argue against *naql* Abu Zayd refers to Quran verses that criticize the blind adherence to the forefathers: 2:170 + 7:28, 5:104, 31:21, 43:22–24.

561   Abu Zayd, *Mohammed und die Zeichen Gottes*, 169–70.

562   " [...] dynamische, soziale und historische Wirkungskraft." (Abu Zayd, *Politik und Islam*, 93)

563   Abu Zayd, *Politik und Islam*, 93.

564   Kermani, "From Revelation to Interpretation," 173.

565   Cf. chapter V, Zayd, 2 where we discuss how he applies Gadamer's hermeneutics.

566   Q 3:7/8.

567   Q 4:82.

568   Abu Zayd, "Research Profile."

569   Abu Zayd, *Gottes Menschenwort*, 168 (article: "Rethinking the Quran").

570   Subcategories are: most clear: *al-naṣ*, least clear: *al-zahir*, metaphorical: *al-mu'awwal*, ambiguous: *al-mujmal* (Abu Zayd, "The Textuality of the Quran, from Islam and Europe"). He refers to these categorizations via al-Suyuti's, *Al Itqan fi Ulum al Qur'an*, Cairo, 1952.

discriminate the spirit or direction of the Quran.[571] Consequently he differentiates fundamental (*asāsiyya*) verses from exceptional (*istithnā'iyya*) verses.[572] The fundamental verses seem in one respect similar in nature to the clear verses, namely in that their nature is such that the other (ambiguous or exceptional verses respectively) are to be read in their light. In addition these fundamental verses entail some kind of stable entity which transcends all times and hence gives hints of the overall direction of the Quran. In that case Abu Zayd's shift from *clear* to *fundamental* and from *ambiguous* to *exceptional* enables an altered set of criteria for a categorization of Quran verses. Fundamental verses are those, which mention universal matters. However, he implies that contingent verses also carry hints of the basic ideas that are promoted by the Quran. Punishing crimes in order to protect society can for example be a general principle, without the necessity of applying the punishment practices that circulated in the seventh century Arab peninsula.

1.3 Determine Meaning and Significance

Kermani in his analysis of Abu Zayd's book, *mafhūm an-nās*, asserts that the distinction between *meaning* and *significance* employed by Hirsch goes back to Frege.[573] For Frege *Sinn* emerges in the context of perception, whereas *Bedeutung* is the process of reference, which is fixed by the object it describes.[574] For Hirsch *meaning* is the authorial intent which is fixed, whereas *significance* emerges in a particular context. What they have in common is that *Bedeutung* (Frege) and *meaning* (Hirsch) are of fixed character, while *Sinn* (Frege) and *significance* (Hirsch) are contextual.

However Abu Zayd incorporates the terminologies put forward by Hirsch (Frege), for him *maghzā* (*significance* or *sense*, in German works translated as *Sinn* (and *Aussagekraft*)[575] is dynamic, while *ma'nā* (meaning, in German rendered *Bedeutung*) constitutes a stable referential relationship between word and object.[576] This unchangeable element, namely the stable referential relationship, transcends all times. For the interpretation process *meaning* is by itself not something contingent that needs to

---

571   Abu Zayd mentions with sympathy Ibn Rushd's and Arabi's distinction of further semantic levels of meaning within Quran verses.

572   Y. Rahman derives the Arabic terms from Abu Zayd's, *Dawa'ir al-Khawf*, 1999, 123 (cf. Rahman, Y. *The Hermeneutical Theory of Naṣr Ḥāmid Abū Zayd*, 20–1). Abu Zayd himself writes in *Politik und Islam*, 170: "Die Unterscheidung zwischen dem Besonderen und Allgemeinen in der Bedeutung der Texte ist immer sehr wichtig."

573   „Hirschs von Abū Zayd zitierte Unterscheidung zwischen Sinn und Bedeutung geht auf Gottlieb [sic! Korrekt: Gottlob] Frege zurück: vgl. ‚Über Sinn und Bedeutung' in: Zeitschrift für Philosophie und philosophische Kritik, NF 100 (1892), 25–50.", 12–3)." (cf. Kermani, *Das Konzept* wahy, 12–3)

574   Frege writes: "Es würde die Bedeutung von "Abendstern" und "Morgenstern" dieselbe sein, aber nicht der Sinn." (Frege, "Über Sinn und Bedeutung," 1) Although from Kermani emerges the impression that *Sinn* and *Bedeutung* were understood in the same way by Frege and Hirsch, there is in fact a difference.

575   Hildebrandt translates Abu Zayd's term *significance* (as used in his text: "The Textuality of the Quran") as *Aussagekraft* (power of expression). Cf. Abu Zayd, *Gottes Menschenwort*, 89.

576   Hildebrandt, *Neo-Mu'tazilismus?* 389. He refers to Abu Zayd's 1992 *iskaliyat al-qira'a wa-aliyat at-ta'wil.*

be discarded in today's comprehension, but simply defines a word and the affixed linguistic description. Having said that, we will see that Abu Zayd comes in some cases to the conclusion that contingent elements, which surround or produce the meaning of the past must today be discarded. An example is the Quran's reference to slavery,[577] which Abu Zayd claims does not exist anymore.[578] In any case, the meaning itself remains attached to its designated object as specified in the time of the initial discourse. In contrast, *significance* is of a dynamic, changeable character, which is often clothed in the linguistic tool of metaphor (*magāz*).[579] The exegete approaches the text with the aim to tease out the significance for today, which then can be formulated in contemporary terms and contexts and hence be applied to current social conditions. In order to find the most appropriate application, the current social circumstances need to also be studied and identified. In Abu Zayd's words the code of the Quran then needs to be "recoded" into the "cultural and linguistic context of the interpreter."[580]

1.4 *Practice of* ta'wīl *and Reassessment of* turāth [581]

The practice of discerning significance is *ta'wīl*.[582] In Abu Zayd's words, *ta'wīl* leads to 'the other side of the text' (*al-wagh al-āhar li-n-naṣ*),[583] 'which cannot be separated from the text.'[584] The Quran is by its nature in need of *ta'wīl* in order to find the significance of the text's meanings for today's *umma*. Acknowledging the function of the Quran as creative tool for humankind to evolve God's creation, *ta'wīl* takes on the role of an existentially creative and necessary practice. It is indispensable since the text would otherwise lose significance and become meaningless. Abu Zayd says: "Das Wort *ta'wīl* kommt von ʾāla, also zurückkehren. [...]. Das geht weiter als *tafsīr*, das nur eine Vorstufe ist, dem *ta'wīl* folgt. *ta'wīl* ist also der Versuch, zum Sinn zu gelangen, zur Struktur, zu den Beziehungen etc. *ta'wīl* führt einen in tiefere

---

577 "Es ist auch nicht nuetzlich, am Sinngehalt der islamischen Position zur Sklaverei festzuhalten, wie sie aus den Texten deutlich wird. Sie kann nur als historisches Zeugnis dienen, mehr nicht." (Abu Zayd, *Politik und Islam*, 170)

578 Abu Zayd asserts e.g. that slavery does not exist any more and therefore verses referring to it must carry a meaning beyond this immediate context. Cf. Abu Zayd, *Mohammed und die Zeichen Gottes*, 174.

579 Hildebrandt, *Neo-Muʿtazilismus?* 389–90.

580 Abu Zayd, *Gottes Menschenwort*, 89. ("[...] kulturellen und sprachlichen Kontext des Interpreten.")

581 Hasan Hanafi advised Abu Zayd to use *ta'wīl* as equivalence to the term *hermeneutics* used in Western scholarship. Cf. Abu Zayd, "Über die Hermeneutik und Gadamer und das arabisch-islamische Erbe."

582 To subjective thinking and *ta'wīl* the Sunni majority attached a negative connotation (from the 4th century (AH) onwards). It was associated with the interpretation of *Shia* exegetes called *Bātinīya*. They believed in a secret meaning within the Quran which ought to be extracted. In the fight between the Sunnis and Shiites, *ta'wīl* became the negative term associated with the Shia point of view and *tafsīr* was linked to 'righteous' Sunni exegesis.

583 Wild, "Die andere Seite des Textes," 257. Er zitiert aus Abu Zayd, *mafhūm an-nās*, 11.

584 Abu Zayd, *Gottes Menschenwort*, 89. ("die andere, nicht von ihm [text] zu trennende Seite des Textes")

semantische Beziehungen als die Erklärung."[585] While *ta'wīl* is the concrete practice, *ta'wiliya* means the theory of hermeneutics: "*ta'wīlīla* ist meiner Meinung nach die Hermeneutik. Es ist die Theorie des Verstehens, das heißt, die philosophischen und sprachlichen Regeln des Textstudiums."[586] This is based on Abu Zayd's understanding of the Quran as having emerged from dialectical encounters between the Divine and humankind.[587] For Abu Zayd a hermeneutic of the Quran must therefore incorporate contextualization, literary archaeology into the understanding and use of language and expressions of the first audience, discourse analysis, plus theories of communication and comprehension.

With regard to *ta'wiliya* today Abu Zayd hopes to find inspiration in hermeneutical theories developed in the West and especially by Hans-Georg Gadamer. But a hermeneutic should also be derived from Islamic heritage *(turāth)* of which a mature understanding must be gained.[588] This leads to a re-reading of the Quran which is not new in the sense of being an entirely modern practice which is largely alien to Islamic tradition. It is novel because it is developed by those who intend a broadening of perspectives and expanded spectrum of thought which does justice to the challenges of contemporary times. This demand emphasizes the distinction between *tafsīr* and *ta'wīl*. Abu Zayd promotes the positive re-labelling of the term *ta'wīl*, and refers to an Islamic example of a constructive relation between *tafsīr* and *ta'wīl* as expressed by as-Suyūtī, "*Tafsīr* ist bei ihm die Erklärung der Worte, während man mit *ta'wīl* zum Sinn gelangt."[589]

In general, Abu Zayd blames Islamic tradition for its concentration on *tafsīr* and its opposition to Shiism, Sufism and Mu'tazilism. Their marginalization did not only lead to neglect *ta'wīl*, it also excluded some innovative ideas developed by the dismissed groups. According to Abu Zayd traditional interpreters were more inclined to cement their interpretations as absolute truths.[590] For Abu Zayd, there are no absolutely binding claims to truth in the realm of interpretation: individuals must strive to discover meaning for themselves. So Abu Zayd argues for an individual perception of truth and promotes a plurality of exegetical methods which also allows for a constructive evaluation of a variety of Islamic approaches.[591] It is important here to realize that Abu Zayd argues for his views on the Quran and exegesis from within Islamic heritage, just as his intellectual influence al-Khuli did. Referring to al-Khuli's *Manāhij 'Tajdīd* (1961)

---

585   Abu Zayd, "Über die Hermeneutik und Gadamer und das arabisch-islamische Erbe."
     – "The word *ta'wīl* comes from āla, which is 'to return.' […]. This goes beyond *tafsīr*, which is only a preliminary stage, onto which *ta'wīl* follows. *ta'wīl* therefore is the attempt to reach the meaning, the structure, the relations, etc. *ta'wīl* leads one into deeper semantic relations as the explanation."

586   Abu Zayd, "Über die Hermeneutik und Gadamer und das arabisch-islamische Erbe."
     – "*ta'wīlīla* is in my opinion hermeneutics. It is the theory of understanding, that is, the philosophical and linguistic rules of text interpretation."

587   Hildebrandt, *Neo-Mu'tazilismus?* 387.

588   Hildebrandt, *Neo-Mu'tazilismus?* 390–1.

589   Abu Zayd, "Über die Hermeneutik und Gadamer und das arabisch-islamische Erbe."

590   Wild, "Die andere Seite des Textes," 259. (see Abu Zayd, *mafhūm an-nās*, 251)

591   "[As a result,] he felt more inclined to criticize many traditional opinions in the sciences of the Qur'an and to suggest new ideas on the basis of the dialectical […] interaction between socio-cultural contexts and the text/Qur'an." (Y. Rahman, *Hermeneutical Theory of Naṣr Ḥāmid Abu Zayd*, 25)

Abu Zayd cites and formulates al-Khuli's motto: "'the first step for any real innovation is to fully analyze tradition' (*awwalu tajdid qatlu l-qadimi bahthan*) [al-Khuli 1961: 82; 128; 180]. Otherwise, the result will be loss rather than reconstruction (*tabdid la tajdid*) [al-Khuli 1961: 143]."[592] It is exactly Abu Zayd's knowledge of the heritage that makes his thinking remarkable and potentially influential for inner-Islamic reform.

1.5 Reading in the Spirit (maqsad) and Two Dimensions of the Quran

The two dimensions of the Quran are the "normative dimension" (or the "religious-spiritual level") and the "historical-situative" dimension of the Quran. The overall Quranic spirit (*maqsad*) finds expression in the fundamental verses with their "normative" elements of the Quranic content. Such normative elements are of timeless nature.[593] On the other hand the "historical-situative" elements arise from prevailing circumstances, and hence the historical-situative dimension of the Quran is established upon exceptional verses. In this dimension the Quran does for example not yet imply gender equality, due to the historical and cultural conditions and practices which amount to limitations to gender equality. In verses setting up the historical-situative dimension "social circumstances of the past are grasped, partly criticised, adapted or also confirmed."[594] Hence these verses need to be read in the context of seventh-century Arabia and analysed in the light of social conditions, culture, linguistic implications, and so on. For the interpretation of the Quran, Abu Zayd regards the "Qur'an and the authentic traditions of the Prophet,"[595] as reliable material with which to reconstruct the understanding achieved by the first audience of the revelation. In his demands for the archaeological study of the context of revelation conditions he resembles Taha Husayn's claims for the study of the *jāhili* (pre-Islamic) society. If a study of the *jāhiliyya* was to be undertaken one must consult "the most reliable and authentic source for understanding pre-Islamic social and religious life."[596] Although for Husayn the Quran was a source for understanding the time of revelation, it was still a limited source.[597] The Quran does not represent pure historical facts, but it represents a reflection or echo of some of the conditions of the past.

Abu Zayd asserts that when viewing the Quran not as eternal but as created "the message it contains has to be understood in that context. This view leaves room for the reinterpretation of religious law, because God's word has to be understood according to the spirit not according to the letter."[598]

---

592   Abu Zayd, *Reformation of Islamic Thought*, 55.

593   Abu Zayd, *Mohammed und die Zeichen Gottes*, 149.

594   Abu Zayd, *Mohammed und die Zeichen Gottes*, 150. („werden gesellschaftliche Verhältnisse der damaligen Zeit aufgegriffen, teilweise kritisiert, adaptiert oder auch bestätigt.")

595   Abu Zayd, "From Islam and Europe," (Cf. the German version "Die Textualität des Koran" in Abu Zayd, *Gottes Menschenwort*.)

596   Abu Zayd, *Reformation of Islamic Thought*, 54.

597   Hildebrandt, *Neo-Muʿtazilismus?* 209.

598   „Wenn der Koran nicht ewig ist, dann ist er in einem ganz bestimmten Kontext erschaffen worden, und die Botschaft, die er enthält, muss in diesem Kontext verstanden werden. Diese Sichtweise lässt Raum für die Neuinterpretation des religiösen Gesetzes, denn das Wort Gottes muss in seinem Geist, nicht in seinem Wortlaut verstanden werden." (Abu Zayd, *Gottes Menschenwort*, 86–7)

2. Gadamer and Abu Zayd

Since Abu Zayd studied in the USA he continued to engage with the thought of H.G. Gadamer.[599] It is not my task to analyse whether Abu Zayd's reception of Gadamer is adequate or holistic, but to show what the main ideas are that Abu Zayd has received from him and which he incorporated into his view of Quranic interpretation.

From Gadamer derives the general notion of a critical but appreciative attitude towards tradition which influences our perception of the world. For Quranic exegesis this means that the reader brings these influences into the process of understanding. In addition there exist vast layers of previous Quranic interpretations, which can influence one's understanding.[600] With the awareness of pre-concepts and the influences of tradition comes the understanding that no comprehension is absolutely objective. In contrast, schools and thinkers in Islam have through many centuries proclaimed an ideology-free and absolutely objective understanding (in fact many 'absolute' understandings) of the Quran.[601] Such claims assume utter independence from history and tradition. In opposition to these claims Abu Zayd refers to Gadamer who "teaches us humility." Abu Zayd asserts: "Wir sollen uns darüber bewusst sein, dass wir uns in einem Disput mit der Gegenwart und der Vergangenheit befinden, und wie immer auch die Art der Rezeption aussieht, zu der wir uns entscheiden, so ist es nicht die absolute Wahrheit. Ich glaube, dass wir alle diese Lektion von Gadamer begreifen müssen."[602]

However, in the context of exegesis of revealed scriptures the need felt by exegetes to derive a normative understanding is understandable. So if Abu Zayd does not believe in the possibility of making absolute truth claims, which alternative does he offer? Abu Zayd does allow for the idea that some sort of truth in the understanding process is generated. He reflects on Gadamer's description of the encounter between

---

599   Abu Zayd specifically engaged with *Wahrheit und Methode*. In that period Abu Zayd read also various other works by Heidegger, Ricœur, Jacobson et al. and he found similarities between their interests and those of Islamic scholars like Ibn Arabi, Jurjani, and others. He found that for him the borders between Islamic and Western philosophy started to melt.

       As minor remark it might be worth mentioning, that within the Ankara School the Heidelberg scholar is called "Imam Gadamer" which indicates high respect paid towards him by modern Muslim thinkers. (Cf. Spiewak, "Allahs scheuer Bote: Ömer Özsoy," 3). Also Rahman realized the importance of Gadamer's thought on the tight links between legal and theological hermeneutics. Therefore he reflected briefly on the implications, also those arising from both Gadamer's and Emilio Betti's philosophies.

600   Abu Zayd, "Über die Hermeneutik und Gadamer und das arabisch-islamische Erbe." Reflecting on Gadamer Abu Zayd states "I have an ideology and I profess it, and so I observe it and limit its influence on me. In this important point I am [to] Gadamer very thankful."

601   cf. Abu Zayd, *Politik und Islam*, 59–61.

602   Abu Zayd, "Über die Hermeneutik und Gadamer und das arabisch-islamische Erbe." – "We should be conscious of the fact, that we are in a dispute with the present and the past, and whatever the kind of reception we agree upon looks like, it is not the absolute truth. I think, we all have to understand this lesson of Gadamer."

reader and art work which results in the emergence of individual truths.[603] Abu Zayd in this way can make use of the notion of relative truth.[604]

Another parallel between Abu Zayd and Gadamer is that both claim that entering the understanding process will leave one changed. Gadamer holds that "to reach an understanding with one's partner in a dialogue is not merely a matter of total self-expression and the successful assertion of one's own point of view, but a transformation into a communion, in which we do not remain what we were."[605] It is remarkable that Gadamer and Abu Zayd both attribute life changing forces to the engagement not only with human beings, but also with art, text and music. In addition to this, Abu Zayd attributes importance to the linguisticality with which humans express their thoughts and beliefs about the world. He emphasizes that the way we use language can change the way we live and understand the world. It can change the world.[606]

It is important to note that he makes a distinction between one's own knowledge (e.g. pre-concepts, expectations) and the otherness of what is found in the text. This is reminiscent of Abu Zayd's request for distinguishing human and divine sphere,[607] human knowledge and divine will. Despite this differentiation, Gadamer and Abu Zayd

---

603 A similar point is made by Hildebrandt, who explores influences on Abu Zayd. He recognizes that Gadamer understands truth to be "in opposition to a stagnated form [and transforms] into a space-and-time-bound, hence relative issue." („[...] die aus dem Kunstwerk herausgelesene Wahrheit im Gegensatz zu einer feststehenden Form [wird] zu einer orts- und zeitgebundenen, also relativen Angelegenheit.") (Hildebrandt, *Neo-Mu'tazilismus?* 389). Hildebrandt refers here to Abu Zayd's article *Iskaliyat al-qira'a wa-aliyat at-ta'wil* (*The Problematic of Reading and the Method of Interpretation*), Kairo (*al-Hai'a al-misriya al amma li-l-kitāb*), here cited after 2nd edition: Beirut/Casablanca (*al-Markaz at-taqafi al-arabi*) 1994, 38–42.

604 Felix Körner illustrates the reception of Gadamer's hermeneutic by representatives of the *Ankara School*. He describes how truth claims are results of individual encounter. "Dealing with texts cannot be split up into three separate acts of understanding, interpreting and applying. Just as in the case of a musician, actualising the text is identical to 'interpreting' it. Interpreting a text is to understand its truth claim in the interpreter's own perspective." Körner, "Turkish Theology Meets European Philosophy," 807. Körner's discussion of the *Ankara School* shows that Abu Zayd is not alone amongst modern Muslim theologians in considering Gadamer's approach.

605 Gadamer, *Truth and Method*, 341.

606 For example he points out that the gender-friendly use of language in English is a reflection of the changed perception on gender and the drive towards real gender equality. In Abu Zayd's book *Islam and Politics: Critique of the Religious Discourse* I find indications for this idea of transformation. To this transformation Abu Zayd links the hope that the interpreter will adequately refer to the present realities, hence change attitude towards the surrounding environment. He assumes that rational Quran exegesis leads to a more adequate relationship between humankind and present time. He even rests his hopes for an emergence of ethics on this theory. He says: "If rationality is broadened to include all human creative faculties of cognition, [...] it will also lead to humanistic spirituality in addition to universal ethics." (Völker, *Rationalität und Islam*, 95)

607 Abu Zayd does not support the distinction between the human and divine sphere to such an extent that one might think humans were unable to communicate with God. This latter thought was mainly developed by the scholars 'Ašᶜarī, Schafii and al-Ġazālī. Abu Zayd is opposed to this so called 'ideology of the middle' (*al-idiyulugiya*

plead for the merging between our current understanding and the otherness of the text and both locate this event in the living dialogue. The human mind interacts with its subject of interpretation and lets the subject speak (Gadamer: "*Sprechenlassen*", "*Zur Sprache kommen lassen*") through the interpreter. The meaning is not detached from the interpreter. Still, the interpreter is not a mere tool but takes part in the production of meaning vis-à-vis the text.

Some might argue that Abu Zayd's attempts to free the Quran from old layers of interpretation would contradict Gadamer's demand for the recognition of pre-conceptions. But Abu Zayd does not want to radically free Quranic exegesis from the history of former interpretations; to the contrary, he wants to consider them and their techniques and evaluate them with regard to their modernizing potentials. He intends to examine their compatibility (if possible) with what he believes to be an adequate approach to the Quran. Also, he pleads for keeping the mind open to non-Islamic hermeneutical and literary approaches that could enable refreshing understandings of the Quran. Former interpretations are of course products of their time. Only a new hermeneutic can do justice to the fact that many Muslims live in contemporary also non-Islamic contexts.

3. Exegesis and Hermeneutics

Although Abu Zayd does not offer a comprehensive exegesis of the Quran, he does provide thematic interpretations of selected Quranic verses. Examples of his interpretations will illustrate the application of aforementioned terminology and methods. Let us recall what those were. The underlying principle of all exegesis is the rational approach. This includes a critical reassessing of heritage and tradition (*turāth*), and the practice of *ta'wīl* beyond *tafsīr*. The practical steps leading to *ta'wīl* are the categorization of fundamental and exceptional verses, the distinction between meaning and significance, and the reading of the Quran towards its *maqsad*, namely justice. Abu Zayd applies a literary reading.[608] In chapter III we were introduced to his interpretation

---

 al wasatiya) that does allow a very pessimistic view towards history. (Cf Völker, *Rationalität und Islam*, 70; Kermani, *Das Konzept* wahy, 99)

608 The literary reading entails amongst others the study of etymology, metaphorical expressions, comparing historical genres, historical language comprehension, and the discerning of voices of the Quranic discourses. In addition, Abu Zayd emphasizes the "artistic effects" of the Quran's "poetic language" (Abu Zayd, "The Qur'anic Concept of Justice," §6). However he points out that the Quran should not be categorized as pure artwork. (Abu Zayd, *Reformation of Islamic Thought*, 55). Kermani explains: "Each work of art conveys information through a system of signs. This places it as a 'text' within a specific language system, despite the fact that works of art include both verbal and non-verbal texts. Hence each artistic text 'behaves as a kind of living organism which has a feedback channel to the reader and thereby instructs him.' It conveys 'different information to different readers in proportion to each one's comprehension'" (Kermani, "From Revelation to Interpretation," 173). The Quran's divine origin must be kept in mind at all times, without developing an over-emphasizing of its sacredness. The text must remain approachable for human reason. Although the Quran is of polyphonic structure, its voices must be understood as tools of the Divine to communicate its message. Abu Zayd prefers to speak of the Quran as discourse, as we have discovered already in chapter II. He says: „Um ganz exakt zu

of *waḥy* as found in his book *mafhūm an-nās*.[609] I will now look at some examples of Abu Zayd's interpretation by concentrating on the following themes:[610] Justice, *fiṭra*, gender equality and verses regarding polygamy, clothing, superiority, and beating.

3.1 Justice

Justice is the "central Qur'anic concept."[611] To arrive at this conclusion it helps to analyse the *jahl* which Islam came to oppose. As we have seen above, by applying archaeological linguistics Abu Zayd shows that *jahl* meant at that time "lack of controlling emotions." This lack allowed for injustice and was primarily responsible for the stagnation of culture and society. Hence essential principles of Islam were "the appeal to reason and the rejection of injustice and the *jahl*."[612] Abu Zayd concludes hence the purpose of the Quran: It is a manual for how to oppose *jahl* and aspire towards justice.

---

sein, sollte man sagen: Der Koran ist eine Komposition aus diversen Diskursen," and „[m]it 'Stimmen' sind hier schließlich keine realen Stimmen gemeint, die sich verbal äußern, sondern fiktionale Stimmen, die einen bestimmten Sinn transportieren. Bezogen auf den Koran als Offenbarungstext mag das zunächst etwas verwirrend sein – aber nur, wenn man die Rede vom Koran als Wort Gottes wörtlich nimmt; wenn man den Koran durch und durch als eine Rede Gottes versteht, der als einziger Sprecher zu seinen Zuhörern spricht. Dem ist aber nicht so. Der Koran in seiner Gesamtheit ist die Kommunikation zwischen dem Göttlichen und den Menschen. Darum ist streng genommen sogar der Begriff 'Diskurs' dem des Textes vorzuziehen." "To be completely accurate, one should say: The Quran is a composition of various discourses, and "with 'voices' is finally not meant real voices, which express themselves verbally, but fictional voices, which transport a certain sense. Referring to the Quran as a text of revelation, this may initially be a bit confusing – but only, if we take the speech of the Quran to be literally; if one understands the Quran through and through as a speech of God, who speaks as only speaker to his audience. But this is not so. The Quran in its entirety, is the communication between the divine and the human. Therefore, strictly speaking, the term 'discourse' is to be preferred from the term 'text.'" (Abu Zayd, *Mohammed und die Zeichen Gottes*, 66)

609   Given that in chapter II, Abu Zayd 3 (Humanity and Historicity) we have discovered his stance on interpreting Quranic terms referring to metaphysical entities like *the preserved tablet* (and the *throne of God* etc.) as metaphors, (cf. Zayd, *Politik und Islam*, 166; Abu Zayd, *Gottes Menschenwort*, 94–5) these interpretations of *waḥy* and *al-lawḥ al-maḥfūz* are not repeated here.

610   I mainly draw on following sources *Politik und Islam*, "The Qur'anic Concept of Justice," *Mohammed und die Zeichen Gottes*, and his article "Historizität. Der missverstande Begriff" (*mafhum ‚al-Tarikhiya' al-muftara ‚alaih*), which can be found in Abu Zayd, *Gottes Menschenwort*.

611   Abu Zayd, "The Qur'anic Concept of Justice," §33.

612   "Eine der Hauptursachen för die allgemeine Stagnation waren damals zweifellos die auf Ungerechtigkeit (*djahl*) basierenden sozialen Beziehungen. Zu den wesentlichen Prinzipien, die der Islam zur Überwindung dieser Realität einsetzte, gehörte die Berufung auf die Vernunft und die Ablehnung der Ungerechtigkeit und des *djahl*." "One of the main causes of the general stagnation were at that time undoubtedly the social relations which were based on injustice (*djahl*). Included in the essential principles, which Islam utilized in overcoming this reality, was the appeal to reason and the rejection of injustice and the *djahl*." (Abu Zayd, *Politik und Islam*, 59)

The Quranic concept of justice has many facets. One is its cosmological scope, which Abu Zayd tries to prove by reading 16:90 and 3:18. The first verse reads: "Surely God bids to justice and good-doing and giving to kinsmen; and He forbids indecency, dishonour, and insolence, admonishing you, so that haply you will remember."[613] According to this verse, God ordains 'justice' (*ʿadl*) and 'good conduct' (*iḥsān*).[614] The latter Abu Zayd understands as 'doing the utmost possible good.'[615] This doing of the good and the order of justice are not addressing a specific object. Abu Zayd concludes "that absence of a specified grammatical object gives the verb 'ordain' a scope of semantic infinity."[616] This semantic infinity seems to imply the nature of *iḥsān* and *ʿadl* as unrestricted or unlimited. Abu Zayd identifies a semantic relation between *iḥsān* and *ʿadl*. He locates *iḥsān* "on the highest grade of God's service, even higher than the ordinary rank of faith. If *iḥsān* and *ʿadl* are so associated, the position of *iḥsān*, should semantically be attributed to *ʿadl*."[617]

Another characteristic of God's justice is its balance. Thus is expressed in verses 55:7–9 which describe God's justice in "the metaphoric image of 'scale' [*mizan*]" according to which all creation is balanced. The verses go: "and heaven – He raised it up, and set the Balance. (8) (Transgress not in the Balance, (9) and weigh with justice, and skimp not in the Balance.)." It is said that God brought balance which humankind ought to preserve. That the Quran uses poetic language, describing God's justice as *mizan* indicates for Abu Zayd: "[The implication in such a poetic style is] that *mizan* does not symbolize only justice on earth, but it could also symbolize Divine Justice manifested in everything."[618] Abu Zayd concludes from the poetic nature of the term *mizan* the universality of God's justice, its manifestation in all creation.[619] He specifies this poetic nature of the term *mizan* as metaphor. Abu Zayd explains: "In Sure 11

---

613   Q. 16:90.

614   "The Qur'ān also uses the term *ʿadl* but relatively rarely (only fourteen times in the sense of justice or equity) and in a much broader fashion. While God's words are described as *ʿadl* in q 6:115, more common is the use of *ʿadl* or its verbal derivatives to mean equal treatment of wives or disputants (q 4:3, 58, 129; 5:8; 42:15; 49:9)." (Brockopp, "Justice and Injustice," EQ); *Iḥsān* is one of the Quranic terms for piety (compare with the concept *taqwa*, which is emphasized by Rahman). (Kinberg, "Piety," EQ)

615   *Iḥsān* appears in various forms in seventy Quranic verses. Cf. Sachiko/Chittick. *The Vision of Islam*, 269.

616   "It is remarkable in this verse that the order to do justice and to do the best is not addressed to any addressee not to man nor to the believers, as is the case in other verses, which signify an overall comprehensive, or rather cosmological, ordinance. The absence of a specified grammatical object gives the verb 'ordain' a scope of semantic infinity." (Abu Zayd, "The Qur'anic Concept of Justice," §35.)

617   Abu Zayd, "The Qur'anic Concept of Justice," These two sentences imply numerous ideas. First it is reminiscent of the Muʿtazila notion of justice being the second highest principle of God (after *tawḥīd* / unity). Abu Zayd introduces this idea however through the argument that *iḥsān* is a connotation of *ʿadl*, hence adds an ethical dimension – namely moral conduct – to the term.

618   Abu Zayd, "The Qur'anic Concept of Justice," §42.

619   Abu Zayd, *Mohammed und die Zeichen Gottes*, 184: "Das Ausbalancieren, das Geben des "rechten Maßes" und ganz allgemein der Topos der Gerechtigkeit sind zentral fuer die Weltsicht des Korans." – "The Balancing, giving the "right measure" and, more generally, the topos of justice are central to the worldview of the Quran."

beispielsweise wird die Verpflichtung des Kaufmanns, sein Handelspartner nicht zu betrügen, als Beispiel für die moralische Pflicht per se aufgeführt: 85. O mein Volk! Gebt rechtes Maß und Gewicht und enthaltet den Leuten nichts vor und richtet auf Erden kein Unheil an." This confirms that Abu Zayd means by the poetic nature of a term that it is a metaphor or linguistic expression which refers beyond the immediate connotation. This leads us to think about the metaphorical reading of ambiguous verses. Abu Zayd evidently reads metaphors such as the preserved table or the throne of God, and other anthropomorphic descriptions of God in a symbolic way. Those terms then do refer to a (supposedly) real fact, but they do not refer to the object they literally denote. With regard to anthropomorphism and angels, Abu Zayd even goes beyond the metaphorical understanding, by suggesting that these ideas are remains of polytheistic beliefs: "Wir finden einen Nachhall dieser vielen Götter in den Engeln oder auch in Gottes Attributen."[620] Abu Zayd agrees with those theologians (e.g. the Muʿtazila) who find that a literal reading of God's attributes leads to a polytheistic notion,[621] or in other words it violates the principle of *tawhīd* (oneness).

3.2 Doing Justice in Accordance with fiṭra

One way for the Quran to oppose *jahl* was to invoke *fiṭra*, which Abu Zayd defines as "divine law inherent in every individual soul."[622] It is the human inner state which ought to resemble God's spirit of ultimate justice. Ideally *fiṭra* will carry into society through each individual's thought and practice. In a way that recalls Rahman's exegesis. Abu Zayd explains the "inner nature" of the Quran as the covenant between God and humankind which constitutes God's justice towards creation. The Quran is a reminder (*dhikr*) of God's name and that humankind ought to praise God,[623] and a memento of the pacts established between humankind and God throughout human history. This treaty between God and mankind constitutes the inner state of *fiṭra* ("the divine law inherent in every individual soul.")[624] It is the state within each individual that remembers to adhere to God. Living up to the expectations of *fiṭra* means to do justice to this inner state. Violating *fiṭra* means to violate one's own inner state, and subsequently the pact. Each individual will be judged upon the failure or success to live up to *fiṭra*. It is important here to remark that doing justice in this context means to be just towards one's own self, and not towards other humans. It does not yet imply inter-human, hence social justice.

To support his understanding of justice, Abu Zayd refers to the fall narrative in 7:23 in which Adam and Eve admit having done "injustice to our own souls [...]." Abu Zayd writes: "Judgement is then not based on arbitrary authority, but it is the outcome of

---

620 Abu Zayd, *Mohammed und die Zeichen Gottes*, 101: "In Sura 11, for example, the obligation of the merchant, not to cheat on his trading partner, is displayed as example for the moral duty per se: 85 O my people! Give right measure and weight and do not deprive people and do no evil on earth. We find an echo of these many gods in the angels or also in the attributes of God." Abu Zayd believes that Islamic theologians were inspired to the discussion of God's attributes by Christian disputes about Jesus's nature (Cf. Abu Zayd, ibid., 80–1).

621 Abu Zayd, *Mohammed und die Zeichen Gottes*, 101.

622 Abu Zayd, "The Qur'anic Concept of Justice," §10.

623 Abu Zayd, *Gottes Menschenwort*, 138.

624 Abu Zayd, "The Qur'anic Concept of Justice," §10.

every individual's self-awareness or unawareness of his own inherent soul. The story of Adam and Eve as portrayed in the Quranic narrative sets this example." Humans are absolutely responsible for all injustice done to *fiṭra*: "The concept of self-injustice, *ẓulm al-nafs* is always associated in the Qur'an with confirming the Divine justice and strongly negating any sense of injustice to be attributed to God [...]."[625] Abu Zayd indicates here that the Quran consciously shifts responsibility for injustice to the individual and away from God. God is of course ultimately just and will judge the individual upon her treatment of *fiṭra* in this context. If injustice occurs it is imposed by mankind upon itself, or in the case of individuals upon their own soul.

Abu Zayd's emphasis of this Quranic co-occurrence of the terms self-injustice (*ẓulm al-nafs*) with God's ultimate justice has two implications. First it shows the difference between fallible humankind and infallible God, and secondly it reflects the freedom of choice in decision making that is given to all humans. Hence it serves as argument against determinism. The combination of these two implications entail that humankind is able to be unjust to its own *fiṭra* because it is given free will. However, Abu Zayd is very careful with making decisive statements about whether the Quran promotes determinism or not. For him the Quran has dynamic character and cannot be frozen into definite answers to particular questions, and "der Koran ist nun einmal kein theologisches Traktat!"[626]

3.3 Gender Equality in Fundamental Verses

Although Islam aims at installing a just society, it is at the same time often subject to controversial critique of its alleged gender inequality. The legal and social situation of women, however, differs from one Muslim country to another. Abu Zayd does not focus on specific cases, although he sometimes refers to cases from his home country, Egypt. Instead he puts forward a style of interpretation that would administer the Quranic principle of justice.

As we have seen, Abu Zayd believes the Quran's spirit to aim at an ideal, which is justice. He maintains that an aim (*maqsad*) of the Quran is the ideal of equality, which incorporates not only economic justice but also gender egalitarianism, as aspects of God's justice. "If we communicate with the Quran rightly, we see that the ideal of equality may not yet be realised, but it is in root already entailed, and we can develop this ideal beyond the existing condition."[627] In support of his assumption that the *maqsad* includes gender equality, Abu Zayd argues that the fundamental verses

---

625 Abu Zayd, "The Qur'anic Concept of Justice," §13. He refers to e.g. Q. 2:57; 3:117; 7:60–2, 91,177; 9:36,70; 10:44; 16:33,118; 18:49; 29:40; 30:9 in which injustice is attributed not to God but to other factors. As examples of verses that speak against original sin and pro self-responsibility Abu Zayd mentions Q. 2:48, 14:51, and 16:111 (Cf. Abu Zayd, *Mohammed und die Zeichen Gottes*, 209).

626 "The Quran is once and for all not a theological treatise!" Abu Zayd understands that verses, which seem to hint at predestination (e.g. Q. 7:70, 46:22, and 6:34–35) were revealed in the context of "provocation and answer, not a context, in which norms or theses of theology or weltanschauung shall be established." (Abu Zayd, *Mohammed und die Zeichen Gottes*, 84–5) Verses regarding determinism must be read in their complex contexts.

627 Abu Zayd, *Mohammed und die Zeichen Gottes*, 155: "Wenn wir mit dem Koran richtig kommunizieren, sehen wir, dass das Ideal der Gleichheit zwar noch nicht realisiert,

addressing the creation and fall of humankind, eschatological verses mentioning salvation or punishment, and religiosity in general establish the basic notion of the Quran, namely to support and promote equality.[628] Two examples for this fundamental equality are: First, Adam and Eve are created from one soul (*nafs*) as 49:13 has it.[629] Secondly, Abu Zayd shows that the fundamental Quranic verses as mentioned above in the *fiṭra* debate state equal responsibility for the fall.[630] The fundamental character of gender equality is supported by the importance and generality of verses in whose context males and females are addressed equally. Again, the fundamental verses point towards the Quran's normative dimension, whereas the exceptional verses point towards the historical-situative dimension. If the Quran wanted to establish an inequality amongst humankind and specifically genders, it would have done so through mentioning humankind as unequal in its creation, or in other fundamental affairs.

After the fundamental verses are identified and their support for equality and justice is ascertained, the exceptional verses, which diverge from the fundamental spirit, can be identified. Those then must be understood as contingent phenomena, and not read literally but contextually. However, we need to keep in mind that the exceptional verses at least contain hints towards the normative spirit or direction of the Quran.[631] Abu Zayd writes that there are "scores of indications, which point into the direction of gender equality. I call them indications, because this equality is not fully realised, but the Quran directs beyond the existing state into this direction."[632] Viewing the Quran as a product of culture and language means to acknowledge that it contains reflections on the state of mind and life of the pre-Islamic people. In other words the Quran plants seeds in the heart of the first audience which need to develop over time into its ideal of equality through the following generations of Muslims. In many cases, these exceptional verses brought improvement and Abu Zayd believes that they were meant to lead towards gender equality, since equality is an improvement.[633] These small changes seem to aim at an unhurried re-education of an entire culture, that otherwise confronted with a total "overthrow," would not be able to cope with or would even refuse such sudden changes.[634] Examples of these small changes can be found in the exceptional verses, which Zayd tries to contextualise in order to filter out the *ratio* of their message. Zayd finds that the Quran had to contest pre-Islamic practices, such as burying female babies, granting men unlimited numbers of women, lacking inheritance or divorce rights for women and leaving women in total financial

---

aber im Ansatz schon enthalten ist, und können dieses Ideal über das Bestehende hinaus weiter entwickeln."

628   Abu Zayd, *Mohammed und die Zeichen Gottes*, 151+160.

629   Abu Zayd, "The Qur'anic Concept of Justice," §19. Cf. Abu Zayd, *Mohammed und die Zeichen Gottes*, 149.

630   Abu Zayd, "The Qur'anic Concept of Justice," §12.

631   Abu Zayd, "The Textuality of the Qur'an."

632   ("[...] eine Menge weiterer Hinweise, die in Richtung der Geschlechtergleichheit deuten. Ich nenne es Hinweise, weil diese Gleichheit nicht voll realisiert wird, sondern der Koran über das damals Bestehende in diese Richtung weist." (Abu Zayd, *Mohammed und die Zeichen Gottes*, 156)

633   Abu Zayd, *Mohammed und die Zeichen Gottes*, 156–7. Abu Zayd refers explicitly to Q. 2:229–232.

634   Abu Zayd, *Mohammed und die Zeichen Gottes*, 150.

dependency from males.[635] Against this background "the position of women expressed in the Qur'an, in general, is relatively and historically speaking progressive."[636] Exceptional verses have to be read in different contexts such as 'context of description' or 'context of contest.'[637] Since exceptional verses are to be read in differing contexts they do not serve as optimum material for establishing religious decrees.[638]

Even exceptional verses contain some hint towards the general direction of the Quran. Abu Zayd interprets verses regarding polygamy, clothing, superiority, beating, and heritage in their historical context and concludes that a literal reading can barely find application today since circumstances have changed. For example Abu Zayd shows how the Quran restricts the number of wives. If the Quran wanted to establish polygamy as the ideal marital system, it would not have made the effort to restrict the number to four. Abu Zayd finds that the implementation of this allowance is highly contextualised. The verse was revealed at a time in which many orphans were unprotected and marrying them would allow guardianship and relief from misery.[639] It can be concluded from Abu Zayd's reading that polygamy was not decreed by a fundamental verse; hence it is not an ideal marital model. Referring to an example of a saying of Muhammad, Abu Zayd even considers that polygamy ought to be forbidden.[640] He asserts one can occasionally go beyond the Quran like the early Muslims who practised individual insight in contrast to blind obedience.[641] By this stance we are again reminded that Abu Zayd calls for the primacy of reason.

From the verses which are often consulted in the discussion about women's clothing, Abu Zayd concludes that the text calls females not to use a special new kind of clothing, but their own clothing (in this case robes: *jalābīb*) to cover themselves.[642]

---

635 Abu Zayd, *Mohammed und die Zeichen Gottes*, 158. See for the issue of 'divorce,' ibid, 156; for 'burying females,' ibid, 157. Cf. Abu Zayd, *Politik und Islam*, 97 on the issue 'heritage' and 'dependence.' Y. Rahman writes that the 'context of contest' is "a context where the Qur'an was intended to oppose and change a given situation." He refers to Abū Zayd, *Dawa'ir al-Khawf*, 207–11 (Y. Rahman, *The Hermeneutical Theory of Naṣr Ḥāmid Abu Zayd*, 183)

636 Abu Zayd, "The Qur'anic Concept of Justice," §18. He refers here to verses Q. 30:21–2, and 16:72.which state that differences amongst languages and skin colours are product of God's wisdom (cf. Abu Zayd, *Mohammed und die Zeichen Gottes*, 149).

637 Y. Rahman, *The Hermeneutical Theory of Naṣr Ḥāmid Abu Zayd*, 184. He takes these terms from Abu Zayd, *Dawa'ir al-Khawf*, 212.

638 Abu Zayd, *Mohammed und die Zeichen Gottes*, 160.

639 "Wenn man sich diesen Vers genauer anschaut, merkt man: Im Vordergrund steht hier gar nicht der Wunsch des Mannes nach Polygamie, sondern die Notlage der Waisen." (Abu Zayd. *Mohammed und die Zeichen Gottes*, 152. He refers to Q. 4:2–3)/ cf. Abu Zayd, *Mohammed und die Zeichen Gottes*, 151–2. Referring to Q. 4 Abu Zayd asserts: "The name of the chapter is misleading, because Muslims realized the subject matter rather than the content of the chapter when they decided to name it *al-Nisa'* (women). If the content were taken into consideration, it would have been named 'Justice' *(al-'Adl)*." (Abu Zayd, "The Qur'anic Concept of Justice," §16–7)

640 Abu Zayd refers to a non-Quranic narrative depicting Muhammad as refusing Ali, his daughter's (Fatima) husband, to marry a second woman in order to spare Fatima from hardship.

641 Abu Zayd, *Mohammed und die Zeichen Gottes*, 158.

642 For example Q. 33:59 "O Prophet, say to thy wives and daughters and the believing women, that they draw their veils close to them; so it is likelier they will be known,

This had the function of recognition and protection from harassment, which was at that time practised towards female slaves who were generally not allowed to wear the *jalābīb*, and treated as lacking rights. Slave women and free women were easily recognized by their dress and against this background Muslim women should also use a specific dress to be recognized as *muslima*. Since in most countries slavery is abolished and legal equality of physical integrity is granted to both women and men, veiling in these contexts seems no longer applicable.[643] Even though Abu Zayd accepts the interpretation that a specific dress code might have helped to distinguish Muslim women from others, he still thinks that this measurement was for a temporary purpose. One cannot conclude that Muslim women today have to dress differently, apart from dressing decently which the Quran also calls for.[644]

Often discussed in controversies regarding Islam is he alleged superiority of men over women. One particular verse (4:34) offers grounds for this perception by stating that men are the 'managers' of women.[645] This is, Abu Zayd claims, only a description or observation of the current socio-cultural state in seventh-century Arabia.[646] Nevertheless, it is often used by orthodoxy also today to indicate that men should be superior to women. Abu Zayd says that the difficult term *qawwāmūna* (which is often translated as "having authority and responsibility") must be understood as 'having financial strength and responsibility.'[647] Such business was usually in the hands of males, so if the males had more financial means they need to give to their wives and provide financial security. If today the financial strength is provided by the woman then the responsibility is in her hands.[648]

---

and not hurt. God is All-forgiving, All-compassionate." in Abu Zayd, *Mohammed und die Zeichen Gottes*, 161. He refers also to Q. 24:31.

643   Abu Zayd, *Mohammed und die Zeichen Gottes*, 162.

644   "Was der Koran gebietet, sind Anstand und eine gewisse Schamhaftigkeit in der Präsentation des eigenen Körpers in der Öffentlichkeit. Dieses Gebot gilt aber nicht nur für Frauen, sondern auch für Männer, und damit ist kein bestimmter Dresscode verbunden." – "The Quran dictates decency and certain modesty in the presentation of one's own body in public. This requirement applies not only to women but also to men; this does not imply a certain dress code." (Abu Zayd, *Mohammed und die Zeichen Gottes*, 161)

645   The verse reads: "Men are the managers of the affairs of women for that God has preferred in bounty one of them over another, and for that they have expended of their property. Righteous women are therefore obedient, guarding the secret for God's guarding. And those you fear may be rebellious admonish; banish them to their couches, and beat them. If they then obey you, look not for any way against them; God is All-high, All-great."

646   Abu Zayd, *Mohammed und die Zeichen Gottes*, 160.

647   Abu Zayd, *Mohammed und die Zeichen Gottes*, 159.

648   Y. Rahman, *The Hermeneutical Theory of Naṣr Ḥāmid Abu Zayd*, 184. Abu Zayd also refers to another part of the sura which is often used to 'prove' the superiority of men over women: "God has given to some more than others and with what they spend out of their own money." However Abu Zayd points out that the phrase "God has given to some more than others" must also be read in the above described context of financial strength. In addition the sentence does not identify whether which gender has been given more by God. 'What is given' (*infiq*, Engl.: expenditure) Abu Zayd also interprets as monetary means. In some translations one can find an artificial addition to the sentence: "for the women," hence it reads "spend out of their own

The other part of the verse is even more controversial: "If you fear high-handedness from your wives, remind them [of the teachings of God], then ignore them when you go to bed, then hit them." Some feminist exegetes translate the word Arabic word *daraba* as "to keep aloof." However, Abu Zayd reads the word in its literal sense of "to beat." He states that this practice is culturally conditioned and does not present a Quranic ideal. It must be understood as a product of its 'social reality' in which "exists no equality" yet.[649]

A contextual interpretation of the verse might not seem to carry any implications for today's believers. But as we have seen, Abu Zayd believes that even the exceptional verses carry messages about justice. In this particular verse this message can be detected in lacking the mentioning of gender which leaves open the interpretation that whoever has the monetary means must take care of the spouse. Abu Zayd's interpretation shows that in this verse the seed is planted for the notion of equal rights under equal circumstances. Nonetheless, there remains the interpretation of the part of the verse that mentions the beating. Does Abu Zayd imply that this part is simply historically conditioned and that it does not entail any lesson we could learn from today? If so, he applies radical criticism, rejecting a part of the scripture as non-applicable and hence false in the eyes of the contemporary reader. But until now he has not alluded to such a possibility of radical criticism. If a verse was, as he sometimes suggests, merely an observation of the practices of the time, then one could justify discarding it. But this particular verse is not formulated as an observation but as an imperative. In the end Abu Zayd does not deliver a satisfying solution. Even if Abu Zayd asserts that one can "often also extract a message from verses, which a priori do not seem to fit into contemporary time [...],"[650] it seems to be not always the case that exceptional verses have something to say to today. Hence the option remains open to actually discard the beating verse in total for the sake of following the Quranic principle of justice. After all Abu Zayd says 'we have the right to go beyond the Quran with its own ideals.'[651]

In some aspects of the Quranic language Abu Zayd detects an improvement towards gender equality. As suggested above, sura 4 ought to be read in a specific historical context in which many orphans were deprived of their properties because they lacked protection (hence the allowance for polygamy). In the same context the Quran establishes a progressive rule regarding heritage. Abu Zayd analyses verse 4:11 where it says: "God charges you, concerning your children: to the male the like of the

---

money (for the women)." (Es muss in "üblichen Übersetzungen ergänzt werden, dass dieses Vermögen für die Frauen auszugeben ist." [Abu Zayd, *Mohammed und die Zeichen Gottes*, 159]) Here the linguistic feature of not using a specific gender in the Quranic wording helps to enable a modified understanding in changed contexts. This means that even if at that time women were not earning money outside the household, they might do so today and moreover might be the main earner. If one understands the sentence to indicate male gender in superiority over the females, Abu Zayd also here suggests reading it at least as observation of the situation at the time of revelation and not as a universal decree. Cf. Abu Zayd, *Mohammed und die Zeichen Gottes*, 160.

649   Abu Zayd, *Mohammed und die Zeichen Gottes*, 151+160.
650   Abu Zayd, *Mohammed und die Zeichen Gottes*, 174. Cf. also Abu Zayd, *Gottes Menschenwort*, 89.
651   Abu Zayd, *Mohammed und die Zeichen Gottes*, 165.

portion of two females [...]."[652] He observes that the Quranic language is revolution-
ary in the sense of calling the female share a measure: "Der Anteil der Frau bildet die
Berechnungsgrundlage für das, was dem Mann zukommt, nicht umgekehrt."[653] This
verse war revealed into a world described and dominated by male terminologies, and
establishes a significant improvement of valuation. Now, items –assigned to females –
can be used as measurements of general orientation.[654]

Comparison

In this chapter I attempted to explain main interpretation methods applied by Rahman,
Arkoun and Abu Zayd. I also selected concrete interpretation examples in order to
discern in how far their treatment of the Quran supports their reform ideas.

First it becomes apparent that their expectations of Quranic interpretation differ.
Rahman believes that the Quran delivers a coherent and sufficient message for setting
up a just society. Arkoun and Abu Zayd do not affirm that the Quran ought to be the
basis for a general social order. While Rahman pleads for a Quranic *weltanschauung*
to be the basis for an ideal society, Arkoun and Abu Zayd demand the separation of
state and religion. However both Arkoun and Abu Zayd affirm the importance of
religion for society, but formulate such in terms of sociological function and meaning
for the individual

The differences in these expectations lead toward distinct aims regarding what
the three thinkers hope to achieve through interpretation. Rahman believes that all
verses in the Quran potentially bear messages of significance for today. Hence the
entire Quran needs to be scrutinized and each verse to be read in the spirit of Quran
and interpreted in light of its main rationale, justice amongst humankind. Arkoun on
the other hand analyses the Quran with regard to its psychological implications. He
is interested in how the Quran works with symbols in the attempt to change social
dynamics. These mechanisms Arkoun reckons are still working today, especially in the
search for a Muslim identity. Abu Zayd concentrates on how the first audience might
have understood the messages, in order to conclude that the significance of specific
verses may be perceived differently today, since circumstances have changed. He even
suggests that some verses need to be discarded, or in his terms, that one needs to go
beyond some of the exceptional verses by following the overall spirit of the Quran.

---

652   Arberry, *The Koran Interpreted: A Translation*, 78.
653   Abu Zayd, *Mohammed und die Zeichen Gottes*, 153: "The proportion of the woman
      makes the basis of calculation for that, which belongs to the man, not vice versa."
654   „Der Koran halbiert also nicht den Anteil der Frau, sondern er begrenzt den des
      Mannes und ordnet an: Ein Mann erhält den doppelten Teil dessen, was die Frau er-
      hält – aber nicht mehr! Das sind linguistische Feinheiten, die einem erst bei genauer
      Lektüre auffallen, die uns aber die Richtung anzeigen, in die uns der Koran führen
      will. Solche Details helfen uns, das koranische Verständnis von Gerechtigkeit zu
      erkennen." "The Quran does not halve the proportion of the woman, but it limits the
      proportion of the man and the Quran proclaims: A man receives double the amount
      of what the woman receives – but no more! These are linguistic subtleties that only
      become obvious upon closer reading, but they show us the direction, into which the
      Quran wants to lead us. Such details help us to recognize the Quranic concept of
      justice." (Abu Zayd, *Mohammed und die Zeichen Gottes*, 153.)

A good example of the need to discard a verse is the failure of all Abu Zayd's other interpretation methods when faced with the "beating verse."

All three recognize the importance of understanding the circumstances of revelations in order to reconstruct how the first audience might have understood the messages. Rahman and Abu Zayd assert that the revelations came to oppose an unjust society and hence both argue that the primary goal of the Quran is to improve social situations. For Arkoun the "concept of revelation" entails elements of liberation which originally intended to free the people from tribal codes and transform them into a group which is now responsible to a higher principle (namely that of God and the covenant). However I find that the path leading to Arkoun's conclusions from his reading of the selected verses is obscure. We see that in Arkoun's and Abu Zayd's interpretation of the Quran they seem influenced by the basic notion, namely that the Quran brought a positive message that still bears significance for contemporary societies.

None of the three speak of certainties in 'getting it right,' in the sense of actually capturing the divine will. Rahman and Abu Zayd nevertheless argue that interpretations that violate what they have perceives as the spirit of Quran, must be erring. Rahman, although he believes that a nation state inspired by the Quran has the best chance to establish an ideal society, says that one must always practice *taqwā* and never speak of certainties. We are reminded that he refuses the notion that one could know to be elected by God to be amongst the knowing ones.

Looking at concrete examples of interpretation we find that Rahman tries to establish the ideas of equality through the reading of the Quran. Every reading of Rahman is geared towards supporting his basic idea that the Quran promotes justice and does not allow for the belief in determinism. This reading becomes problematic once Rahman deals with contrary verses, such as those we discussed with reference to determinism and free will. We find that he fails to address the problem that, according to his reading, the Quran says some people lack the capacity of faith. This seems, at least, to violate Rahman's principle of justice, because it allows for the idea that people lack this capacity for reasons outside their control. However he grants that the source of the Quran is the same for other scriptures (he refers to Judaism and Christianity), hence his account has some potential for inter-religious dialogue, at least amongst the three major monotheistic religions.

Nonetheless, we see that Rahman argues for his reform ideas exclusively from within an Islamic perspective. This seems due to his idea that the Quran brings the ideal guidance for societies. The idea that every decision must be geared towards what the Quranic spirit suggests might imply a kind of exclusivism to Rahman's thinking. One wonders why he does not address the possibility of clashes of values that emerge from the different understandings of the scriptures that according to him have the same origin. Arkoun and Abu Zayd are not so much exposed to this critique since they do not claim any kind of ultimate religious comprehensiveness for the role of the Quran.

Rahman does not find much support in the Quran for his concrete reform ideas. This is because there is not enough material in the Quran to provide the details of how to run a society. However, he interprets the term *shūrā* as a sufficient basis for a democratic structure. Abu Zayd, however, debates whether the principle of *shūrā* as it was practised in seventh-century Arabia could be developed into a modern mode. And he does not see the need to seek support for democracy in the Quran. This is because he first of all regards the Quran as a spiritual text not as a manual for today's society. Like Arkoun, Abu Zayd uphold the primate of universal human rights.

Which are the concrete interpretation techniques the three thinkers employ?

Rahman's innovative re-interpretation of the exegesis principle 'abrogation' (*naskh*) comes down to him reading the Quran in light of its spirit. In that he is consistent with his own premise, that each verse potentially entails a message that contributes towards the guidance of humankind. Rahman often relates to the experiences and situations of the Prophet during the time of revelation, in order to conclude the meaning of specific verses. Hence he relies often on secondary literature, particularly with biographical material (*sīra*). At the same time he is very critical of the traditional reliance on secondary literature, which had led Islamic scholarship of the past to neglect the Quran.

Abu Zayd also reads the Quran along with such secondary literature. We have seen how Abu Zayd tries to reconstruct Muhammad's revelation experience by consulting hadith literature. Rahman and Abu Zayd seem a bit torn between their use of secondary literature and their proclamation of the centrality of the Quran. Both rely on secondary sources in the course of reconstructing the original circumstances of revelations. However intensely they promote reading the Quran in its own light, they do not belong to the 'Quran alone' movement. Arkoun is also sceptical about the chronologies of the Quranic verses, but in practice he too relies on them. In addition he doubts the infallibility of the *ṣaḥāba*'s memories and hence must be sceptical about the hadith. Nevertheless he promotes the idea that we should consider all material that could shed light on the original circumstances (semiological environment). All three thinkers therefore have an unclear relationship with secondary literature on the Quran. In other words, their call to understanding the Quran first of all in its original meaning for the first audience necessitates the use of secondary literature.

The degree to which they refer to Quranic material differs. Rahman and Abu Zayd refer to numerous verses in their interpretation of specific themes of the Quran. Both also put forward suggestions for categorizing verses. Rahman's distinction between *ideal* and *contingent* finds echo in Abu Zayd's categorization of verses into *fundamental* and *exceptional*. A difference though is that Rahman speaks of the two aspects of each verse, while Abu Zayd speaks of two types of verses. However in their interpretations they do not warrant their specific selection of verses, other than recognizing their relative relevancy. Arkoun justifies the importance of certain verses with reference to their chronologies. However, considering that he is sceptical about the scholarly chronologies, his verse selection also seems a little arbitrary.

All three refer to the Quranic use of (pre-Islamic) words and how their definitions might have been altered through this different use (e.g. *qadar*, *waḥy*, and *shūrā*). In addition, they embrace the belief that it is part of the Quranic didactic to give these terms a new meaning throughout the course of history.[655]

In the end, none of them puts forward an entirely systematic interpretation. However, Rahman's interpretation as established in *Major Themes* seems the most comprehensive. Arkoun does not even intend to deliver a systematic interpretation, although he calls for one. Abu Zayd's interpretations are mostly scattered around in his essays; he does not collect them in one work.

---

655   They are different but similar in nature to the pre-Islamic meaning. They are similar enough to be understood by the audience but are invested by slightly new meanings, so a change of comprehension occurs in the listeners.

Chapter VI – Conclusion

The challenges faced by religions in a changing world are numerous, and over time the Islamic faith has undergone various modifications. They might be initiated from within or imposed from outside. As a result the perception of what 'being a Muslim' entails changes over time. For all three of the thinkers I have studied, such modifications are essential for a religion that desires to have significance today. Religion, they contend, needs to adapt to the social and mental dynamics of reality. Stagnation of religious thought is likely to make religions irrelevant for society. Rahman, Arkoun and Abu Zayd acknowledge the powers of social change and their impact on religious thinking. As a result they contribute to the discussion about what Islam is and what it has to offer for Muslim societies today. However sceptical all three thinkers are with the range of answers given to the challenges of modernity from within Islamic circles, they affirm that religion has a place in society. Even more, and this is of chief interest to this inquiry, the three intellectuals maintain that Islam can add to the improvement of the human condition.

Not only are Rahman, Arkoun and Abu Zayd hopeful that Islam will continue having significance, they believe that Islam in itself carries power for transformation. They locate this force for change also within the Quran. In order to release this power, the three thinkers reckon, a certain approach to the Quran is required. The versions of this approach, as offered by Rahman, Arkound and Abu Zayd, are the subject of this thesis.

All three thinkers arrive at distinct views. Rahman and Abu Zayd believe that, in general, dynamical modification is a prerequisite for society to develop closer towards what God intended for creation. The main goal of creation, they say, is that of striving towards a just society. According to Abu Zayd humankind ought to contribute to the completion of God's creation. And for Rahman humankind ought to develop towards the fulfilment of God's ideal, justice on earth. Revelation and Muhammad's ministry were only the beginning of a long journey. Humankind is the central actor within creation and so it is understood as the central addressee of revelation, prophecy and religious guidance. Arkoun, from his socio-psychological perspective, sees that the Quran contains ideas that can lead to individualisation, and the development of an autonomous and responsible civil society. But to unleash these as 'positive' dynamics from within the Quran, much still needs to be done. Arkoun at all times admits though, that his envisaged project of deconstruction is only the first of a chain of necessary amendments to the larger project of a global humanistic solidarity.

The three thinkers establish that understandings of religion and scripture impact societies on numerous levels (e.g. that of values, and mentalities). This is why they feel an up to date engagement with the Quran, its content and history, and Islamic tradition is paramount for any rethinking of Muslim life today.[656] They promote an intellectual engagement with the Quran's history, interpretations and contents. Such commitment to the Quran ought to go beyond the mere aim of formulating religious doctrines. In contrast, it must be directed at finding ways of dealing with a seventh-century text

---

656 Here their approach to encounter challenges of modernity differs from those answers given by Muslims who believed that religion is the main factor that prevents development of a society.

that claims to be relevant for today's society. Rahman, Arkoun and Abu Zayd then develop ideas about the future of Islam, as it might be established on the basis of what the three thinkers believe to be a valid understanding of the Quran's nature.

The intellectuals examined in this study formulate ideas about the improvement of the human condition. Although they spent much of their work debating Islamic tradition, I have looked less into their critique of Islamic thought than into their hopes derived from the Quran and Islam. The question I have addressed is: How does each thinker understand the Quran and can this understanding lend support to their reform ideas? My investigation has come across numerous ideas of how the three wish to initiate changes in scholarship and society. In these final reflections I will focus on those aspects which seem most significant in view of the contemporary challenges facing Islam. I also attempt to point out parallels and differences in the approaches and conclusions Rahman, Arkoun and Abu Zayd put forward.

Different Expectations towards the Quran

I found that although Rahman, Arkoun and Abu Zayd affirm the importance of understanding the Quran, they vary significantly in their expectations of what the Quran actually offers. The way they view the nature of the Quran determines to what degree they rest their reform hopes on scripture. For example, Rahman's quite uncritical acceptance of traditional narratives of post-revelation transmission and compilation of the Quranic text, allows him to trust in the infallibility of the Quran's wording and authority. Hence the Quran and its interpretation become leading factors for society. In fact, the state that rules society ought to be Islamic. In contrast, Abu Zayd, who acknowledges the difficulties and obscurities concerning the history of the Quran's text, leaves it to faith whether one considers the scripture infallible or not. That he does not believe the Quran to deliver answers for all questions, I suggest, can be regarded as one consequence of his historical critical view. But much more, and Abu Zayd's work clearly supports this: it is not the Quran's primary aim to address all matters of life. Here Rahman's and Abu Zayd's expectations towards the outcome of reading the Quran as a guideline, differ drastically. This difference is of course supported by Abu Zayd's underlying notion that Quran interpretation and any form of religiosity derived from it ought to remain private.

It is here to mention that Arkoun and Abu Zayd do not advocate for the necessity of leading a religious life, and more specific an Islamic life, in order to establish a just and humanistic society. They only argue that the Quran delivers possible tools for this establishment. They do not however believe that the Quran delivers the only means by which a society develops towards humanistic ideals of justice.

Ideas on religiosity, Arkoun and Abu Zayd reckon, should not become norms for society that are imposed on the people by a religious state. And here we discover a parallel of Abu Zayd's to Muhammad Arkoun's thought on religion and state. Arkoun's critical stance, on the evolution of the Quran allows him to reject any certainty that the Quranic words actually represent the original Quranic discourse. For this reason he does not promote any kind of particular religiosity based on the Quran. Even though Arkoun's criticism goes beyond that of Abu Zayd, he upholds that the Quran contains definite dynamics that are worth reconsidering today. As a result of their critical awareness of the human history of the Quranic text, Arkoun and Abu Zayd call for a secular state. Both reason that considering Islam as only source of Muslim identity leads to the distortion or reduction of Islam. Even though Arkoun and Abu Zayd diverge much from Rahman's outlook on the Quran as source for the conduct of society, I have found that even though Rahman proposes an Islamic state system, in his overall thought, the identity of the human as a just and righteous person (not exclusively as a Muslim person) seems paramount. Rahman proclaims that although religion informs identity and contributes to the formulation of values and norms, religion ought not to be the sole source. Still, any 'outside source' which is worth of considerations, needs to comply with the overall scheme of the Quran concerning the just society, as sketched by Rahman.

We find that none of the three's claims for a particular state system, be it religious (Rahman) or secular (Arkoun, Abu Zayd), is able to find support in the Quran by way of/through their Quran interpretation. This seems to come down to the fact that the Quran does not deliver comprehensive material for the creation of a modern state. Abu Zayd (and implicitly Arkoun) recognize this fact and do not claim to deduce all their reform principles from the Quran. Rahman, on the other hand, does appeal to Quranic terms such as *shūrā* in support of modern democratic principles. However it is questionable if this is possible without ignoring the actual practice of *shūrā* at the time of Quranic revelation, and the actual concept alluded to by the. Abu Zayd claims that since the Quran in none of its fundamental verses calls for a specific state system, there is no divinely ordained system. While neither Abu Zayd nor Arkoun can build upon Quranic material in order to justify secularism, still Rahman and Abu Zayd nonetheless argue for democratic structures since those lead to more equality, which conforms to the overarching Quranic ideal of justice. Abu Zayd and Arkoun basically argue for a secular democracy since such a system is based on the autonomous citizen who can make responsible and reflective decisions. In this line of thought, all three thinkers commonly believe in the necessity of education. They argue for an education that combines the best knowledge of the Muslim and non-Muslim realm, or in Arkoun's terms, a holistic education that manages to include the rational discerning of religious beliefs. All three call for the liberation of religious thinking from purely political agendas. At the same time they acknowledge the importance of the state's role in providing education. At the forefront Rahman and Arkoun call for a reformation of state-led education structures and curricula.

Quranic Text in Human Realm

Overall this thesis shows that all three thinkers discuss criteria for the founding of an autonomous populace. In this line of discourse they introduce humanity as the main addressee of revelation. Rahman understands that the Quran's original function is to guide humankind towards a just lifestyle, which eradicates inequality, and establishes social and economic fairness. His understanding of the purpose of the Quran is utterly practical and essentially reality-related. In addition Rahman relies much on the literature on Muhammad's biography in his Quran interpretation. He reads the Quran through the filter of the experiences of the Prophet, who is understood as a fallible human being. However, according to Rahman Muhammad's fallibility did not distort the Quranic messages, but gave them an essentially human expression. This is because the revelations passed through Muhammad's heart, mind and tongue and the Prophetic speech is then a human speech designed to address humankind. Both, Rahman and Abu Zayd emphasise the humanity of Muhammad and his contributions to revelation and prophecy. Nevertheless, both scholars have in common that although they emphasise the fallibility and humanity of the Prophet, they nowhere consider any 'mistakes' by the Prophet in the process of transmitting the divine messages. Understandably such a consideration would not be helpful to their overall project and in addition there is no way of claiming that any of the Prophet's oral statements do not represent the original divine message.

One consequence of a critical view onto the Quran, or a literary reading in the case of Abu Zayd, seems to be the rejection of a literal interpretation of the 'preserved tablet.' With that, most expressively Rahman and Abu Zayd deny the idea of a direct line of authority that originates in the inscrutable divine sphere. Related to the denial of reading the term 'preserved tablet' literally is the acknowledgement of the history and createdness of the Quran. This acknowledgement includes for one the claim that Quranic revelation took place in a specific time and space, and secondly that Quranic text has a history. All three thinkers reflect on this but they put forward different views. The notion of the createdness of the Quran is supported by the three thinker's views on its evolution as either closely linked to the Prophet's mind (Rahman, Abu Zayd) or as a product of diverse oral discourses (Arkoun, Abu Zayd). Furthermore the idea of the createdness of the Quran is sustained by Rahman's and Abu Zayd's metaphorical interpretation of the Quranic term 'preserved tablet.' With their understanding of the tablet, Rahman and Abu Zayd bring the notion of a pre-existing Quran into the human realm. Here a shift of authority occurs, since Rahman and Abu Zayd – in slightly different accounts – think of the Quran as born and preserved in the human heart. Rather than an inscrutable divine reality, the tablet is understood as the inspiration that serves as source of human creativity. This way both argue against accounts of Islam that conclude from the existence of 'the tablet' that the fate of humankind is predetermined. In their metaphorical interpretation they follow the argument of the Mu'tazila who thought that the belief in an entity as eternal and divine as God would involve idolatry. For Rahman and Abu Zayd this 'bringing down to human realm' represents the fact that Muslims today can discern its meaning.

Also common amongst them is the recognition that the Quran contains reflections of the pre-Islamic time and the social circumstance of the revelations. Muslims engaging with the Quran today have to deal with these historically contingent elements. The three thinkers propose different strategies. Rahman grants each verse the potential to entail messages for all times, but his reading in the light of the Quranic ideal of justice allows for a relativization of verses that seem to contradict the Quranic spirit. Abu Zayd makes a similar distinction of verses as Rahman (contingent/ideal) and calls for going beyond the Quran with the Quran, by which he means that the messages from fundamental verses outweigh those of the exceptional ones. Arkoun's Quran understanding permits an even more liberal approach to the text. This is because his reluctance to affirm the divine origin of the text opens up the Quran to a psychological reading, which tries to show how its narratives and linguistic features had through the centuries the power to form various expressions of Islam. From this, the impression arises that for Arkoun the text is a compilation of motivating forces which can either contribute to social developments for the betterment of the human condition or to its disadvantage. He generally hopes that the liberating forces in the Quran could be unleashed for the improvement of the human condition. However I have shown that his treatment of the Quranic text does not conclusively support this notion.

Let us return to the three thinkers' views on the Quran which express that the Quran is a human product that must necessarily be communicated amongst humans. It is a text for humankind. In Rahman's and Abu Zayd's thinking, the Quran's authority lays not so much in its coming from a divine source, but in the fact that it attempts to guide the people in the name of justice. It is not to be underestimated that by acknowledging the active participation of Muhammad in the revelation process, they enter dangerous grounds in the eyes of traditionalists who view the Prophet more passively. Both then had to suffer the consequence of having to live in exile from their home countries until the end of their lives. Arkoun on the other hand does not enter this discourse about the possible contributions by Muhammad, other than mentioning that of course Muhammad's psyche must have had played a role in how the message was first understood and distributed (which also earned him the accusation of heresy). Arkoun's socio-psychological reading of the dark beginnings of Islam is expressed in far less confessional tones than those of Rahman and Abu Zayd. Nonetheless, Arkoun's reading allows for the notion that the original Muslim community can somehow serve as a model for today's Muslim societies.

Umma and *'Ulama'*

Intriguingly, I discovered that all three intellectuals' stances on the exemplary of the original Muslim community both resemble and differ from fundamentalist and revivalist accounts, which consider the original *umma* as model for a contemporary Muslim society. First of all Rahman, Arkoun and Abu Zayd note to different degrees the significance of how the first *umma* understood and reacted to the revelations. The general idea is that the first *umma* was the opening part in the chain of humankind, which ought to be led by the Quranic revelations. This first community resembles the whole of humanity, which is the ultimate addressee of the divine messages. All three thinkers admit that the reactions by the first community to the revelations are reflected in the Quran. Abu Zayd stresses that through individual opinion making they engaged with Muhammad's message in a critical way. Arkoun and Abu Zayd emphasise how the Quran had to connect to the horizon of these addressees in order to slowly transform their understanding of the Divine and its instructions. According to Rahman and Abu Zayd this means that also today's *umma* should engage with the Quran critically and individually. The Quran is designed to be understood. The call for rational engagement with the Quran as a text is in line with the three thinkers' call for access to education for all citizens.

One obstacle to what the three thinkers might term 'a proper view' onto the Quran is in their eyes the influence of the *'ulama'*. Rahman, Arkoun and Abu Zayd in different ways call for a de-monopolization of religious authority. They argue for an understanding of the Quran that is less depending on religious authorities. Hence, they call for a more individual engagement with the Quran. This individual approach is deemed necessary by all three thinkers who, as we have shown, try to 'bring down' the Quranic messages to the level of human understanding. In addition the individual engagement must be enabled through proper education that is accessible for all citizens. This way the monopoly over Quran interpretation as claimed by Muslim clerics – whom Arkoun calls the "managers of faith" – can be challenged. Rahman takes a different view, which still promotes the influence of a well-trained *'ulama'* (practising innovative *ijtihād*). But he subjects their proposals for establishing norms for Islamic societies to democratic voting. It is the sovereign deciding on those values which ought to be imposed through law. In contrast to Rahman, Arkoun and Abu Zayd plead for a separation of religious authorities from state affairs. However, Arkoun hopes that theologians will receive the same interdisciplinary training in historical and critical studies as do non-Muslim scholars. This way he hopes for an improved education of religious authorities which then will have a better understanding of the situation and needs of contemporary societies. Arkoun's proposal allows education and critical scholarship to influence religious thinkers. This means that they will have to apply a new culture of argumentation, which challenges a narrowly-conceived religious reasoning. For Abu Zayd, who calls for a secular education, the *'ulama'* have only the function of spiritual proposers. Also Abu Zayd hopes they would be well-informed about the state of contemporary societies. Then they suggest interpretations, but it is up to the individual to follow them. So in different ways all three challenge the status quo of religious authorities.

Last Remarks

At last I would like to reflect on the findings of analysing the exegetical methods applied by Rahman, Arkoun and Abu Zayd. This study has shown that Rahman, Arkoun and Abu Zayd constantly call for: human freedom, free will, free thinking, free speech, and political freedom. These calls to freedom are consistent with their rejection of determinism. As we have seen, all three believe that the essential prerequisite to enable self-responsible decisions is education. I have argued, however, that Rahman does not have a consistent view of free will and human equality. Although he establishes that the Quran assumes that all humans are able to make the right decisions, and to find to the right path, he cannot explain why some people apparently lack the capacity of faith. In addition to this, Rahman's preference for reading certain verses metaphorically while reading those literally which he finds supportive of his argument, does not represent a coherent exegetical policy. Nor does it conform to his idea of the overall spirit of the Quran, in the light of which everything must be read.

I have found not only that the exegesis of Rahman lacks consistency, and that Arkoun's exegesis is often obscure, but also that Abu Zayd's proposed interpretation methods fail on occasion, for example in discerning the meaning of the 'beating verse.' The only way to deal with this verse seems to be, according to Abu Zayd, a kind of radical criticism, namely the 'going beyond the Quran with the Quran.' In simple terms this stance resembles also Rahman's idea that if the content of a verse violates the underlying spirit of the Quran it needs to be understood as a merely contingent message. Other than this radical step of discarding a verse's significance for today, Abu Zayd's interpretation techniques do not resolve such problematic readings.

My study has also revealed an ambivalent relation of the three thinkers to the use of secondary Islamic literature when dealing with the Quran. Rahman, Abu Zayd and Arkoun refer to secondary literature such as *hadith, sunna* and *sīra* to varying degrees. However, given their scepticism about the reliability of such literature, they all three have in common that they do not explain their criteria for selecting these references. It might be that their emphasis on the centrality of the Quran makes it difficult for them to accept the need for referencing secondary literature. On the other hand Rahman and Abu Zayd clearly refer to materials that give accounts of the experiences of the Prophet in the moment of revelation and of the circumstances of Prophecy. Arkoun also shows an ambivalent relationship to both traditional and modern chronologies of the revealed verses. He identifies the chronologies as man-made speculations but on the other hand bases on them the selection of verses which seem important to his socio-psychological reading of the Quran.

What, then, is the basic idea that emerges from studying Rahman, Arkoun and Abu Zayd? It is that with their views on the Quran as a text for humanity they bring the needs and dynamics of humanity into the focus of their thinking. In this way they transform the notion of religion as a practice to serve the Divine into thinking of religion as a tool for humankind to develop their potential within God's creation. And this main goal – the improvement of the human condition – shaped their approach to the Quran and Islam. In a word, the philosophies of Rahman, Arkoun and Abu Zayd promote human solidarity in the greater scope of a world civilisation.

Bibliography

Abu Zaid, Nasr Hamid. "The Textuality of the Qu'ran." *Middle East NGO.* <http://www. mengos.net/index.php?option=com_content&view=article&id=136:nasrtextuality& catid=49:articles&Itemid=70>. Lecture held in Academic Session: Islam and Europe: in the Past and Present. (Dorpskerk in Wassenaar, Friday, September 20th, 1996). Original language: English.

Abu Zaid, Nasr Hamid, interview by Stefan Weidner and Ahmad Hissou. "Über die Hermeneutik und Gadamer und das arabisch-islamische Erbe." *<www.nefais. net/2010/07/06/interview-abu-zaid>*. Netzwerk Fachjournalisten islamische Welt, (June 7, 2010). Translated from Arabic into German by Larissa Bender.

Abu Zayd, Nasr Hamid. "A Critical Commentary." *In History and Memory in Contemporary Islam – Between Enlightenment and Apologetics.* Berlin: Friedrich Ebert Stiftung, 2009. 29–30. Original language: English.

—. *Ein Leben mit dem Islam.* Freiburg: Herder, 2001. Based on interviews by Navid Kermani and Chérifa Magdi with Abu Zaid, translated and edited by Magdi Chérifa and assembled by Navid Kermani into a biography.

—. *Gottes Menschenwort. Für ein humanistisches Verständnis des Koran.* Freiburg: Herder, 2008. Translated from English and Arabic into German by Thomas Hildebrandt (Ed.)

—. "Im holländischen Exil." *Südwestrundfunk.* Beate Hinrichs. October 23, 2006. Translated from English into German by SWR. <http://www.swr.de/-/id=1754248/ property=download/12ofrap/index.rtf>.

Abu Zayd, Nasr Hamid, interview in English by Katharina Völker. *Interview 2009* (September 4, 2009).

—. *Mohammed und die Zeichen Gottes. Der Koran und die Zukunft des Islam.* Freiburg: Herder, 2008. Based on interviews by Hilal Sezgin. Translated from English into German by Hilal Sezgin.

—. *Politik und Islam: Kritik des religiösen Diskurses.* Translated from Arabic into German by Chérifa Magdi. Frankfurt: dipa, 1996.

—. *Reformation of Islamic Thought.* Amsterdam: Amsterdam University Press, 2006. Original language: English.

—. "Research Profile." *University of Leiden.* <www.uvh.nl> (accessed July 26, 2010). Original language: English.

—. *Rethinking the Qur'an: Towards a Humanistic Hermeneutics.* Amsterdam: Humanistics University Press, 2004. Inaugural lecture delivered on May 27, 2004 for Ibn Rushd Academic Chair, for Islam and Humanism, established by the University of Humanistics, Utrecht, The Netherlands. Original language: English.

—. "Spricht Gott nur Arabisch?" *Die ZEIT-online – Reihe: Der Islam und der Westen 4.* May 2003. <www.zeit.de/2003/05/Abu_Zaid?page=all>. Shortened version of lecture held on 15th January 2003, as Bucerius/ZEIT-Fellow at Wissenschaftskolleg zu Berlin. Translated from English into German by Sophia Pick and Navid Kermani.

Abu Zayd, Nasr Hamid. "The Dilemma of the Literary Aproach to the Qur'an." *Alif: Journal of Comparative Poetics* (Department of English and Comparative Literature,

American University in Cairo and American University in Cairo Press), no. 23 (2003): 8–47. Original language: English.

—. "The Qur'anic Concept of Justice." *polylog: Forum for Intercultural Philosophy.* 2001. <http://them.polylog.org/3/fan-en.htm>. Original language: English.

Abu Zayd, Nasr Hamid. "Women in the Discourse of Crisis (Extracts)." *Peoples Rights – a Quaterly Women's Rights Journal,* no. 2 (August 1996). Extracts from the book "Women in the Discourse of Crisis" are translated from Arabic into English by Marlene Tadros.

Adang, Camilla. "Belief and Unbelief." *EQ.* <http://www.brillonline.nl/subscriber/entry?entry=q3_COM-00025> (accessed May 17, 2010).

Akhtar, Shabbir. *The Quran and the secular mind: a philosophy of Islam.* New York: Routledge, 2008.

Al-Jabri, Mohammed Abed. *Kritik der arabischen Vernunft. Naqd al-'aql al-'arabi. Die Einführung.* Translated by Sarah Dornhof Vincent von Wroblewsky. Berlin: Perlen, 2009.

Amirpur, Katajun and Ludwig Ammann, ed. *Der Islam am Wendepunkt. Liberale und konservative Reformer einer Weltreligion.* Freiburg: Herder, 2006.

Amirpur, Katajun, ed. *Unterwegs zu einem anderen Islam. Texte iranischer Denker.* Translated by Katajun Amirpur. Freiburg: Herder, 2009.

Arberry, Arthur John. *The Koran Interpreted: A Translation.* New York: Simon & Schuster, 1996.

Arkoun, Mohammad. "The Notion of Revelation: From Ahl al-Kitāb to the Societies of the Book ." *Die Welt des Islams,* no. 28 (1988): 62–89.

—. "Violence." *EQ.* (accessed December 2, 2010).

Arkoun, Mohammed. "Islam." *EQ.* (accessed June 28, 2011).

Arkoun, Mohammed. "Present-Day Islam Between its Tradition and Globalisation." In *Intellectual Traditions in Islam,* edited by Farhad Daftary, 179–221. London: I.B.Tauris , 2000.

Arkoun, Mohammed. "The State, the Individual, and Human Rights: A Contemporary View of Muslims in a Global Context." In *The Muslim Almanac: The Reference Work on History, Faith and Culture, and Peoples of Islam,* 453–457. Detroit: Gale Research Inc., 1995.

Arkoun, Muhammad. "A Return to the Question of Humanism in Islamic." (unpublished essay).

Arkoun, Muhammad. "Algeria ." (unpublished essay).

Arkoun, Muhammad. "Auf den Spuren humanistischer Traditionen im Islam." In *Interkultureller Humanismus,* 145–175. Schwalbach am Taunus: Wochenschau Verlag, 2009. Translated from English into German.

Arkoun, Muhammad. "Contemporary Critical Practices and the Qur'an." *EQ,* 2001.

—. "Curriculum Vitae." *Ibn Rushd Fund for Freedom of Thought.* <www.ibn-rushd.org/English/CV-Arkoun.htm>.

—. *Islam: To Reform or to Subvert?* London: Saqi Essentials, 2007.

—. *Rethinking Islam: Common Questions, Uncommon Answers.* Boulder: Westview Press, 1994.

Arkoun, Muhammad. "Revelation Revisited." (unpublished essay).

Arkoun, Muhammad. *The Reflexive History of Thought Seen as a Problematisation of Truth.* (unpublished essay).

Armajani, Jon. *Dynamic Islam: Liberal Muslim Perspectives in a Transnational Age.* Lanham: University Press of America, 2004.

Arts, Wilhelmus Antonius and Loek Halman, ed. *European Values at the Turn of the Millennium.* Leiden: Brill, 2004.

Azmi, Shaykhul-Hadeeth (Maulana) Fazlur Rahman. *Shabe Bara'at – The Fifteenth of Sha'baan in the light of Qur'aan & Hadeeth.* <http://www.central-mosque.com/fiqh/shabebaraat.pdf>.

Baum, Gregory. The Theology of Tariq Ramadan: A Catholic Perspective. Notre Dame: University of Notre Dame Press, 2009.

Berry, Donald L. "A Life in Review." In *The shaping of an American and Islamic Discourse,* edited by Earle H. Waugh and Frederick M. Denny, 37–45. Atlanta: Scholars Press, 1998.

—. *Islam and Modernity Through the Writings of Islamic Modernist Fazlur Rahman.* New York: The Edwin Mellon Press, 2003.

Böwering, Gerhard. "Recent Research on the Construction of the Qur'ān." In *The Qur'ān in its historical context,* edited by Gabriel Said Reynolds, 70–87. London and New York: Routledge, 2008.

Brockopp, Jonathan E. "Justice and Injustice." *EQ,* 2011.

Brown, D.W. "Sunna." *EI.* 2010. <http://www.brillonline.nl/subscriber/entry?entry=islam_COM-1123> (accessed November 11, 2010).

Brown, Daniel. *The Triumph of Scripturalism: The Doctrine of Naskh and its Modern Critics.* Vol. 17, in *The Shaping of an American and Islamic Discourse,* edited by Earle H. Waugh and Frederick M. Denny, 49–66. Rochester: Scholars Press, 1998.

Callaway, Rhonda L. "The Rhetoric of Asian Values." Edited by Rhonda L. Callaway and Julie Harrelson-Stephens, 112–121. Boulder: Lynne Rienner Publishers, 2007.

Corsini, Raymond J. *The Dictionary of Psychology.* New York: Brunner/Routledge, 2002.

Cragg, Kenneth. *The Call of the Minaret.* New York : Oxford University Press, 1964.

—. *The pen and the faith: Eight modern Muslim writers and the Qur'an.* London and Boston: Allen & Unwin, 1985.

Denny, Frederick. "Fazlur Rahman: Muslim Intellectual." *The Muslim World,* April 1989: 91–101.

Donner, Fred. "The Quran in recent scholarship: challendes and desiderata." In *The Qur'an in its historical context,* edited by Gabriel Said Reynolds, 29–50. Routledge, 2008.

Esack, Farid. *Qur'an, Liberation and Pluralism: An Islamic Perspective of the Interreligious Solidarity against Oppression.* Oxford: Oneworld, 1997.

Felix Körner, SJ. *Alter Text – neuer Kontext. Koranhermeneutik in der Türkei heute. Ausgewählte Texte übersetzt und kommentiert.* Freiburg: Herder, 2006.

Fourest, Caroline. *Brother Tariq: The Doublespeak of Tariq Ramadan.* New York: Encounter Books, 2008.

Frege, Gottlob. "Über Sinn und Bedeutung." *Zeitschrift für Philosophie und philosophische Kritik,* 1892: 25–50.

Gabrieli, F. "adab." *EI2.* <www.brillonline.nl/subscriber/entry?entry=islam_SIM-0293> (accessed May 25, 2010).

Gadamer, Hans-Georg. *Truth and Method.* London: Sheed & Ward, 1975.

Gleave, Robert. "Arkoun and the 'Sword Verse'." *livitproject.net.* October 1, 2010. <http://www.livitproject.net/blog/arkoun-and-the-sword-verse->.

Goodman, Lenn Evan. *Islamic Humanism.* New York: Oxford University Press, 2006.

Groff, Peter S. and Oliver Leaman. *Islamic Philosophy.* Edinburgh: Edinburgh University Press, 2007.

Günther, Ursula. "Mohammad Arkoun: Towards a Radical Rethinking of Islamic Thought." In *Modern Muslim Intellectuals and the Qur'an,* edited by Suha Taji-Farouki, 125–168. London: Oxford University Press, 2004.

—. *Mohammed Arkoun: ein moderner Kritiker der islamischen Vernunft.* Würzburg: Ergon, 2003.

Günther, Ursula, ed. *Theologie-Pädagogik-Kontext. Zukunftsperspektiven der Religionspädagogik.* Münster, 2005.

Günther, Ursula. "Zum Potenzial von Mohammed Arkouns Ansatz für Dialogkonzepte." In *Theologie-Pädagogik-Kontext. Zukunftsperspektiven der Religionspädagogik,* edited by Ursula Günther, 209–222. Münster, 2005.

Halman, L. C. J. M. & Pettersson, T. "Normative orientations towards the differentiation between religion and politics", in Arts, W. A. & Halman, L. C. J. M. (eds.). *European Values at the Turn of the Millennium.* Boston: Brill (2004), 317–333.

Hashemi, Nader. *Islam, Secularism, and Liberal Democracy. Toward a Democratic Theory of Muslim Societies.* Oxford: Oxford University Press, 2009.

Hassan, Riaz. *Faithlines: Muslim Conceptions of Islam and Society.* Oxford: Oxford University Press, 2002.

Hawting, Gerald R. "Pre-Islamic Arabia and the Qur'an." *EQ,* 2010.

Heit, Helmut. *Die Werte Europas: Verfassungspatriotismus und Wertegemeinschaft in der EU?* Münster: Lit, 2005.

Hendrich, Geert. *Islam und Aufklärung.* Darmstadt: Wissenschaftliche Buchgesellschaft, 2004.

Hildebrandt, Thomas. *Neo-Mu'tazilismus? Intention und Kontext im modernen arabischen Umgang mit dem wieder entdeckten rationalistisch-theologischen Erbe des Islam.* Leiden: Brill, 2007.

Hoffman, Valerie J. "Qur'anic Interpretation and Modesty Norms for Women." Edited by Earle H. Waugh and Frederick M. Denny. *In The shaping of an American and Islamic Discourse.* Atlanda: Scholars Press, 1998. 89–121.

Inglehart, Ronald and Pippa Norris. *Sacred and Secular: Religion and Politics Worldwide.* Cambridge: Cambridge University Press, 2004.

Karlekar, Hiranmay. *Bangladesh: the next Afghanistan?* London: Sage Publication, 2005.

Kaufmann, Franz-Xaver. *Religion und Modernität: sozialwissenschaftliche Perspektiven.* Tübingen: Mohr, 1989.

Kermani, Navid. *Das Konzept wahy – Offenbarung als Kommunikation.* Frankfurt/ Main: Peter-Lang, 1996.

—. *Gott ist schön. Das ästhetische Erleben des Koran.* München: Beck, 2000.

Kermani, Navid. "Revelation in its Aesthetic Dimension." In *The Qur'an as Text,* edited by Stefan Wild. Leiden: Brill, 1996.

Kinberg, Leah. "Piety." *EQ.* 2011. <http://www.brillonline.nl/subscriber/entry?entry=q3_SIM-00326> (accessed May 25, 2011).

Körner, Felix. *Alter Text – neuer Kontext.* Freiburg: Herder, 2006.

Körner, Felix. "Turkish Theology Meets European Philosophy: Emilio Betti, Hans-Georg Gadamer and Paul Ricoeur in Muslim Thinking." *Revista Portuguesa de Filosofia,* no. 2 (2006): 905–809.

Kraemer, Joel L. *Humanism in the Renaissance of Islam: the Cultural Revivial during the Buyid Age.* Leiden: Brill, 1992.

Krawulsky, Dorothea. *Eine Einführung in die Koranwissenschaften.* Bern: Peter Lang, 2006.

Küng, Hans and Karl-Josef Kuschel. *A global Ethic: the Declaration of the Parliament of the World's Religions.* Chicago: Council for the Parliament of the World's Religions, 1993.

Kuran, Timur. *Islam and Mammon. The Economic Predicaments of Islamism.* Princeton: Princeton University Press, 2004.

Lund, Michael S. "Human Rights. The Source of Conflict, State Making, and State Breaking." In *Human Rights and Conflict: Exploring the Links between Rights, Law, and Peacebuilding,* edited by Julie Mertus and Jeffrey W. Helsing, 39–63. Washington: United States Institute of Peace, 2006.

M.S. Asimov, C.E. Bosworth, ed. *History of Civilizations of Central Asia.* Vol. IV. Paris: Unesco Publishing, 1998.

Marshall, Paul and Nina Shea. "Afgan Blowback." *Assyrian International News Agency.* <http://www.aina.org/news/20110408123220.htm>.

Martin, Richard C. "Inimitability." *EQ.* 2008. <http://www.brillonline.nl/subscriber/entry?entry=q3_COM-00093> (accessed May 19, 2008).

Mertus, Julie and Jeffrey W. Helsing, ed. *Human Rights and Conflict: Exploring the Links between Rights, Law, and Peacebuilding.* Washington: United States Institute of Peace, 2006.

Mirbabaev, A.K. "The Islamic Lands and Their Culture." In *History of Civilizations of Central Asia,* edited by M.S. Asimov and C.E. Bosworth, 31–43. Paris: Unesco Publishing, 1998.

Müller, Tim. "Individual Religiosity and Attitudes towards the Involvement of Religious Leaders in Politics. A Multilevel-analysis of 55 Societies", in: World Values Research 2 (2009): 1–29.

Murata, Sachiko and William C. Chittick. *The Vision of Islam.* New York: I.B.Tauris, 2006.

Nagel, Tilman. *Allahs Liebling: Ursprung und Erscheinungsformen des Mohammedglaubens*. München: Oldenbourg, 2008.

Neuwirth, Angelika and Michael Marx. "Corpus Quran Project." <http://corpus.quran. com/search.jsp?q=truth&s=1&page=1>.

Neuwirth, Angelika. *Der Koran als Text der Spätantike: ein europäischer Zugang*. Berlin: Verlag der Weltreligionen, 2010.

Nielsen-Sikora, Jürgen. "'Verfassungspatriotismus' in der Europäischen Union?" In *Die Werte Europas: Verfassungspatriotismus und Wertegemeinschaft in der EU?*, by Helmut Heit, 178–191. Münster: Lit, 2005.

Oevermann, Ulrich. "Modernisierungspotentiale im Monotheismus und Modernisierungsblockaden im fundamentalistischen Islam." In *Religiosität in der säkularisierten Welt. Theoretische und empirische Beiträge zur Säkularisierungsdebatte in der Religionssoziologie*, edited by Manuel Franzmann, Christel Gärtner and Nicole Köck, 395–428. Wiesbaden: Verlag für Sozialwissenschaften, 2006.

Okakura, Kakuzo. *The Book of Tea*. 1906. <http://www.gutenberg.org/cache/epub/769/ pg769.txt>.

Özsoy, Ömer. "Erneuerungsprobleme zeitgenössischer Muslime und der Koran." In *Alter Text – neuer Kontext. Koranhermeneutik in der Türkei heute. Ausgewählte Texte übersetzt und kommentiert*, edited by Felix Körner, translated by Felix Körner, 16–28. Freiburg: Herder, 2006.

Özsoy, Ömer. "Rede, nicht Text." In *Alter Text – neuer Kontext. Koranhermeneutik in der Türkei heute. Ausgwählte Texte übersetzt und kommentiert*, edited by Felix Körner, translated by Felix Körner, 78–98. Freiburg: Herder, 2006.

Paçaci, Mehmet. "Der Koran und ich – wie geschichtlich sind wir?" In *Alter Text – neuer Kontext*, edited by Felix Körner, translated by Felix Körner, 32–69. Freiburg: Herder, 2006.

Soanes, Catherine and Angus Stevenson, ed. "paideia noun." *The Oxford Dictionary of English (revised edition)*. 2005. http:<//www.oxfordreference.com/views/ENTRY. html?subview=Main&entry=t140.e55731> (accessed May 26, 2010).

Rahman, Fazlur. "Aql." *www.MuslimPhilosophy.com*. <http://www.muslimphilosophy. com/ei2/aql.htm>.

—. *Avicenna's Psychology*. London: Oxford Univeristy Press, 1952.

—. *Islam*. London: Weidenfeld & Nicolson, 1966.

—. *Islam and Modernity: Transformation of an Intellectual Tradition*. Chicago: The University of Chicago Press, 1982.

—. *Major Themes of the Qur'an*. Minneapolis: Bibliotheca Islamica, 1980.

—. *Major Themes of the Qur'an.*[2] Edited by Ebrahim Moosa. Chicago: The University of Chicago Press, 2009.

—. *Prophecy in Islam*. London: Allen & Unwin , 1958.

Rahman, Fazlur. "Roots of Islamic Neo-Fundamentalism." In *Change in the Muslim World*, edited by P.H. Stoddard, 23–39. Syracuse: Syracuse University Press, 1981.

—. "Some Issues in the Ayyub Khan Era." Edited by Niyazi Berkes and D.P. Little. *In Essays on Islamic civilization: presented to Niyazi Berkes*. Leiden: E.J. Brill, 1976.

Rahman, Fazlur. "The Islamic Concept of State." Edited by J.J. Donohue and J.L. Esposito. Oxford: Oxford University Press, 1982.

Rahman, Yusuf. *The Hermeneutical Theory of Naṣr Ḥāmid Abu Zayd: An Analytical Study of His Method of Interpreting the Qur'ān.* Montreal: (unpublished PhD thesis), 2001.

Renner, Erich. "Kulturtheoretische und kulturvergleichende Ansätze." In *Handbuch Kindheits- und Jugendforschung,* edited by Heinz-Hermann Krüger and Cathleen Grunert, 175–201. Wiesbaden: Verlag für Sozialwissenschaften, 2010.

Rippin, Andrew. "Occasions of Revelation." *EQ.* <http://www.brillonline.nl/subscriber/entry?entry=q3_COM-00157> (accessed April 17, 2010).

Rubin, U. "Nūr Muḥammadī." *EI.* 2010. <http://www.brillonline.nl/subscriber/entry?entry=islam_SIM-5985> (accessed November 22, 2010).

Saeed, Abdullah. "Fazlur Rahman: a framework for interpreting the ethico-legal content of the Quran." In *Modern Muslim Intellectuals and the Quran,* edited by Suha Taji-Farouki, 37–66. London: Oxford University Press, 2004.

—. "Contemporary Trends in Islam: A Preliminary Attempt at a Classification." *The Muslim World,* July 2007.

Schuchardt, Beatrice. *Auf der Grenze: postkoloniale Geschichtsbilder bei Assia Djebar.* Köln: Böhlau, 2006.

Sonn, Tamara. "Fazlur Rahman's Islamic Methodology." *The Muslim World,* 1991: 360–363.

Spiewak, Martin. "Allahs scheuer Bote: Ömer Özsoy." *Die Zeit,* March 2007.

Strohmaier, Gotthard. *Avicenna.* München: Beck, 2006.

Sukidi. "Naṣr Ḥāmid Abū Zayd and the Quest for a Humanistic Hermeneutics of the Qur'ān." *Die Welt des Islam,* 2009: 181–211.

Thielmann, Jörn. *Nasr Hâmid Abû Zaid und die wiedererfundene hisba. Scharî'a und Qânûn im heutigen Ägypten.* Würzburg: Ergon, 2003.

Tibi, Bassam. *The challenge of fundamentalism: Political Islam and the New World Disorder.* Berkeley: University of California Press, 1998.

Troll SJ, Christian. "Es fehlt eine zeitgemäße Hermeneutik des Korans." *Die Tagespost,* December 23, 2006.

—. "Plurality of Religion – Plurality in Religion (Christianity and Islam). Part II: Islam. Islamic Voices on Social, Cultural and Religious Pluralism." *sankt-georgen.de.* Philosophisch-Theologische Hochschule Sankt Georgen. October 16, 2002. <http://www.sankt-georgen.de/leseraum/troll14.html>.

Twardella, Johannes. *Religös-philosophische Profile. Positionsbestimmungen jüdischer und islamischer Intellektueller im Säkularisierungsprozess.* Hildesheim: Georg Olms, 2006.

United, Nations. "Arab Human Development Report." *<http://www.arab-hdr.org/>.*

United, Nations. "Human Development Report." *<http://hdr.undp.org/en/reports/global/hdr2011/>,* 2011.

Valentin, Joachim. "Rationalität im Islam? Theologische Hintergründe aktueller Konflikte." *Stimmen der Zeit,* no. 2 (2005).

—. "Is There Rationality in Islam? Theological Backgrounds of the Current Conflicts." *Stimmen der Zeit*, February 2005: 75–89.

Völker, Katharina. *Rationalität und Islam: Die Vernunftforderungen des islamischen Literaturwissenschaftlers Naṣr Hamīd 'Abū Zayd in der Koranexegese.* Frankfurt: MA thesis, J.W. Goethe University: Library Publication, 2007.

—. "A Danger to Free Research and Teaching in German Universities? The Case of Muhammad Sven Kalisch." In *The Teaching and Study of Islam in Western Universities*, ed. by Paul Morris, William Shepard, Toni Tidswell, Paul Trebilco, 175–85. New York: Routledge, 2013.

—. "Mohammad Arkoun: The Quran Rethought – Genesis, Significance, and the Study of the Quran." *Journal of Religious Culture*, ed. by Edmund Weber et al., no. 189. Frankfurt am Main: Goethe-University, Institute for Religious Peace Research, 2014. (http://web.uni-frankfurt.de/irenik/relkultur189.pdf)

—. "Parameters of Teaching Islam *Freely.*" In *Freedom of Speech and Islam*, ed. By: Erich Kolig, 209–224. London: Ashgate, 2014.

—. "Two Accounts of Quranic Revelation – Fazlur Rahman and N.H. Abu Zayd on Muhammad's *Contribution.*" *Journal of Islam and Christian-Muslim Relations.* Eds. University of Birmingham (UK) and Monash University (Australia). London: Routledge, 2015: 271–286.

—. "Nasr Hamid Abu Zayd." In *International Handbook of Philosophy of Education* (Dordrecht: Springer), forthcoming 2017.

—. "The Humanistic Heritage of Muhammad Arkoun", in: *Philosophical Investigation* – Journal of Faculty of Letters and Humanities (Tabriz: Tabriz University Press, No. 17, 2016), 203–227.

von Kügelgen, Anke. *Averroes und die Arabische Moderne. Ansätze zu einer Neube-gründung des Rationalismus im Islam.* Leiden: Brill, 1994.

Wakin, Jeanette. *Remembering Joseph Schacht (1902–1969).* January 2003. <http://www.law.harvard.edu/programs/ilsp/publications/wakin.pdf> (accessed November 25, 2010).

Waugh, Earle H. and F.M. Denny, ed. *The shaping of an American and Islamic Discourse.* Atlanta: Scholars Press, 1998.

Webb, Gisela. "Angel." *EQ.* 2010. <http://www.brillonline.nl/subscriber/entry?entry=q3_COM-00010> (accessed November 8, 2010).

Welch, A.T., R. Paret and J.D. Pearson. "al-Kur'an." *EI2.* <http://www.brillonline.nl/subscriber/entry?entry=islam_COM-0543> (accessed April 4, 2010).

Wielandt, Rotraud. *Offenbarung und Geschichte im Denken moderner Muslime.* Wiesbaden: Franz Steiner Verlag, 1971.

Wielandt, Rotraud. "Wurzeln der Schwierigkeit innerislamischen Gesprächs über neue hermeneutische Zugänge zum Korantext." In *The Qur'an as Text*, edited by Stefan Wild, 257–282. Leiden: Brill, 1996.

Wild, Stefan. "Die andere Seite des Textes: Nasr Hamid Abu Zaid und der Koran." *Review in: Die Welt des Islam*, no. 33 (1993): 256–261.

Wild, Stefan, ed. *The Quran as Text.* Leiden: Brill, 1996.

Willems, Ulrich. "Religion als Privatsache? Eine kritische Auseinandersetzung mit dem liberalen Prinzip einer strikten Trennung von Politik und Religion." Edited by Michale Minkenberg and Ulrich Willems. *In Politik und Religion.* Opladen: Westdeutscher Verlag, 2002.

Wright, Peter Matthews. *Modern Qur'anic Hermeneutics.* Chapel Hill : (unpublished PhD thesis), 2008.

Zwettler, Michael. *The oral tradition of classical Arabic poetry: its character and implications.* Columbus: Ohio State University Press, 1978.

THEION

Herausgegeben von / edited by Wilhelm-Ludwig Federlin, Edmund Weber und / and Vladislav Serikov

Band 1 Wilhelm-Ludwig Federlin: Kirchliche Volksbildung und Bürgerliche Gesellschaft. Studien zu Thomas Abbt, Alexander Gottlieb Baumgarten, Johann David Heilmann, Johann Gottfried Herder, Johann Georg und Johannes von Müller. 1993.

Band 2 Hans Christoph Stoodt / Edmund Weber (Hrsg.): Interreligiöse Beziehungen: Konflikte und Konvergenzen. 1993.

Band 3 Hans Christoph Stoodt / Edmund Weber (Hrsg.): INTER LEGEM ET EVANGELIUM. 1994.

Band 4 Sylvia Mangold: Ādi Śaṅkarācāryaḥ. G. V. Iyers Filmkommentar zur Religionsphilosophie Śaṅkaras. 1994.

Band 5 Cheriyan Menacherry: Christ: The Mystery in History. A Critical Study on the Christology of Raymond Panikkar. 1995.

Band 6 Wilhelm-Ludwig Federlin (Hrsg.): Sein ist im Werden. Essays zur Wirklichkeitskultur bei Johann Gottfried Herder anläßlich seines 250. Geburtstages. 1995.

Band 7 Matthias Benad / Edmund Weber (Hrsg.): Diakonie der Religionen 1. Studien zu Lehre und Praxis karitativen Handelns in der christlichen, buddhistischen, Hindu und Sikh Religion. 1996.

Band 8 Byong-Ro An: Die Religiosität der Koreaner in Deutschland. 1997.

Band 9 Friedrich Weber: Sendrecht, Policey und Kirchenzucht. Kirchenrechtsbildung und religiös-ethische Normierung in Ostfriesland und Emden bis Ende des 16. Jahrhunderts. 1998.

Band 10 Peter Schmidt: A. C. Bhaktivedanta Swami im interreligiösen Dialog. Biographische Studien zur Begegnung von Hinduismus und Christentum. 1999.

Band 11 Stephan Nagel: Brahmas geheime Schöpfung. Die indische Reformbewegung der "Brahma Kumaris". Quellen, Lehre, Raja Yoga. 1999.

Band 12 Steven Ballard: Rudolf Otto and the Synthesis of the Rational and the Non-Rational in the Idea of the Holy. Some Encounters in Theory and Practice. 2000.

Band 13 Thea Mohr: Weibliche Identität und Leerheit. Eine ideengeschichtliche Rekonstruktion der buddhistischen Frauenbewegung Sakyadhita International. 2002.

Band 14 Bärbel Beinhauer-Köhler / Matthias Benad / Edmund Weber (Hrsg.): Diakonie der Religionen 2. Schwerpunkt Islam. 2005.

Band 15 Wilhelm-Ludwig Federlin / Markus Witte (Hrsg.): Herder-Gedenken. Interdisziplinäre Beiträge anläßlich des 200. Todestages von Johann Gottfried Herder. 2005

Band 16 Young-Sik Park: Konvivenz der Religionen. 2006.

Band 17 Roswitha Möstl: Naraseva – Moderne Hindudiakonie. Erscheinungsformen, Konzepte, Strategien, religiöse und weltanschauliche Begründungen.Diakonie der Religionen 3. 2006.

Band 18 Thea Mohr / Edmund Weber (Hrsg.): Universelle Kultur des Helfens. Im Hinduismus, Buddhismus, Islam, Judentum und in den Naturwissenschaften. Diakonie der Religionen 4. 2006.

Band 19 Edmund Weber: Hindu India. Another Approach to its Multiflorous Religious Culture. Collected Essays. 2006.

Band 20 Karl Dienst: „Zerstörte" oder „wahre" Kirche: Eine geistliche oder kirchenpolitische Entscheidung? 2007.

Band 21 Tharwat Kades: Der Dialog zwischen Christen und Muslimen im Spannungsfeld von Tradition und Moderne. 2008.

Band 22 Karl Dienst: Zwischen Wissenschaft und Kirchenpolitik. Zur Bedeutung universitärer Theologie für die Identität einer Landeskirche in Geschichte und Gegenwart. 2009.

Band 23 Marijke Metselaar: Die Nestorianer und der frühe Islam. Wechselwirkungen zwischen den ostsyrischen Christen und ihren arabischen Nachbarn. 2009.

Band 24 Natalia Diefenbach-Popov: Das russisch-orthodoxe Kirillo-Belozerskij-Kloster zwischen Macht und Spiritualität. 2009.

Band 25 Karl Dienst: Politik und Religionskultur in Hessen und Nassau zwischen ‚Staatsumbruch' (1918) und ‚nationaler Revolution' (1933). Ursachen und Folgen. 2010.

Band 26 Hüseyin Kurt/ Edmund Weber (Hrsg.): Die Zukunft der Muslime in Deutschland. Tagungen der Kommunalen Ausländer- und Ausländerinnenvertretung der Stadt Frankfurt am Main (KAV) und der Arbeitsgemeinschaft der Ausländerbeiräte Hessen (agah). Eine Dokumentation ausgewählter akademischer und politischer Beiträge. 2011.

Band 27 Wilhelm-Ludwig Federlin / Sven Lichtenecker / Vladislav, Serikov / Gülhan Şirin (Hrsg.): Was ist Religion? Beiträge zur Religionsforschung. Edmund Weber zum 70. Geburtstag. 2011.

Band 28 Karl Dienst: Kirchenreform als Strukturreform. Die Kirche muß anders werden: Aber wie? 2011.

Band 29 Edmund Weber: Religion und Religionskultur. Gesammelte Aufsätze. 2013.

Band 30 Wolfgang Gantke / Vladislav Serikov (Hrsg.): Das Heilige als Problem der gegenwärtigen Religionswissenschaft. 2015.

Band 31 Katharina Völker: Quran and Reform. Rahman, Arkoun, Abu Zayd. 2017.

www.peterlang.com